D1015685

ACCOUNTABLE LEADERSHIP

ACCOUNTABLE LEADERSHIP

A Resource Guide for Sustaining Legal,
Financial, and Ethical Integrity
in Today's Congregations

Revised and Expanded

Paul Chaffee

Jossey-Bass Publishers
San Francisco

This publication is designed to provide accurate and authorita-
tive information in regard to the subject matter covered and
is made available with the understanding that the author and
the publisher are not engaged in rendering legal or professional
services. If legal advice or expert assistance is required, the
services of a competent professional should be sought.

Substantial discounts on bulk quantities of Jossey-Bass
books are available to corporations, professional
associations, and other organizations. For details
and discount information, contact the special sales
department at (415) 433–1740; Fax (800) 605–2665.

For sales outside the United States, please contact your local
Simon & Schuster International Office.

Jossey-Bass Web address: http://www.josseybass.com

 Manufactured in the United States of America on Lyons
Falls Turin Book. This paper is acid-free and 100 percent
totally chlorine-free.

Library of Congress Cataloging-in-Publication Data

Chaffee, Paul, date.
    Accountable leadership : a resource guide for sustaining legal,
    financial, and ethical integrity in today's congregations /
    Paul Chaffee. — 1st ed., rev. and expanded.
        p. cm. — (The Jossey-Bass religion-in-practice series)
    Includes index.
    ISBN 0–7879–0364–7 (cloth : acid-free paper)
    1. Christian leadership. 2. Parishes. 3. Church management.
    4. Pastoral theology. I. Title. II. Series.
    BV652.1.C 1997
    253—dc21   96-45857

FIRST EDITION

HB Printing 10 9 8 7 6 5 4 3 2 1

The Jossey-Bass
Religion-in-Practice Series

CONTENTS

PREFACE

The most important thought I ever had was that of
my individual responsibility to God.

—Daniel Webster

ELECTED, APPOINTED, VOLUNTEERED, AND HIRED, the leaders of a local congregation are responsible for the operations and health of the institution as well as the personal safety of members, guests, and property. Since the 1960s, life in the worshiping community has become more complicated for everyone. "How we used to do it" is rarely adequate anymore and often inappropriate. Roles, rules, and organizational structures keep evolving, and congregations have begun holding their leaders accountable in new ways. To a great extent, the resulting tumult and our frequent confusion and anxiety mirror an out-of-control social culture.

Throughout the sixties, institutional identity crisis was everyday news in the religious community. We entered the seventies with "future shock" on our lips, and life kept getting more complex. The eighties brought a series of body blows to most faith communities, including the public scandal of sexual abuse, an epidemic of litigation, dramatically evolving expectations of leaders, and a much more intricate legal and financial environment. The turmoil in worshiping communities has not abated in the nineties. But one finds new reasons for good cheer, including a growing set of superb resources that, thirty years ago, nobody had the vaguest idea we would need.

Against this backdrop, *Accountable Leadership* explores the ethical, legal, and financial responsibilities of lay and clergy leaders in religious congregations. The information it surveys and its relevance to corporate decision making cut across traditions and groupings. When their congregations are sued, Methodists and Muslims are equally disconcerted. Basic standards of accountability apply similarly to the president of the local synagogue and the trustee of an independent community fellowship.

Priests, rabbis, and ministers all share legal reporting responsibilities regarding child abuse.

Accountability issues shared by religious communities are the subject here. Surveying a variety of practical concerns, each chapter offers suggestions and then points the way to more detailed information. Over four hundred resources are referenced in these chapters.

Why publish another book about books? Of the thousands of religious publications to hit the press each month, only a small portion provide the down-to-earth information needed by local leaders seeking to make informed decisions. Even denominational publications leave aside many practical issues congregational leaders daily address.

Similarly, seminaries appropriately place priority on scripture, theology, ethics, history, and human services—a stunning challenge by itself. Little time is left to pay attention to finance and management, institutional liability, or legal reporting requirements. Contract law, employee relations, and conflict resolution receive only passing attention.

Yet every congregation's leaders, whether prepared or not, must deal with these issues each day. When not prepared, they fly blind. They do a valiant job much of the time but deserve better training and access to available resources. Without leaders committed to a steep learning curve, congregations suffer. Too many religious facilities are poorly used and maintained; too often our business and safety practices are grossly inadequate. People in pain or conflict, even in danger, too seldom receive the protection and nurture which we hope to find in the worshiping community.

This knowledge vacuum has inspired a burgeoning industry of research, publishing, training, and consulting ventures that give congregations specific resources and tools to handle a much more complex world than our parents faced. The story of the major players in this pioneering work and the ways their organizations serve specific congregational needs is the subtext in these pages. Almost all the referenced materials have been written since the late eighties (and many more are in the planning, not always from expected sources).

This book itself, in its revised edition, is part of a new series from a major publisher in the secular nonprofit world. This series recognizes that practical, congregationally based issues regularly parallel those in the rest of the nonprofit sector. The religious and secular nonprofit communities are like cousins who never see each other; this series and other publications like it will bring about some family reunions.

Most of this new activity is research driven. Fewer and fewer articles from experienced pastors sharing their wisdom are being printed in the leadership arena—except where these leaders have systematically studied a particular issue as it occurs in their own backyard. This new activity also tends to be not secondary research (writing about other writers, as I do here) but primary research: statistical research, implementation of new models and methodologies, and systematic study of actual congregations to see if we can understand how to improve their effectiveness.

The most important story within this story is the emergence of congregational studies as a bona fide academic discipline. Its most important text, *Handbook for Congregational Studies* (1986), remains a classic. (An enlarged second edition is due in 1998.)

Congregational studies' becoming a discipline is good news for several reasons. It focuses on the most serious needs of congregations and offers real solutions. Though inspired by the Alban Institute, the development is gaining recognition within theological higher education, building badly needed new bridges between the pew and the ivory tower. The movement is inspiring seminaries to get into primary research themselves and be less dependent on the printed word. And congregational studies offers a wonderful laboratory environment in which to test the headier theories of scripture, theology, and ethics.

It is easy to despair over failures in the religious community, and this book examines some of those sterner realities. I cannot hear the tragic stories any longer, though, without thinking of the incredible ferment and cross-fertilization going on in congregational studies to address these issues. Bright, caring, engaged members from all sorts of faith traditions are offering congregations access to a new growing edge and ways to create an environment where safety, healing, and vitality predominate.

If we often miss the mark in our congregations, it remains that thousands of worshiping communities do provide a safe, wholesome, imaginative environment where miracles happen. For congregations large and small, urban and rural, conservative and liberal, this book gathers together some of best information and resources supporting such miracle work.

Audience

Accountable Leadership was written for two audiences: individuals preparing for leadership roles within a worshiping community and current practitioners who want a quick way to unpack the complex developments cropping up in the religious community over the past twenty-five years.

As I have noted, seminary students preparing for parish ministry typically bypass this subject matter. For most of this century it has been assumed that if the traditional theological curriculum is absorbed thoroughly, the practical, more utilitarian responsibilities of congregational life can be learned on the job. But new realities tear at the old assumptions. For instance, thousands of clergy are being terminated each year by unhappy governing boards, thousands of congregations are being sued each year, and congregations across the interfaith spectrum are confronting abuse within their own memberships.

It is crucial to the survival and health of religious communities that we learn to face these tough new circumstances rather than run from them. Religious leadership has always been an awesome challenge, after all, and tackling this material is much easier than mastering Greek or Hebrew. What is unconscionable is sending seminarians "into the field" without some background and guidance about the practical complexities of leading a faith family. The literature for such an education is being researched and written daily, but nowhere else is it surveyed comprehensively. *Accountable Leadership*, then, is for seminarians who want an overview of the vocation from an operative point of view.

The burden of lay leadership is not weighed down with the complexities of ordination. However, most religious communities make too little provision for training lay leaders, and the information here is as important to them as to clergy. A number of churches and synagogues bought copies of the first edition for all of the members of their governing boards.

This book is also intended for practiced leaders who see the value of a resource reference. The dozens of issues addressed here typically turn up on your doorstep without a manual. What do you need to know before committing the congregation to a $20,000 paint job? Look under "Contracting with Service Providers." When a child reports being abused, what is your legal responsibility? Look under "Zero Tolerance for Abusive Behavior." When one of the congregation's trustees, someone between jobs perhaps, asks the pastor for a church loan, what is the appropriate response? Look under "Responsible Financial Management." The suggested resources take you the next step of the journey when more information is needed.

The book may be most important to a group within the pool of seasoned leaders, those who climb the ladder of authority and find themselves responsible for groups of leaders—the bishop or conference minister, the elder or district superintendent. Unless these people have mastered the vast and still emerging literature, they should find this road map useful, a practical guide for staying at least one step ahead of the problems.

Overview of the Contents

Part One of *Accountable Leadership* contains chapters on leadership, law, and the governing board, all aimed at providing some sense of what it means to be accountable when you become a leader in a congregation. Part Two (Chapters Four, Five, Six, and Seven) begins by exploring ways to approach administration as empowerment rather than a burden. Chap-

ter Five, on finances, is one of the longest because so many issues insist
on our attention when we deal with money in the worshiping community.
After discussing the numbers, I turn to relationships with service providers
and professionals. Part Three (Chapters Eight, Nine, and Ten) examines
the invisible violence of abuse behind closed doors, concluding with a
chapter about healing the wounded congregation.

A number of issues mentioned in passing in the 1993 edition receive
more substantial attention this time. Fired clergy, troublesome members,
new church-state issues, the stormy ride of the 1993 Religious Freedom
Restoration Act, the legal issues involved with the congregation as
employer and pastoral counseling, and disturbing trends in reduced giving all are examined in more depth. I also detail a few of the ways that
government (from city hall to the IRS) is squeezing congregations financially. New literature unpacking dozens of issues relating to clergy sexual
abuse has grown enormously and is surveyed. Along the way, we will
observe how systems analysis, which studies the relationships between the
parts and the whole of any system, such as a congregation, is showing up
in several arenas, usually with new insights and good suggestions.

In 1996, William McKinney, a leading light in the development of congregational studies, took a leap of faith and accepted one of academia's most
formidable assignments—he became a seminary president. In an interview
when he arrived at Pacific School of Religion in Berkeley, McKinney said:

> We must remember that our calling is not only to produce skilled grad-
> uates but to equip the church for its ministry. And by this I don't mean
> just more courses in evangelism, stewardship, community leadership,
> religious education and preaching, as important as these may be.
>
> The questions facing our churches are far more fundamental. . . . Can
> we form—and reform—religious communities that truly empower men
> and women for ministries in family, workplace, and public life? Can we
> form—and reform—religious communities that help modern people dis-
> cover the claims and rhythms of biblical religion for their daily living?

From where I sit, Rev. McKinney has his finger on the salient questions,
and it is for each of us to live with the challenge. "There is no love which
does not become care," said a theologian. This book is designed for individuals who love the worshiping community and who seek the tools
enabling us to better care for one another.

Acknowledgments

First to be thanked are the hundreds of people who created the resources
surveyed in the following pages, their willingness to go where others had

not gone before, to ask new questions and teach us a renewed wisdom for leading accountably.

The several dozen supporters thanked in the first edition will always hold deed to a plot of land in my heart: Mineo Katagiri, Peter Keck, Ed Dantzig, Paul Hammer, Frank Heffernan, Paul Wankle, and John Deckenback all helped in the work's early stages. Roger Ridgway provided the ear that helped call forth the words, Annie Maisie Blend the encouragement and prayer, and Ralph Bertsche and Patricia Hetter Kelso the idea for the capital ownership that helped finance it all. James and Judy McKenney provided research, counsel, and support each step of the way. William Hulteen Jr., Jack Kelley, and Loren Mead shared generously from their particularly rich backgrounds to improve the text.

Many have offered expertise, critique, and encouragement. They include Gary Arnold, James Austin, Ronald Barton, William Bassett, James Berkley, Julie Bloss, Sheron Brunner, William Caldwell, James Cobble Jr., May Cotton, David and Anne Delaplane, Marie Fortune, Neil Gaston, David Goetz, Martin and Jan Haseman, Fred Hofheinz, Manfred Holck Jr., A. Robert Jaeger, John Lanehart, Speed Leas, Craig Brian Larson, Karen Lebacqz, Ritchie Lowry, Rennie Mau, Marvin Myers Jr., Debra Oliver, Joyce Parchman, David Philapart, David Roozen, Kibbie Ruth, Peter Rutter, Lyle Schaller, Adam Schneider, Bradley Sonderman, John Stanford, Bron Taylor, Barbara Thurman, Douglas Walrath, Robert Welch, James Wind, and the members of St. John's United Church of Christ in San Francisco.

For this revised edition, special thanks go to Gary Arnold, James Cobble, Nancy Myer Hopkins, and Loren Mead; to the agencies around the country that assisted in updating statistical data; to Jossey-Bass Publishers for being interested in the religious community; and to Sarah Polster, whose editing so improved this manuscript.

Gratitude is too small a word for what I owe Jan Chaffee, my partner and spouse and the light of my life. We have walked every step of this journey together and both feel blessed by the privilege. Each of our families is a gathering of blessings and has influenced this effort, particularly our parents, all four of them masters at making love more than a word to use. God bless you all.

San Francisco, California   PAUL CHAFFEE
January 1997

REFERENCE

McKinney, William. Interview. *Pacific School of Religion Bulletin,*
     Fall 1996, pp. 1–3.

THE AUTHOR

PAUL CLIFFORD CHAFFEE grew up in Asia, the son of Presbyterian missionaries, and received his seminary training at Pacific School of Religion. Before ordination in the United Church of Christ, he taught English literature at Emory and Henry College and served as a staff member for the Woodrow Wilson National Fellowship Foundation, the California Council for the Humanities, and the University of Southern California.

He has served a number of parishes in San Francisco and was church coordinator at the San Francisco Council of Churches for two years. *Accountable Leadership* was inspired by his parish ministry experience and eight years of research and writing for the property and casualty insurance program of the United Church of Christ. He is now executive director of the Interfaith Center at the Presidio in San Francisco.

PART ONE

BECOMING AN ACCOUNTABLE LEADER

BEHOLD, I DO NOT GIVE lectures or a little charity.
When I give, I give myself.

—Walt Whitman, *Song of Myself*

COURAGE AND
THE RESPONSIBILITIES
OF LEADERSHIP

THE BOY SAMUEL, falling asleep in the Holy of Holies, heard his name called. He answered by running across the Temple in Shiloh to find Eli, his blind mentor (1 Samuel 3:1–4). Three times came the call, and three times the child ran to Eli. Finally getting the point, Eli directs the child, tells him what he *needs to know* in order to respond. As the biblical text explains, "the word of the Lord had not yet been disclosed to him." The next time you hear the call, advises the old man, answer, "Here I am, Lord—your servant awaits you."

These were spiritually arid times, a generation without vision, and the religious leadership of Israel was failing. Blind Eli, slow to teach Samuel, failed as well to train his sons to be accountable leaders, and their behavior was the scandal of the nation. Where the elders failed, God chose a child to lead the people.

The boy Samuel recognizes and responds to the fourth call. God makes a request. Samuel's first task is to tell his mentor the truth. He must convey God's harsh judgment to the highest religious leader of the land, and, no surprise, it frightens him. He lies in bed through the dark hours of the night wrestling with the unexpected responsibility. In the morning light, he walks out of the Temple, and Eli calls out to him. The child is tongue-tied. But Eli, finally showing some courage, insists on hearing the entire message. The truth is spoken, and the children of Israel take their first step back into an authentic relationship with God.

Finding the Courage to Lead

The call to leadership need not be nearly so dramatic. It may be a telephone call from a nominating committee member or the simple realization that if *you* do not pick up a certain responsibility, no one will. It may feel lonely, as it did to Samuel in the wee hours of the morning. You may struggle with the commitment before saying yes. Throughout the biblical text, this struggle is dramatically reenacted. Many leaders avoid leadership at first, running away before being able to turn back and accept the challenge.

Moses resists the voice in the burning bush with quick excuses, and Jonah heads in the opposite direction when God calls. Jesus prays that he might not drink the cup, and Peter weeps after realizing how quickly raw fear has dissolved his loyalty to his master. Yet each of these leaders eventually was able to cut through the fear, to fulfill the call he heard.

Finding the courage and direction to be a leader is a spiritual matter and happens in different ways. The biblical record suggests that women sometimes are the quickest to learn. Young Esther, without a word of protest, joined the Persian king's harem, a pagan boudoir from whence she invaded the throne room and liberated her people. When the angel appears to young Mary to tell her a baby is coming, she understands the call in her heart and takes seriously the instruction to "fear not," instead to experience the joy accompanying the charge.

In accepting the call, you join a company of millions of courageous women and men through the centuries who have broken through their fears and been willing to shoulder specific responsibilities in service to God, the worshiping community, and its mission. In each of our traditions, these leaders are the saints on whose shoulders we stand. Their example instructs us when we learn to say, with Samuel, "Here I am, Lord—your servant awaits you."

At the same time, an uneducated enthusiasm can harm you. Abandon your fear but not your foresight. Religious communities can be as volatile as any other kind of family, and religious leaders, especially when ordained, are an almost inevitable target. Conflict comes with the territory, so learning how to deal with it, not running away, is critical.

Everyone knows how much more complicated the world has become in the past fifty years. Congregations, sentimentally regarded as guaranteed safe harbors, often reflect our unruly culture. At their best, congregations offer an ordered, healthy place for people to know each other, grow, and be productive and faithful. At their worst, they can provide petty tyrants a corner of influence, with plenty of people getting hurt in the process.

One-third of all churches forced their last pastor to resign. Norris Smith, full-time congregational consultant for the Southern Baptist Convention, opened the door to this sad story. His research in the early 1990s indicated that 116 Southern Baptist pastors were fired each month in 1988, up from 88 a month four years earlier (LaRue, 1996).

Research by Alban Institute senior consultant Speed Leas suggests that 6,000 clergy terminations annually is a conservative guess. Leas's study of six mainline denominations revealed 1.275 terminations per 100 practicing clergy. Southern Baptist congregations, with less denominational influence in the local setting than most traditions, experience a higher rate. The Baptist Sunday School Board estimates that 225 Baptist clergy are fired each year; with around 38,700 clergy serving parishioners, that comes to 7 percent a year ("Figures," 1996). With 350,000 congregations employing over 400,000 clergy, a calculation of 1.5 terminations per 100 suggests 6,000 such situations each year, or 60,000 in a decade.

When Leas and Smith were doing their initial work, little in the way of support or resources was available to those whose pastorate ends with a board moratorium to be "out of your office by Monday evening." In 1993, *Christian Ministry*, *Clergy Journal*, and *Leadership* all gave considerable ink to the issue of "forced exits," in each case relating the traumatic story of one or more pastors forced to leave a position.

These same periodicals and others have done considerable homework since then. Terminating a pastor is appropriate for sexual misconduct, financial malfeasance, serious doctrinal disagreement, or continuing incompetence. Most pastoral terminations, however, result from power struggles. In a 1994 Disciples of Christ study (Meece, 1994), 40 percent of clergy polled said that "undesignated power brokers" within the congregation have pressured them to resign at one time or another.

Often a clique of three or four (officers or former officers) takes things into its own hands, pressuring the pastor to leave and, after the deed is done, sweeping as much under the rug as possible. Eighty percent of the time, most congregation members are uninformed or misinformed about the real issues when they suddenly lose their pastor (Goetz, 1996). After one pastor is pushed out, it becomes much easier to do the same thing again, so many congregations become "repeat offenders." Denominations are only beginning to track this tragic tendency, and none has yet done much to turn it around.

These harsh realities will not deter the person who feels deeply called to a religious vocation, but they should inspire appropriate preparation. The following suggestions can be as useful to lay leaders as to clergy who find their leadership challenged.

SUGGESTIONS FOR PROSPECTIVE LEADERS

o Take conflict resolution workshops and survey the available literature described later in this text.

o Before accepting leadership positions, ask about any history of conflict in the group. In particular, ask those who formerly had the responsibility you are assuming, such as former pastors. Also talk to those who have stayed out of the leadership track but have been around for a while.

○ Build strong, healthy relationships, especially with those you serve, your denominational supervisor, and your support circle. All of them can help you handle problems before they escalate into conflict and crisis.

○ Pastors are wise to develop pastoral relations committees to have a safe arena in which problems can be addressed.

Clergy fired from congregations with denominational ties turn to their bishops and conference ministers about half the time when they are in trouble, and about half of such pleas receive significant help. Too often, however, the denominational officer has little real clout. It is easier to discipline a pastor than a congregation, and congregations, not clergy, pay the denomination's bills. So do not be optimistic about help on this front. Those leading independent congregations are particularly out on their own.

Ten years ago, the fired pastor had few places to turn. That has changed. In the journal *Leadership,* Wes and Judy Roberts periodically list agencies and programs that can provide comfort and support to clergy in distress. Their most recent article, "Who Cares for Pastors?" (1995), identifies three dozen such agencies. Barbara Gilbert's article "Where Can Clergy and Their Spouses Go for Help or Renewal?" (1993) also lists three dozen programs. Only six agencies are listed by both Gilbert, with her liberal connections, and the Roberts, with mostly evangelical associations. So be sure you know an agency's theological point of view and counseling approach before seeking its services.

In acknowledging the difficulties, however, let us not skew our perspective. Most pastors do not get fired, and only rarely are volunteer officers asked to step down. You can reduce your likelihood of facing such struggles by addressing the issues in this book. Leading a congregation is a daunting task, to be sure. Pastors and treasurers, youth workers and choir directors, all know the fear in the middle of the night Samuel experienced so long ago. At the same time, an educated excitement and the long-term satisfaction of local leadership can carry you through the fear like a raft on a white-water river.

Rest assured, you are not alone. Many, many others share the quest, and as never before, we have a growing body of information and good resources. Grasping the nature of your responsibility and how to respond accountably and ethically can be learned with dispatch.

That is fortunate since no one has much time for leadership training. In the past, learning about leadership could be the fruit of long experience. Before joining a governing council, one had time to become well established in the community and seasoned for the task. Nominating committees today cannot afford such leisurely attitudes. New members may relocate within several years, so they need to be tapped earlier in their tenure and prepared accordingly. Some congregations lose 30 percent of their membership annually and still manage to grow.

What Accountability Means

Accountability is the obligation one assumes in accepting the prerogative to lead the community in one way or another, make decisions, and act in its behalf. The word *accountability* comes from the fourteenth-century word *accounts,* meaning a record of money received and paid. King James II of England made the first recorded use of the word in 1688, when he said to his people, "I am accountable for all things that I openly and voluntarily do or say."

In short, being accountable means being answerable for your actions. It does not necessarily mean that you will succeed. James lost his throne within a year of making his pledge—due to religious quarrels! Nevertheless, accountability offers something better than success. It provides a measure of whether you are doing the best you can in the circumstances, important information however well you do.

Basic standards of accountability spring to mind when we consider what is expected of a good leader. The confidence that congregations vest in leaders assumes they will be faithful, informed, honest, fair, and responsible. Leaders need a clear understanding of the congregation and its organization. Combining prudence and imagination, they need to be able to work well with others, taking initiative, studying issues, leading groups, and making decisions.

A leader is expected to make trustworthy decisions and act ethically, a rigorous standard considering the novel ethical complexities we live with today. But some commonsense questions can quickly clarify the ethics of your response to most situations: Is your response honest? Is it legal? Does it promote your congregation's values and your own? Will you feel good about it afterward?

A strong, clear ethical point of view is important but, by itself, inadequate. Like Samuel, leaders *need to know* certain basic information. Ignorant leadership is dangerous leadership.

The first step concerns knowing yourself, whatever your faith family and your abilities. Never have the opportunities for personal growth and leadership development been greater in this country's religious community. Along with the spiritual resources in your own tradition, in its scripture and approach to the inner life, you can find a feast of retreats, workshops, books, tapes, periodicals, new research, consultants, and institutes that can support you in knowing yourself as you lead others. The *depth* of your exploration is the primary issue here, not how many journals you read or workshops you attend.

Knowing yourself is not entirely a spiritual matter. The Myers-Briggs Type Indicator, for instance, is a widely used test to learn about your "personality type." More useful but less widely known are the *perceiver interviews* that the Gallup organization has been developing with the company that bought it, Selection Research, Inc. (SRI), in Lincoln, Nebraska. This interview approach has been used in various professions for twenty-five years. Now it is being applied to religious leaders. Essentially, the process seeks to identify people "who make a significant difference in the lives of other people," a cardinal characteristic of powerful leadership (Rebeck, 1993, p. 671). SRI/Gallup interviews look for ability, motivation, and work-style: Can the person lead? Will the person lead? And how will the person lead?

In addition, SRI/Gallup works with individual denominations to identify a dozen or so characteristics or "gifts" held high by the corporate body. For the Church of the Nazarene, for instance, gifts hoped for in a pastor include focus, esteem, loyalty, empathy, caring, command, and business thinking. Perceiver interviews are not psychological, do not focus on personality type or particular flaws, and are not aimed at finding either the brightest or most experienced. Instead, these interviews assume that everyone has gifts and that some gifts are particularly useful in pastoral leadership. The goal of the interview is to fit an individual with specific talents to a specific job.

Knowing yourself, then, is the first step. Equally important is learning *the scope and details of the role you are assuming*. What are you agreeing to do? How will you be held accountable in the task? Elected, appointed, ordained, employed, or volunteering, being able to answer for decisions and action goes with the territory. So knowing what is expected, what is allowed and disallowed, and what is encouraged are all helpful. Many churches and temples maintain short "job descriptions" for all their officer and leadership roles.

Along with specific responsibilities comes the charge to support the welfare of the community as a whole. Together, laity and clergy, volunteers and staff, share the task of maintaining a community that at a minimum, is safe from abuse. Building an effective program, defining and working toward congregational goals, assuming legal responsibility, and overseeing risk management—these concerns fall on the shoulders of lay and ordained alike.

Joy and enormous satisfaction can be the fruit of authentic account-able leadership. Our work will never be faultless, biblical examples sug-gest. Yet the experience of being an effective vessel, an agent for God's pleasure, offers a deeper joy than all that glitters in the ego's eye. Accept-ing this gift is a learning experience, and all the learning we manage along the way can help.

Before I propose some standards of accountability that apply to all lead-ership, the implications of *ordaining* certain leaders deserve our attention.

Vesting Trust in Ordained Leaders

Most effective leadership is shared leadership. Nevertheless, distinctions need to be made between clergy and lay leaders. Some of these differences concern practical matters. In Protestant and Jewish settings, for example, the clergy tend to be employees and the laity employers, each side of the table calling for appropriate ethical, legal, and financial standards.

The greatest difference between clergy and laity comes from the per-sonal trust and authority vested in the clergy by the laity. Ordination and the pastoral role confer a form of power on clergy. It may be shunned by those uncomfortable with authority, but it is not escaped. Like any power, it comes with special responsibilities. Power is easily wasted and abused, often by well-intentioned clergy who have failed to examine the ethical imperatives of the role.

Until the mid-1980s, professional accountability in the worshiping community was rarely an issue. But today's crisis in leadership account-ability in most sectors of public life has not spared the religious institu-tion. Television and the press have found a bonanza in stories about fraud or sexual misconduct by clergy.

The religious community is responding. New books and articles address clerical standards. Religious magazines and seminary journals focus on eth-ical, legal, and financial responsibilities that exist throughout the worship-ing community. Seminaries are revamping their fieldwork so students become acquainted with issues of professional ethics in the worshiping com-munity. The causes of pastoral stress and burnout are better understood today. We know much more about the professional religious vocation—who is attracted, personality types that fit best, how much pay to expect.

Marriage turns out to be the number one enhancer of pastoral ministry, followed by preaching, a fulfilled sense of call, and the satisfactions of pas-toral care (LaRue, 1995). The issues that may vex and frustrate ministers and rabbis include congregational politics, financial shortfalls, and staff-board relations. For some clergy, sermon preparation and counseling create stress rather than meaning, and most pastors have enormous difficulty in seeing administrative responsibilities as part of their ministry.

Whether we are cataloging the satisfactions or the aggravations of the ministerial calling, the salient issue in both cases turns out to be the quality of our relationships. When they are good, all is well. When they sour, beware. Preventive maintenance for religious leaders suggests approaching friendship as a spiritual discipline.

Identifying Ethical Principles and Standards of Care

In the past, the high intentions and ethical correctness of religious leadership were assumed as a matter of course. Too many failures make such assumptions impossible any longer. Today, we need to clarify and communicate what we expect of responsible leadership. Two extremely valuable, underutilized systems exist to guide this clarification.

Establishing a *code of ethics* is one remedy, particularly useful because it provides ground rules for decision making. Deciding never to steal, for instance, is a personal guidepost for decisions. A code of ethics sets out principles that distinguish good and bad behavior in a particular community. Endorsing this code educates members about the behavior expected within the community.

The ethical illiteracy staining so much contemporary culture suggests that the religious community no longer adequately understands, models, or educates people ethically. It becomes doubly important for congregations to return to their own ethical wellsprings periodically for inspiration and instruction, to do the hard work of discovering the personal and corporate meanings of goodness and evil.

In this learning process, cooperate with whatever allies you find along the way. Goodness deserves all the help it can get! An important secular voice crying out in the ethical wilderness is the Josephson Institute of Ethics, a research and educational organization. It produces resources full of practical advice for returning ethics to U.S. culture. A number of these resources focus on young people, and the institute's tapes and books are excellent for inciting interest in ethical matters.

Along with *ethics,* the idea of *standards* is useful for accountable leaders. While ethical principles distinguish right from wrong and usually apply to everyone, the need to live up to certain standards may only apply to some. Failing to live up to a certain standard may be disappointing without being unethical. Both standards and ethics are important. Taken together, they represent the best strategy for avoiding the pitfalls of leadership.

Standard of care is a phrase from the law that applies to individuals vested with trust. Explicit standards of care apply whenever a person practices medicine or law, manages a financial asset, sells real estate, or in any other way assumes formal responsibility for a task requiring special trustworthiness. Accepting a leadership role in a congregation means receiving trust from your community. The task comes with high standards—the highest, one might hope. Yet defining these standards is not so easy. Honesty and good intentions are not nearly enough.

In the 1970s, pioneering work began raising the conscience and consciousness of the religious community on a number of fronts surveyed in this book. The proposed standards of care that follow distill this valuable work from one perspective. They are offered as guidelines for strengthening leaders and protecting them from the dangers of their role. Feel free to use them as a first draft of your own list.

SUGGESTED STANDARDS OF CARE FOR
CONGREGATIONAL LEADERS

1. With dedication and faithfulness, an accountable leader holds up the best interests of the community, offering a level of trustworthiness and faithful care expected of prudent leaders in similar circumstances.

2. An accountable leader is conscious of the power of the role, respecting and consistently living within the ethical boundaries that accompany such authority.

3. An accountable leader stays informed about the rules and records that order the community's life, the resources that may enrich it, and the requirements of the state.

4. An accountable leader creates a safe environment and safe institutional habits for the benefit of members, guests, and friends.

5. An accountable leader tells the truth.

6. An accountable leader gives special attention to all financial matters, abstaining from personal gain in congregational affairs and championing honesty.

7. An accountable leader oversees relationships, building and nurturing them both within the community and with strangers, guests, service providers, partner institutions, and the state.

8. An accountable leader leads, taking responsibility along with other leaders to move the community forward carefully.

9. An accountable leader nurtures self-respect in all, beginning with himself or herself.

Standards 1 and 2 are attitudinal. The first concerns a leader's care and commitment to the faith and the congregation. Caring for yourself more than for the family of God does the community little good, eventually becomes obvious, and breeds resentment and cynicism. Dedication, by contrast, is the fruit of a faithful life.

The second standard concerns a leader's attitude toward the role being assumed and is even more important than the first. It is abusive to cross the boundaries defined by our roles and take personal advantage of someone through the authority and power conferred by a leadership role. Stepping over appropriate boundaries betrays the trust the role confers. This is one standard with specific ethical implications.

Without these two attitudinal standards, the gifts of leadership easily become destructive. Embraced, they protect the community and guide its leaders.

The next six standards are all behavioral. Doing what they require does not guarantee anyone's success but ignoring any of them can be disastrous. Staying informed, standard 3, is where the task of leadership begins and the learning never ceases. Standard 4, the commitment to safety, receives plenty of lip service and not nearly enough actual attention. Congregations often are not nearly as safe as their members assume. The final third of the book explores how to make good our commitment to protect God's people.

Telling the truth, standard 5, may be the most obvious standard of care. It can also be complex and sometimes difficult to honor. Telling everything about everyone would be an ethical travesty, so full disclosure is not the point here. One begins by studying agreements, types of relationship, confidentiality, and the various meanings of truth-telling. Like being informed, learning to tell the truth is a lifelong process.

When the first five standards are observed, standard 6, about money, should not be a problem. In the eyes of the law, financial honesty is one of the most important requirements of leadership.

The next two standards, about relationships and community development, cover a universe. In a sense, maintaining healthy relationships and congregational vitality are goals rather than standards of care. Accountable leaders, however, learn to treat them as personal standards, arenas where they accept some responsibility for moving the membership toward the life it envisions. The importance of sharing leadership becomes paramount with these two standards. Sharing power, inspiring responsibility in all, seeking to balance, harmonize, and make fruitful the many in the one—these finally are the measure and the gift of good leadership in worshiping communities.

The final standard, like the first two, is attitudinal. Building self-respect is a subject unto itself and an important one given the lack of self-esteem in so many. Taking care of gifts and abilities, attending to personal well-being, clarifying and keeping agreements, all buttress the self-respect to be found in the experience of faith.

An easy, tempting way to stumble with self-respect is overwork. Fatigue and burnout can be contributors to clergy misconduct. Leadership that always has its foot on the accelerator, never the brake, is driving dangerously. Taking care of yourself empowers you to care for others. Wise leaders, realizing we have no scarcity of engaging assignments, keep seeking out new leaders, sharing insights and information, passing power along responsibly.

Living up to one's standards is a lifelong quest. Failing a standard you expect of yourself is a kind of betrayal. Not all such failures are serious, of course. Wearing brown shoes with a gray suit may betray your personal standards and make you uncomfortable, but it is not momentous. Failing to treat people fairly, which may also betray your standards and make you uncomfortable, deserves considerably more reflection than the color of anyone's shoes! Paying attention to standards is not a quest for perfection. But the exercise provides a foundation of accountability that helps keep the community and its leaders safe.

Including specific standards of care in worship services when commissioning leaders helps raise the congregation's consciousness about the quality of leadership the community can expect. Publicly declaring a commitment to high standards frees leaders to do their work well, all the while encouraging new people to bring forward their gifts to the beloved community. Faith is a call, and in spite of our fears, we can learn to be answerable to the call and be fruitful.

Most issues in this book are as applicable to Mormons as to Catholics, to Buddhists as to Baptists. The remainder of this chapter, however, focuses largely on Christian leadership development in North America. This is not to ignore leadership issues in other religions, but it is nearly impossible to talk about religious leadership without working from a specific religious framework, and Christianity is the dominant religion in this country. Non-Christians may learn from the always growing library published by their Christian counterparts. But they will also want to turn to their own traditions when considering the training, health, and evaluation of religious leadership.

Learning How to Lead

Should theological schools attend primarily to scripture, theology, history, and pastoral theology or to institutional dynamics, leadership formation, and management skills? Seminaries traditionally favor the former approach, mirroring the academic approach of colleges and universities. So the curriculum at many seminaries pays relatively little attention to practical issues of leadership and its nurture.

During the 1980s, this began to change. New doctor of ministry programs, aimed particularly at ministers wanting to hone their skills, were initiated at a number of theological schools. Field education today receives much more emphasis on most seminary campuses than it used to, and professors increasingly step away from the ivory tower environment to pay closer attention to the life and mission of actual congregations. Southwestern Baptist Seminary in Fort Worth, Texas, the largest theological school in the world, today has six faculty members teaching church administration. Fuller Theological Seminary in Pasadena, California, devotes a section of its curriculum to leadership training, and Atlanta's Interdenominational Theological Center now has an Institute of Church Administration and Management. In 1996, Claremont School of Theology established the Church Administration and Religious Institutions Study Center. A year earlier, the Claremont faculty decided to require all ministerial students to take a course about bringing administrative issues into a theological, pastoral context.

A strong case can still be made for the traditional academic approach. Seminaries produce hundreds of effective clergy each year by teaching the traditional disciplines. One can applaud this work while pointing to the need for additional skills. Many successful clergy grew up in thriving worshiping communities and enjoy in-born leadership strengths. For those without such advantages, it can be a different story. Many seminary graduates walk into their first job ill prepared to handle day-to-day duties and crises. Diploma in hand, they must begin their learning anew.

Alban Institute publications can help. *The Pastor as Newcomer,* by Roy Oswald (1977), is a hands-on guide for clergy in their first congregations, based on research about life after the "honeymoon." A companion publication is Loren Mead's *New Beginnings: The Pastorate Start-Up Workbook* (1989), a practical primer for beginning an ordained ministry effectively. A longer study examines problems causing new clergy to leave the profession. Titled *Beyond the Boundary: Meeting the Challenge of the First Years of Ministry* (Oswald, Harbaugh, Behrens, and Hudson, 1980), it is based on research in Episcopal, United Methodist, Presbyterian, and Lutheran congregations.

In the midst of this ferment, seminaries rightfully have been particularly concerned about what happens theologically when practical professional issues receive new emphasis. A distinguished series of books funded by Lilly Endowment in Indianapolis criticizes the idea of approaching ministry like other professions. The series begins with Edward Farley's *Theologia: The Fragmentation and Unity of Theological Education* (1983), continuing many books and ten years later with David Kelsey's *To Understand God: What's Theological About a Theological School?* (1993). These writers wish to redefine theology as a source of wisdom, not just a course requirement for a professional. For them, an academic package, a set of skills, and a seminary's seal of approval are inadequate. Theology is re-visioned as the authentic subject matter for understanding and leading a local congregation.

Outside the seminary, considerable interest can be found in clerical leadership. Since the 1970s, dozens of books have been published on the subject. Religious bookstores carry many examples, and you might order one of the following or find it in a library:

Effective Church Leadership: A Practical Sourcebook, by Harris W. Lee (1989), is an extraordinary compendium of information. It is excellent help for clergy and lay leaders who want resources to better understand themselves and the requirements of congregational leadership.

Ministers as Leaders, by Robert Dale (1984), looks at different leadership styles as well as different kinds of followers.

A bracing new approach to management and leadership is found in *The Empowering Church: How One Congregation Supports Lay People's Ministries in the World*, by Davida Foy Crabtree (1989). It suggests that congregations organize themselves to support the ministry of the laity during the week, and the meaning of religious leadership is redefined and deepened.

Twelve Keys to an Effective Church, by Kennon Callahan (1983), is a popular practical approach to leadership training and institutional revitalization. It focuses on twelve characteristics of "effective" congregations. A resource kit and audiotaped version of this book are also available from the publisher.

More recently, a crop of books that examine pastoral leadership from special perspectives has appeared.

James Abrahamson's message is caught in his title: *Put Your Best Foot Forward: How to Minister from Your Strength* (1994). Abrahamson suggests that effective congregations excel in at least one of six areas: worship, relationships, social action, teaching, evangelism, and preserving tradition.

The Contemplative Pastor, by Eugene Peterson (1993), approaches the ministry as a spiritual exercise and cuts to the heart of the pastoral impulse in a refreshing return to why people come together in the name of God.

Giving Birth: Reclaiming Biblical Metaphor for Pastoral Practice, by Margaret Hammer (1995), turns to scripture and church history to explore the metaphor of giving birth as a way to be a religious leader. It is full of insight and wisdom, exploring an organic kind of accountability for the vocation.

Very few books devote themselves entirely to the issue of accountability in the religious community. One of the few is *Organizing for Accountability: How to Avoid Crisis in Your Nonprofit Ministry*, by Robert Thompson and Gerald Thompson (1991). It calls to account the evangelical Christian community in the wake of scandals involving television evangelists. The book's coauthors are attorneys serving Campus Crusade for Christ and consultants in nonprofit legal and tax matters.

Their book is filled with good suggestions. The text shines a bright light on the structure of religious organizations, the responsibilities of decision-making, the law's demands, and ethical standards, particularly regarding money. Though aimed primarily at nonprofits concerned with church issues rather than at congregations themselves, it is an important contribution to the short shelf of resources concerning leadership accountability in the religious community.

In the crowded field of new leadership resources, a 1993 book by Lovett Weems Jr. stands out because it focuses on developing trustworthiness. Weems comes to the task with some special advantages—he is president of a Methodist seminary but came to the position after eighteen years in effective pastoral ministry. Well-read in the bibliography of leadership literature, he offers citations not only from the religious community but from excellent work in the secular nonprofit community, an arena religious leaders usually ignore, to their detriment.

The title of Weems's book reflects its outline: *Church Leadership: Vision, Team, Culture, and Integrity*. Throughout, he brings together issues of administration ("doing things right"), management ("doing the right things"), and leadership ("development and articulation of a shared vision, motivation of those key people without whom that vision cannot become a reality, and gaining cooperation of most of the people involved").

A Primary Resource: Lyle Schaller

When three thousand Protestant leaders were asked who had most influenced their thinking about religion in the United States, 43 percent named Lyle E. Schaller (Jacquet and Jones, 1991). Schaller has written three dozen books about the life and health of the local congregation, edited several dozen others in the Creative Leadership Series, and for thirty years has visited thousands of congregations in more than fifty denominations.

Ordained in the United Methodist Church, Schaller served as Parish Consultant of the Yokefellow Institute in Richmond, Indiana, from 1971 to 1993. Retired from Yokefellow at the age of seventy, he continues his writing and consulting unabated. He works on-site with congregations, based on their own concerns. "Over half" his work is with central-city congregations, many of them in ethnic minority traditions.

Schaller's most specific work on leadership is *Getting Things Done: Concepts and Skills for Leaders* (1986), which addresses both laity and clergy. His concerns for religious leadership, though, are at the heart of all his work. His writing is filled with examples, hundreds of stories gathered over years of consulting. The books run the gamut of issues confronted by the local worshiping community and are excellent choices for a congregation's library.

Anyone so successful for so long is not without his critics, particularly those attesting to his importance without affirming all of his priorities. Daniel Olson and Gary Peluso are fairly critical in twin articles in *Christian Century* (Olson, 1993; Peluso, 1993). Inexplicably, neither author talked to the unusually accessible Schaller. So each study depends exclusively on the books, "not on what I do," as Schaller said shortly after the articles were published.

The sad reality is that a bias against hands-on ministry endures in the theological academy. Schaller has never been awarded an honorary doctorate from a seminary, a quiet but stunning measure of the academic prejudice against his hands-on approach and his abiding focus on the dynamics of congregational life. Thank goodness his contribution is available to everyone. Most of his books are available through Abingdon Press in Nashville, including the excellent Creative Leadership Series he edits.

In choosing from the explosion of books about church growth, begin with Schaller. A concern for institutional growth and development infuses all his work. He focuses primarily on the Protestant community, but anyone interested in religious leadership can sit profitably at the feet of this master of the local parish. In spite of a breakneck schedule, Schaller remains accessible. He can be reached at 530 North Brainard Street, Naperville, IL 60563; (630) 355–0817.

Specialized Periodicals

A number of periodicals focus on ordained parish leadership, the best in the United States being *The Christian Ministry, Clergy Journal, Leadership, Net Results,* and *Congregations. Clergy Journal,* the oldest of the five, was founded in the thirties. It remains dedicated to better church management, is full of useful articles about the many aspects of parish ministry, and regularly publishes the work of Julie Bloss and Lyle Schaller, two names that crop up in these pages.

The Christian Ministry, sister publication to *The Christian Century,* emphasizes practical ministerial subject matter, preaching, and a compendium of religious news, "tricks of the trade," and anecdotes.

Leadership is the largest of these journals, a bit more expensive and evangelical than the others, and can be commended for its considerable research into congregational life. *Net Results* has a different focus than the rest, being more preoccupied with the business of church business—issues like improving worship, church growth, taking advantage of computers, and getting local media attention. It is published in cooperation with the evangelism divisions of four denominations and several church-related groups, is full of practical ideas for running a tight ship, and provides another venue for the prolific Lyle Schaller.

The best of the bunch for this reader is *Congregations.* The shortest of the four and subtitled *The Alban Journal,* it comes every other month as a benefit of membership in the Alban Institute (it is not available as a separate subscription). It depends as much on research as opinion and is expert at providing guidance when you want to go further with a subject than a particular article happens to take you.

Ministry Today, a publication from England, receives high marks. Also, most denominations have their own publications for congregational leaders. *Church,* published by Roman Catholics, and *Church Administration,* from the Southern Baptist Convention, are particularly good, covering much the same territory as the nonaffiliated journals. The common element in the denominational arena is care for the local congregation. Unlike most religious publications, these periodicals tend to give less attention to theological differences and conservative-liberal divisions than to research and insight into the subtle dynamics of a worshiping community and its leaders.

Parachurch Resources

Leadership training, group dynamics, management theory, organizational development, fundraising, and the vitality of nonprofit organizations have all become important issues in mainstream culture. In the absence of seminary involvement in lay leadership development, a cottage industry of parachurch organizations has emerged to fill the gap.

The word *parachurch* has been used to characterize everything from religious think-tanks to televangelists. The parachurch movement is much larger than any single organization (and no more prone to bad faith and scandal than any other sector of society). Parachurch groups, both profit and nonprofit ventures, serve the religious community in dozens of ways, usually without being formally connected to a particular denomination.

Congregations with budget troubles, membership loss, conflicted leadership, training needs, and administrative breakdown are turning to these organizations to take advantage of the special expertise they offer. Thousands of consultants, institutes, retreat centers, professional associations, publications, and businesses have emerged to supply congregations with a supermarket of services and products. According to one estimate, three out of four dollars spent on religious leadership development takes place outside of the seminary context (Schaller, 1986, p. 9).

The four groups I will profile here are all well-established parachurch organizations providing excellent value for the dollar invested. Though very different from each other, they are mentioned time and again in these pages because *each is effectively dedicated to bringing home the issue of accountability* in the churches and temples of our land.

The Alban Institute provides training, research, and consultation, along with excellent publications about day-to-day concerns in the life of local congregations. Its catalog is a treasure for leaders of congregations, lay and clergy, and it holds workshops all over the country. It would not be an exaggeration to say that Alban and its founder, Loren Mead, have been prime movers in making the fruit of serious congregational studies available to North American churches. In 1995, the institute had 8,183 individual members, sponsored 42 workshops, sold 112,605 books and reports, and provided consulting to 20 different denominations and 265 congregations and judicatories!

The Center for the Prevention of Sexual and Domestic Violence is another excellent organization. Like the Alban Institute, the center is a pioneering agency, the first organization in the world dedicated to helping religious congregations free themselves from hidden abuse. The center provides consulting and produces excellent teaching resources aimed at exposing and preventing the tragedies of clergy sexual misconduct and domestic violence.

Christian Ministry Resources (CMR) is *the* important source for legal information about clergy, congregations, and denominations. CMR's *Church Law and Tax Report,* written by Richard Hammar, is the only periodical of its kind. CMR also publishes newsletters for congregational secretaries and treasurers. Its books on church copyright law, the congregation as employer, clergy compensation, and annual tax developments are standards in the field, a measure against which anything new must be tested. Despite its name, CMR is essentially an interfaith resource—its subject matter applies to all religious leaders and institutions subject to the laws of the United States of America.

Christianity Today, Inc. (CTI) publishes a family of periodicals about church life from an evangelical Christian perspective. Attractively designed magazines address church history, religious life and culture, leadership, campus life, marriage relationships, and church maintenance and supplies. *Leadership,* aimed at ministers, regularly explores accountability issues. The firm's flagship publication, *Christianity Today,* is evangelical competition to the older, more liberal *Christian Century;* both address religion and culture, often featuring articles about leadership, ethics, and accountability. *Your Church* is an important if undervalued CTI publication, sent free to 180,000 congregations (supported by advertisements for everything from choir robes to church mortgages). The forty-year-old magazine offers a banquet of practical information about property, buildings, their furnishings and maintenance, insurance, new technology, law, and finance. In recent years, under researcher John LaRue Jr.'s byline, *Your Church* has published considerable CTI research on the lives and work of church employees, including pastors. Long considered "an advertising rag," this publication should be mandatory reading for seminary presidents and judicatory officers. Most pastors know how important it is.

Each of these organizations, or each of its component parts, attends to a particular arena. They all pursue original research in specific subject areas, and all deserve their excellent reputations. To these four can be added thousands of others hoping to serve congregations in one way or another. Once the major denominations funded large research offices, but these have all grown small or been disbanded. Parachurch groups are filling the research gap, with one organization—Lilly Endowment—standing apart from all the others.

Lilly Endowment's Unique Contribution

In 1937, Eli Lilly, with his father and brother, established Lilly Endowment with gifts of stock in their pharmaceutical business, Eli Lilly and Company. Lilly's leadership introduced science to an industry then dominated by patent medicines, which claimed to cure every affliction from hangnail to heart attack. Revolutionizing drug manufacturing in the process, Lilly guided the company through the development of insulin for diabetes and into enormous success and wealth.

His influence set *religion* next to *education* and *community* as one of the three central concerns of Lilly Endowment. A leader on the vestry of Christ Church Cathedral in downtown Indianapolis, Lilly contributed financial support, wrote a history of the congregation, and found himself personally fascinated with the problems of character development. The religious curiosity and instincts of this Episcopalian layman, who died in

1977, flowered into hundreds of millions of dollars devoted to religion in the United States.

Most foundations keep the door closed to religious concerns. Lilly Endowment, by contrast, funds research, training, and development to strengthen religion in the United States. In 1991, for instance, 218 grants totaling $28.5 million went to 138 religious institutions, a third of this money aimed at improving the quality of theological education. In 1995, $24.8 million went to 129 grantees. Truly ecumenical, the endowment funds groups as diverse as the Society of Biblical Literature, the Fellowship of Christian Athletes, the National Federation of Priests' Councils, and the Bread for the World Institute on Hunger and Development.

Lilly Endowment grantees publish dozens of books. Its own publications, reporting research results, circulate to religious leaders throughout the nation and to anyone else who requests them. *Progressions: A Lilly Endowment Occasional Report* constitutes a fascinating periodical series. Each issue addresses a particular arena of concern and features half a dozen writers, the cream of the crop of American religious journalists, who survey what Lilly-funded scholars have studied.

Besides theological education, Lilly's religious preoccupations include leadership development, congregational life, and the financial realities religious institutions face. Lilly projects frequently study problems of the nation's different religions.

Lilly is research based, *and* it aims to make a difference with what it learns. Built into the research and data collection is funding for training and development to support individuals and institutions endeavoring to improve the quality of religious life. One of a kind, Lilly Endowment is an unsung partner of worshiping communities.

The assets of Lilly Endowment set it apart from other parachurch groups. Most of them lack a secure income flow and depend on contributions, grants, and fees for services. Many parachurch efforts operate more out of love and concern than an adequate budget. A number succeed, offering good value for services rendered and doing everyone a favor with their work.

Each group has to be evaluated both on its merits and its ability to support *your* interests. Be careful about names and reputations: it is easy to confuse *Church Law and Tax Report,* published by Christian Ministry Resources, with seminars titled "Clergy, Tax and Law," offered by Michael Chitwood. The former is the country's only major periodical on law, litigation, and taxes relating to worshiping communities and their leaders. Chitwood, by contrast, was the subject of an article in the *Dallas Morning News* in March 1992 that raised questions regarding the credentials he advertised (Hammar, 1992, p. 10).

But do not be discouraged from seeking new resources, including consultants. You can usually check a person's credentials with a few phone calls. Whatever difficulty confronts your congregation, good people are available who understand the issue and can offer help.

Developing Character and Trust

In the quest for research, resources, consultants, guidelines, safe systems, and individual and institutional integrity, we make a mistake if we lose sight of the central process—an individual seeking to serve God and care for the worshiping community. Church historian Martin Marty observes, "Religious organizations are scurrying to provide better networks of control, to minimize temptation, to anticipate troubles, to create a climate in which abuse of all sorts is prevented or dealt with. We may need a heavier dose of Aristotle: more concern for ethos, character, and what makes a good person" ("What Others Are Saying," 1992, p. 2).

Indeed, the issue of character in a leader needs more of our attention. Individual definitions of leadership often bypass ethical considerations. A denominational executive might say, "Leadership is an activity that prompts, undergirds, or discourages describable outlook and behavior in the lives of persons, organizations, and communities." A social activist would say, "A leader is somebody people follow."

Both definitions are true, but neither tells us whether the successful leader fitting these definitions is good and faithful or inadequate and corrupt. Neither tells us whether following such leaders means being empowered or manipulated.

The issue of accountability provides an ethical keel to the discussion. The touchstone of accountable leadership is trustworthiness, not success. The breakdown of accountable leadership is betrayal, not failure. This distinction is not a tool for sitting in judgment. After all, most human beings betray and suffer betrayal at various points in their lives. Biblical texts overflow with the problem. Israel's greatest monarch, King David, found occasion to betray his loved ones, friends, and even God. Simon Peter walks into his role as leader of a brand new congregation by dramatically, repeatedly betraying his master. The issue is not who has betrayed anyone else, but how to rediscover, earn, and deserve the trust of others.

For decades, the U.S. public had a particularly high regard for clergy. It peaked in the late 1970s and early 1980s when two out of three people had a high opinion of clerical ethics and honesty. By 1993, that confidence had fallen from 67 to 52 percent, a considerable tumble (Gallup, 1993).

Over a decade of unprecedented religious scandal and a flood of church- and clergy-related litigation have taken their toll. Research in congregations that have suffered clergy sexual misconduct reveal great depths of unexpressed anger. This anger and sorrow is easily displaced, aimed at various unsuspecting targets—the next pastor, the victim of abuse, or "the bishop." Often, the emotional upset is locked up in secrets, so airing it is difficult (Hopkins, 1993).

The first-time pastor, walking into this kind of minefield, flushed with the success of seminary graduation, may think that trust is available for the asking. It is not. It must be earned, often at great expense, often after considerable healing within a badly wounded congregation. Trust remains the currency even when there is none around.

It is like learning to be a good parent. Cultivate honesty, tempered with gentleness. Start out realizing you will not be perfect and that inevitably some will snipe at you. It comes with the job. Be a full participant: do not disappear on clean-up days. Be engaged and get others engaged. A mundane willingness to clean the dirtiest corners occasionally builds trust faster than a season of sermons. Learn to be flexible and develop a variety of skills. Do not stand on the sidelines; lead and lead others to lead. Be reflective about what you do, but do not lose touch with your spontaneity.

Give away the credit, the praise. Appreciate everyone's contribution and give the glory to God. Above all, through prayer, counseling, or the school of hard knocks, learn to relinquish the need to control. As a leadership strategy, control is just one step ahead of chaos. Except when a leader is facing a clear and sudden danger, control erodes trust instead of building it.

The path beyond control is Celia Hahn's theme in *Growing in Authority, Relinquishing Control* (1994). Hahn is editor-in-chief at the Alban Institute and currently responsible for its remarkable journal *Congregations*. Her book offers a developmental analysis of authority that moves from control to trust-building. Authority is as slippery a subject as humility, and anyone with leadership aspirations must wrestle with it, too. Hahn is a helpful guide in the process.

Too many of us, like the biblical Eli, neglect the issues of authority and accountability and lose our trustworthiness. Too few of us love God with the investment of care and achievement we find in someone like Eli Lilly. Understanding accountability encourages us to learn *how* to be trustworthy and fruitful as we share leadership with each other in the worshiping community.

Going the Next Step

This book surveys the broad canvas of congregational leadership and suggests basic guidelines in a number of different arenas. It also aims to help you find more information about any particular subject. At the end of each chapter, you will find the means for contacting the agencies and finding the periodicals and books surveyed in the text.

A little digging in any good religious bookstore or seminary library will usually uncover material on the subjects reviewed here. In some cases— for example, congregational growth—the material surveyed barely cracks open the door to what is available.

Likewise, the agencies and periodicals listed in this book are superb, whether you subscribe to the theological assumptions each represents or not. But they are only a handful of the thousands of religious nonprofit enterprises across the land, each devoted to a particular cause. Desktop publishing, the Internet, and similar new technologies have not been ignored by those who study, love, and work for corporate religious life. So you are likely to find virtual communities, connected through both electronic and print media, full of people who care about the same issues that matter to you.

In short, the levels of your interest, commitment, and need-to-know are the only boundaries to your ongoing education, whatever the subject. Lyle Schaller is a perfect model of such education, with his dozens of books always plowing new ground.

Beyond the resources listed at the end of this chapter and elsewhere in this book, remember that every month sees the publication of new contributions in the arena of religious leadership. It is a fascinating dialogue.

Resources for the Responsibilities of Leadership

Agencies

Alban Institute, Suite 433 North, 4550 Montgomery Avenue, Bethesda, MD 20814; (800) 486–1318.

Center for the Prevention of Sexual and Domestic Violence, 936 North 34th Street, Suite 200, Seattle, WA 98103; (206) 634–1903.

Christian Ministry Resources, P.O. Box 1098, Matthews, NC 28106; (704) 841–8066.

Christianity Today, Inc., 465 Gundersen Drive, Carol Stream, IL 60188; (708) 260–6200.

Church Administration and Religious Institutions Study Center, 1325 North College Avenue, Claremont, CA 91711; (909) 626–3521.

Consulting Psychologists Press, 3803 East Bayshore Road, Palo Alto, CA 94303; (415) 969–8901. (Publishes the Myers-Briggs Type Indicator.)

Institute of Church Administration and Management, 700 Martin Luther King Drive, SW, Atlanta, GA 30314; (404) 688–5960.

Josephson Institute of Ethics, 4640 Admiralty Way, Suite 1001, Marina Del
   Rey, CA 90292; (310) 306–1868.
Lilly Endowment, 2801 North Meridian Street, P.O. Box 88068, Indianapolis,
   IN 46208–0068; (317) 924–5471.

Periodicals

The Christian Century, The Christian Century, 407 South Dearborn Street,
   Chicago, IL 60605; (312) 427–2714.
The Christian Ministry, The Christian Century, 407 South Dearborn Street,
   Chicago, IL 60605; (312) 427–2714.
Christianity Today, Christianity Today, Inc., 465 Gundersen Drive, Carol
   Stream, IL 60188; (708) 260–6200.
Church, National Pastoral Life Center, 18 Bleecker Street, New York, NY
   10012; (212) 431–7825.
Church Administration, Sunday School Board of the Southern Baptist
   Convention, 127 Ninth Avenue North, Nashville, TN 37234;
   (800) 458–2772.
Church Law and Tax Report, Christian Ministry Resources, P.O. Box 1098,
   Matthews, NC 28106; (704) 841–8066.
Clergy Journal, Logos Productions, Inc., 6160 Carmen Avenue East, Inver
   Grove Heights, MN 55076; (800) 328–0200.
Congregations, Alban Institute, Suite 433 North, 4550 Montgomery Avenue,
   Bethesda, MD 20814; (800) 486–1318. (Formerly named *Action
   Information.*)
Leadership: A Practical Journal for Church Leaders, Christianity Today, Inc.,
   465 Gundersen Drive, Carol Stream, IL 60188; (708) 260–6200.
Ministry Today, Richard Baxter Institute for Ministry, 82 Watchhouse Road,
   Galleywood, Chelmsford, Essex CM2 8NH, England.
Net Results, 201 Eighth Avenue South, P.O. Box 801, Nashville, TN
   37202–0801; (800) 672–1789.
Progressions: A Lilly Endowment Occasional Report, 2801 North
   Meridian Street, P.O. Box 88068, Indianapolis, IN 46208–0068;
   (317) 924–5471.
Your Church, Christianity Today, Inc., 465 Gundersen Drive,
   Carol Stream, IL 60188; (708) 260–6200.

Books and Articles

Abrahamson, James O. *Put Your Best Foot Forward: How to Minister from
   Your Strength.* Nashville, Tenn.: Abingdon Press, 1994.

Callahan, Kennon L. *Twelve Keys to an Effective Church.* San Francisco: Harper San Francisco, 1983.

Crabtree, Davida F. *The Empowering Church: How One Congregation Supports Lay People's Ministries in the World.* Bethesda, Md.: Alban Institute, 1989.

Dale, Robert. *Ministers as Leaders.* Nashville, Tenn.: Broadman & Holman, 1984.

Farley, Edward. *Theologia: The Fragmentation and Unity of Theological Education.* Minneapolis: Augsburg Fortress, 1983.

"Figures Show that Church Firings Waste Lives, Witness, Money." *National Christian Reporter,* Oct. 18, 1996, p. 1.

Gallup, George, Jr. "Confidence in Clergy Found Slipping Steadily." *National Christian Reporter,* Nov. 12, 1993, p. 3.

Gilbert, Barbara. "Where Can Clergy and Their Spouses Go for Help or Renewal?" *Congregations,* May/June 1993, pp. 19–22.

Goetz, David L. "Forced Out." *Leadership,* Winter 1996, pp. 40–49.

Hahn, Celia A. *Growing in Authority, Relinquishing Control: A New Approach to Faithful Leadership.* Bethesda, Md.: Alban Institute, 1994.

Hahn, Celia A. "Losing Control—and Gaining Authority." *Christian Ministry,* Jan./Feb. 1995, pp. 11–14.

Hammar, Richard. "Michael Chitwood and 'Clergy, Tax and Law.'" *Church Law and Tax Report,* July/Aug. 1992, pp. 10–11.

Hammer, Margaret L. *Giving Birth: Reclaiming Biblical Metaphor for Pastoral Practice.* Louisville, Ky.: Westminster/John Knox, 1995.

Hopkins, Nancy Myer. "Symbolic Church Fights: The Hidden Agenda When Clerical Trust Has Been Betrayed." *Congregations,* May/June 1993, pp. 15–18.

"How Pure Must a Pastor Be?" *Leadership,* Spring 1988, pp. 12–20.

Jacquet, Constant H., Jr., and Jones, Alice M. (eds.). *Yearbook of American and Canadian Churches, 1991.* New York: National Council of Churches of the U.S.A., 1991.

Kelsey, David. *To Understand God: What's Theological About a Theological School?* Louisville, Ky.: Westminster/John Knox, 1993.

LaRue, John C., Jr. "Profile of Today's Pastor: Ministry Ups and Downs." *Your Church,* July/Aug. 1995, p. 48.

LaRue, John C., Jr. "Forced Exits: Preparation and Survival." *Your Church,* July/Aug. 1996, p. 64.

Lee, Harris W. *Effective Church Leadership: A Practical Sourcebook.* Minneapolis: Augsburg Fortress, 1989.

Mead, Loren. *New Beginnings: The Pastorate Start-Up Workbook.* Bethesda, Md.: Alban Institute, 1989.

Mead, Loren. *The Once and Future Church*. Bethesda, Md.: Alban Institute, 1991.

Meece, Bernie. "You're Outta Here! When the Pastor Must Go." *Disciple,* June 1994, pp. 26–27.

Nimmo, Charlene. "Who's Running the Church and Who Ran Off the Pastor?" *Disciple,* May 1995, pp. 10–11.

Olson, Daniel V. A. "Learning from Lyle Schaller: Social Aspects of Congregations." *Christian Century,* Jan. 27, 1993, pp. 82–84.

Oswald, Roy M. *The Pastor as Newcomer*. Bethesda, Md.: Alban Institute, 1977.

Oswald, Roy M., Harbaugh, Gary L., Behrens, William C., and Hudson, Jill M. *Beyond the Boundary: Meeting the Challenge of the First Years of Ministry.* Bethesda, Md.: Alban Institute, 1980.

Peluso, Gary E. "What Is Lyle Schaller's Vision of the Church?" *Christian Century,* Jan. 27, 1993, pp. 85–87.

Peterson, Eugene H. *The Contemplative Pastor*. Grand Rapids, Mich.: Eerdmans, 1993.

Rebeck, Victoria A. "Gifted for Ministry: Setting Up Pastors for Success." *Christian Century,* June 30, 1993, pp. 670–675.

Roberts, Wes, and Roberts, Judy. "Who Cares for Pastors?" *Leadership,* Summer 1995, pp. 76–78.

Schaefer, Arthur. "Divine Immunity: Should Clergy Be Subject to a Standard of Care?" *CPCU* Journal, Dec. 1987, pp. 217–218.

Schaller, Lyle E. *Getting Things Done: Concepts and Skills for Leaders.* Nashville, Tenn.: Abingdon Press, 1986.

Schaller, Lyle E. *The Seven-Day-a-Week Church*. Nashville, Tenn.: Abingdon Press, 1992.

Smith, Michael. "Pastors Under Fire: A Personal Report." *Christian Century,* Feb. 23, 1994, pp. 196–199.

Thompson, Robert R., and Thompson, Gerald R. *Organizing for Accountability: How to Avoid Crisis in Your Nonprofit Ministry.* Wheaton, Ill.: Shaw, 1991.

Weems, Lovett H., Jr. *Church Leadership: Vision, Team, Culture, and Integrity.* Nashville, Tenn.: Abingdon Press, 1993.

"What Others Are Saying." *National Christian Reporter,* Dec. 18, 1992, p. 2.

2

WHAT THE LAW REQUIRES

THE LEGAL RESPONSIBILITIES of elected or employed officers of religious organizations have become significantly more complicated in the past twenty-five years. Federal, state, and local laws bearing on congregations have multiplied, and in their wake ensues the duty to comply with regulations. Most religious groups are organized as nonprofit corporations, so nonprofit law typically applies to them. As nonprofit law develops, so do requirements placed on the congregation. In 1991, for example, California began *requiring* churches and synagogues (along with businesses) to establish and maintain an active safety program.

Along with new legislation, the threat of litigation has grown, and leaders need to know why and how to respond. Following the explosion of litigation against physicians in the mid-1970s, clergy and congregations found themselves taken to court starting in the 1980s (Schaefer, 1987).

Suing a religious institution was unthinkable thirty years ago. A major factor in reversing this attitude has been sexual abuse. One respected Catholic sociologist suggests that 2,000 to 4,000 Catholic priests, out of 53,000, have sexually abused children ("Clergy Sex Abuse Widespread, Says Priest"), a stunning figure when you remember that the tragedy has emerged with equal ferocity throughout the religious community. In the Roman Catholic case, projections suggest that over $1 billion will be paid in legal settlements by the year 2000.

Alleged abuse is but one of many reasons why hundreds of congregations are taken to court. In the mid-1990s, financial crime replaced sexual misconduct as the primary source of newspaper headlines devoted to religious scandal. Conflict with employees is another factor in the explosion of litigation involving congregations.

Nine hundred churches responded to *Church Law and Tax Report*'s 1996 questionnaire regarding litigation (Hammar, 1996b). Five percent reported being sued within the last five years, figures suggesting that across the nation, over 3,000 congregations are sued annually. Sixteen percent have paid a claim for injury to a member in the past five years.

To complicate matters, ongoing judgments from the courts constantly modify the legal status quo, particularly when attorneys and judges have little legal precedent to turn to for direction. In the 1980s, a number of major issues emerged from this abundant litigation, including the question, "Can I be held personally liable for the debts and court judgments against my congregation?"

If you have not broken the law or been grossly negligent, and if your congregation is legally organized as a nonprofit corporation, the answer to this stark question is usually no. Leaders in unincorporated congregations are much more vulnerable. Corporate structure was created to protect regular members from such liability, and many states protect uncompensated officers and directors from personal liability in cases of "ordinary" negligence. The obvious importance of the question, though, indicates the legal seriousness of leadership accountability.

The central idea behind the modern corporation was created by a thirteenth-century lawyer in Genoa, Italy, who went on to become Pope Innocent IV. His idea is the *persona ficta,* or fictional person. Innocent recognized that only human beings can be held responsible for their actions. But who is to blame for the actions of the group? Can you blame every member of a church if the church bus brakes fail on the way to summer camp? To this day, groups that successfully incorporate are given a *persona ficta* that takes the blame when the group is responsible for harm done to someone. The group purchases insurance in case its fictional person is assessed damages, and everyone can go home and rest easy.

Still, the legal protection enjoyed by a nonprofit corporation should not lull a governing board into a false sense of security. "Director and officers" (D&O) insurance coverage is still valuable, because anyone can be sued for almost any reason, and you want to be able to defend yourself in court. Being exonerated does not pay the legal fees, but good D&O coverage will. This financial protection is much less expensive for the nonprofit than for the for-profit corporation.

We hope that our ethical standards in a worshiping community exceed the law's demand. Most leaders, ordained and otherwise, bring courage and high standards to their calling. They are models of honesty within the worshiping community. From archbishops to local trustees, however, the cold bath of litigation is forcing leaders of religious institutions to re-examine themselves and their institutional ethics. Abuse of power, the temptation to hide the failures of leadership, and a general ignorance of the law continue to harm congregations today as in the past. Later, in Part Three, we examine specific legal risks inherent in employee relations—particularly sexual misconduct and the problem of "ascending" liability. In the process of learning about these matters, we must not bemoan all religious encounters with the law or demonize attorneys. Congregations and most people of faith are loath to let their private conflicts see the light of day, either in the newspaper or in a court of law. But the court sometimes helps those, such as abused children, whom a congregation has failed. Approached wisely, the courts can be your friend. The treasurer of the Episcopal Church stole $2.2 million, and the denomination's insurance was good only for $1 million. Should denomination leaders sue the treasurer? They did and prevailed.

Habits That Protect You

Corporate board members in the business community are legally required to work "in good faith, in a manner such director believes to be in the best interests of the corporation and with such care, including reasonable inquiry, as an ordinarily prudent person in a like position would use under similar circumstances." (This language from the California Corporations Code Section 5231(a) is typical of state requirements for board members.) The same standard of intelligent, loyal care is appropriate for clergy and lay leadership and may, under some circumstances, be legally required.

Richard Hammar's article "The Legal Liability of Church Board Members" (1988) is an excellent discussion of legal responsibility from the perspective of congregational decision makers. More extended discussions of leadership liability are found in Hammar's *Pastor, Church and Law* (1991a) and Richard Couser's *Ministry and the American Legal System* (1993).

In the eyes of the law, loyalty in a church or synagogue leader means that she or he will hold high the best interests of the congregation. This includes a commitment to obey the law and to refuse to profit financially from or through her or his responsibility.

Refusing to profit does not keep leaders hired by the congregation from receiving their salaries, of course; gainful employment is not, in the eyes of the law, profiting through the responsibility. But all employees remunerated by the congregation need to be accountable to the governing board.

Some states, such as California, have a "49 percent" rule, which allows less than half the board members of a nonprofit corporation to provide services to that corporation for remuneration as long as it is done with everyone's full knowledge, in a fair manner consistent with the organization's bylaws and for the organization's best interests. Check your own state law before paying a board member any fee for services.

A congregation's governing body is, generally speaking, legally responsible for most of what happens at the institution, including off-site activities. Leaders are expected to assume this responsibility in good faith. Jim Bakker of the PTL Television Network was sentenced to forty-five years in prison for his bad faith and the consequent fraud. The court said to Bakker, "Good faith requires the undivided loyalty of a corporate director or officer—and such a duty of loyalty prohibits the director or officer. . . . from using this position of trust for his own personal gain to the detriment of the corporation."

The following practices are not all required by the law, but they express good faith and give substance to our desire to be responsible in leadership activity. They can be useful not only to members of the governing body but to anyone doing congregational business.

SUGGESTIONS FOR DECISION MAKERS

○ Remember the purpose and mission of your congregation, and always work for its best interests.

○ Keep handy and become familiar with your constitution and bylaws. They define the critical rules of the game that the congregation has legally accepted for itself. For some congregations, articles of association or articles of incorporation take the place of a constitution.

○ Be known for your faithful attendance at meetings and keep careful records of your work.

○ Being a yes-person all the time is as disastrous as being a no-person all the time. Take responsibility for your own decisions. Without intellectual independence and integrity, a leader devalues his or her role in the community.

○ Brush up your analytical skills! Remember to listen to *all* points of view. Ask questions until you are satisfied that everything is on the table. Be willing to make mistakes and, on discovering them, be quick to correct yourself.

○ Give financial documents and decisions special attention. When you do not understand a financial issue or report, continue asking questions until you do. If you object to a financial decision, voice your concern, and have your vote recorded in the minutes.

○ Let your conscience be your guide when voting, and be willing to disagree.

○ Investigate difficulties, seeking a healing outcome. Sweeping problems under the rug usually guarantees bigger problems in the future.

○ Follow the rules. This includes obeying the law, spending money as designated by appropriate decision-making bodies, and following the strictures of the congregation's founding and corporate documents.

○ Build at least two people into the process that authorizes and tracks money pledged, collected, and disbursed; both should be fully active in the process. The best person to propose a more-than-one policy is the treasurer, to keep feelings from being hurt.

○ Turn to experts when making decisions regarding property, legal matters, and bonds or securities associated with fundraising. Securities law is particularly complex and demanding, with both the agents and the securities requiring registration, unless specifically exempted.

○ Make a habit of talking about important issues to members of the congregation, help keep lines of communication open, and correct false rumors.

○ Learn to be a wise employer. The relationship between clergy and a governing board is complex and in need of ongoing respect and care. Abuse can come from either side of this relationship.

○ Be fair and affirming to other employees, the secretary, choir director, and custodian and to volunteers, vendors, and contracted service providers.

Maintaining a Legal Frame of Reference

Leadership means carrying a greater burden of responsibility *before the law* than other organizational members. This does not mean that you need to become a lawyer, nor does it mean that most decisions made by a governing board need the nod of an attorney. It does suggest the wisdom of knowing the scope of your responsibilities and endeavoring to fulfill them in good faith. Leaders are legally enjoined to be prudent, careful with the authority entrusted to them.

Some specific legal constraints exist that leaders need to know.

SUGGESTIONS FOR OBEYING THE LAW

○ Resist self-dealing, gaining any personal financial profit from your leadership activity. (As noted earlier, this does not preclude being compensated for employment or, in some states, receiving fees for services. Self-dealing, in contrast, employs secrecy and deception and sacrifices organizational interests in favor of personal interests.)

o Bylaws define the scope of leadership responsibility and the procedures for decision making in the community. They deserve to be treated as legally binding. Ignoring bylaws undermines any leader's credibility and record. If existing bylaws do not serve the congregation well, go through the appropriate procedures to amend them.

o Contract law is an elaborate system for keeping promises. Leaders need to know how the contracts work. Breach of a contract creates financial vulnerability. Never sign a contract for the congregation without authorization or without indicating your official role. Legally, the use of the preposition *by* when signing establishes that the signer is acting as an agent and, consequently, is not *personally* liable (as long as signing is within the scope of his or her authority).

o Never voice a congregation's endorsement or support of a political candidate. Joining a candidate's political campaign threatens your nonprofit tax exemption. Endorsing and supporting legislation *is* allowed, however, as long as it does not represent a substantial portion (more than 10 or 15 percent) of the congregation's program or budget. (Be aware that this last guideline, established when Lyndon Johnson was president, is back in the courts. The IRS revoked the tax-exempt status of a congregation that published ads attacking Bill Clinton's candidacy for president. The church is fighting back in the courts, arguing that allowing candidate appearances in front of congregations while forbidding partisan ads about those same candidates is an unfair double standard. Stay posted.)

The Problem of Negligence

A critical factor in accountable leadership is avoiding negligence. Most civil suits against congregations involve injury as a result of allegedly negligent leadership. "Taking care" may come naturally to a faithful person; in the eyes of the court, it is *mandatory* for leaders vested with corporate authority. In some states, directors and officers are held personally liable when they negligently perform their duties.

Here are some examples of negligent leadership:

o To knowingly allow an unsafe condition to exist in the facility or in an activity that causes injury or death

o To write checks against insufficient funds

○ To supervise activities carelessly, so that injury or death results

○ To allow or authorize copyright infringement

○ To make false statements to a potential donor, lender, or extender of credit

○ To terminate an employee for an insufficient or impermissible reason (for filing a workers' compensation claim, for instance, or for refusing to backdate a check)

○ To cause injury through careless driving while on congregational business

Avoiding negligence and having a good sense of the scope of your responsibilities as defined in the organization's bylaws is important, but it cannot substitute for the services of lawyers versed in the legal and taxation issues faced by congregations.

In short, negligence causes accidents, and accidents cause pain and suffering. Lawsuits and severe court judgments may result. One of the purposes to which this book is dedicated is providing information that can help you keep negligence at bay while caring for the people, property, and program of your community.

The Larger Legal Issues

The vitality of over 300,000 local congregations free to believe and worship as they wish is a hard-won, extraordinary benefit of living in this country. We take this freedom quite for granted, and we need to wake up and be vigilant if it is to endure.

Religious freedom in the United States rests on two different principles, which, like the poles of a magnet, are in tension. We can thank the writers of our Constitution for including both principles in the First Amendment to that document. One is found in the establishment clause, which states that "Congress shall make no law respecting an establishment of religion." The second is found in the free exercise clause, which says that "Congress shall make no law . . . prohibiting the free exercise [of religion]." Should ordained clergy get any tax breaks? Yes, if you favor free exercise; no, if you favor the establishment clause.

Should a parent be forced to send his or her child to a physician if it violates the parent's faith? Should an American Indian be allowed to use peyote in worship? Should the Amish people be required to put orange triangles on their buggies? Should religious organizations be exempted from paying property taxes and assessments?

Line up a list of these questions, and you may well find yourself favoring one clause part of the time, the other clause part of the time. The wisdom of having both these difficult clauses becomes clearer. It is a wisdom with fuzzy edges, though, so most church-state issues can and are debated up and down, frontward and backward.

The student of constitutional law and religious freedom enjoys a library of resources and a multitude of issues to study. Something much more immediate, however, calls religious practitioners into this arena. Church-state decisions made by the courts have enormous impact on the day-to-day life of worshiping communities. For the past dozen years, for instance, lawyers have debated whether congregations should have ultimate say over their own property or whether state law and historical commissions should sometimes be the final arbiters concerning the fate of a temple, mosque, or church.

The Religious Freedom Restoration Act

Congress passed the Religious Freedom Restoration Act in 1993, legislation strengthening the rights of religious organizations. The new law was inspired by a 1990 Supreme Court decision that reversed a quarter century of legal precedent and "virtually repealed the first amendment guaranty of religious freedom" (Hammar, 1993, p. 12). Specifically, the court said that the government does not need a good reason—"a compelling governmental interest," in legalese—to act in ways that burden the religious community.

The 1993 act restores the requirement that government have a "compelling" interest before it walks on the toes of the religious community. This gives congregations and their leaders special consideration when they come into conflict with thousands of laws, ranging from employment to zoning.

The new act was tested when St. Peter's, a Catholic church in Boerne, Texas, wished to replace its chapel with a larger sanctuary. City hall said no, claiming the existing beautiful Spanish-style sanctuary was a historical treasure. A lower court sided with Boerne, dubbing the new act unconstitutional. Then on January 23, 1996, the Fifth U.S. Circuit Court of Appeals reversed that decision, and St. Peter's prevailed. On October 15, 1996, the U.S. Supreme Court agreed to hear the case.

The Religious Freedom Restoration Act strengthens the legal position of every member of the nation's congregations, but it is still being challenged and debated. A New Jersey appeals court, for example, has ruled that the standards defining malpractice for psychiatrists, psychologists, and social workers can also be legally applied to pastors serving in a counseling role. This judgment effectively denies the long-held right of privacy surrounding pastoral counseling, a right that previously kept the court out of the pastoral office.

In the New Jersey case, a woman is suing her former priest for having sexual relations with her, a clear violation of New Jersey's professional standards for therapists and nonreligious counselors. Unless reversed by the Supreme Court, this decision means that hundreds of women who have had sexual relations with their ministers, priests, and rabbis have new and strong grounds to sue these clergy for everything they have.

The privacy issue came up again after the secret recording of a Catholic priest hearing confession from an inmate in an Oregon prison in April, 1996. The religious community was outraged, and the priest asked for and received the tape from the prosecutor. Two months later, legislation designed to protect "privileged religious communication" was introduced into Congress by Peter King (R-NY).

In short, all of these issues matter enormously and end up influencing our lives and congregations. And most of them are influenced by various judicial views of the rights of the religious community. Whatever the particular issue, whatever your perspective, the religious community badly needs leaders better educated about church-state relations and better able to communicate with their own constituencies and the public. Often one or two matters, such as abortion or homosexuality, claim the attention of everyone, including the media. Then all sorts of important issues go largely unnoticed.

The Religious Freedom Restoration Act gives religious groups new strength, if it endures. Hammar was pessimistic in a 1995 article on this topic, but his 1996 discussion was much more upbeat. Meanwhile, in July 1996, a federal judge in Maryland said no to the act ("Strikes Another Blow," 1996), and a month later a Wisconsin federal appeals judge said yes ("Ruled Constitutional," 1996). Because so much is at stake and because the nation's judges are in disagreement, the Supreme Court will have to weigh in again. After inspiring the act with its 1990 decision, the court will again face the constitutionality of the "compelling government interest" solution crafted by Congress and the president.

Whether we take it for granted or not, the issue of religious freedom is a living, breathing phenomenon and influences our lives. Even as the meaning of the 1993 act is forged, one decision at a time, there are those in Congress who are promoting a religion Constitutional amendment (Anderson, 1996). If that idea takes off, you will read and hear about it many times before it lands.

Squeezed by the State

Epidemic litigation and constitutional law are two of several legal arenas where an aggressive economy seeks to leverage everything to its own advantage, including worshiping communities.

Another area of ongoing contention concerns the tax privileges that nonprofit institutions receive (privileges detailed in the next chapter). In particular, freedom from property taxes and tax-deductibility of financial donations have kept nonprofits, including most congregations, alive. The Internal Revenue Service, the religiously unaffiliated, and "tax reformers" who fail to see the contributions worshiping communities make to the community-at-large, keep inventing ways to intercept some of the cash flow keeping congregations viable.

Examples abound. As of January 1, 1994, the IRS decided that all gifts to congregations of $250 or more have to generate a receipt if the gift is to be tax deductible to the donor. The net result? Increased paperwork for congregations and much better information for the IRS about how much income religious organizations receive. Alone among nonprofits, religious congregations do not have to report their annual receipts; clearly though, the agents are knocking at the door.

A more proactive attack was made in Colorado. A November 1996 proposal asked voters to end property tax exemptions for nonprofits, including five thousand churches, synagogues, and mosques. The proposal would have allowed exemptions for church-based shelters that provide housing for abused spouses but not for churches that provide free counseling to battered women (Rabey, 1996). The yield to the state of Colorado would have been $70 million a year, with the average homeowner saving about $44 in annual taxes. Fortunately for everyone who participates in this nation's religious communities, Colorado voters roundly defeated the much-debated proposition.

A much subtler approach is the flat tax that Steve Forbes proposed in the 1996 Republican presidential primaries. A flat tax would take a significant tax benefit away from those who donate money to nonprofits, including congregations. Leaders in the nonprofit and religious communities pointed out the disastrous possibilities, but their objections received scant attention in the national debate.

California is particularly imaginative in going after religious money. A 1991 proposal in the Berkeley City Council to tax the offering plate lasted just long enough to generate a roar of ecclesiastical disapproval. In Thousand Oaks, local politicians came close to passing a fire-protection assessment that would have raised one congregation's annual municipal assessments from $760 a year to $5,760. Other, similar attempts have been successful. For example, because local taxes are so hard to pass in California, county and municipal governments now levy "assessments" from property owners, and religious organizations are not exempted. The California Constitution clearly forbids the state from levying property taxes on congregations; assessment is a euphemism that lets local governments do it anyway. In fact, many religious leaders do not object to assessments for local fire and police protection and emergency services, taking the attitude that "we can pay our fair share" for services received.

Nevertheless, the distance between "assess" and "tax" is frighteningly small. In San Francisco, the Community Facilities District 90–1 Special Tax (to make public school classrooms earthquake-proof) exempts space used "exclusively" for worship. All other church property in the city is taxed by the statute at $46 per parcel per year, and congregations with multiple properties pay accordingly, even when a property is being used for a day-care center or a women's shelter.

When asked why the tax was not challenged, the attorney of record for the city's largest religious landowner, insisting on anonymity, said, "We've got so many other problems that this thing just doesn't get much priority. Litigation costs too much to challenge a $46 tax." Taken together, however, San Francisco church, temple, and mosque members are paying over $30,000 a year in tax monies to help public schools. It is a good cause, an illegal tax, and a terrible precedent for the religious community.

Randall Balmer, who writes for the Religious News Service, reports: "I detect considerable resentment of the tax-exempt status of religious organizations these days. It is an issue that arouses the passions of many who believe that tax exemption actually constitutes a form of subsidy for religious organizations, a subsidy borne by all taxpayers" (1993, p. 2). Religious leaders who want to insure the financial future of their institutions will do more than have an opinion and take things for granted. They will participate in public affairs, continue creating programs that benefit the community-at-large, and remind the world that congregations and nonprofits need gentle treatment if they are to continue their important work.

Going the Next Step

Until the 1990s, "church law" meant canonical law, the rules whereby a religious body governs itself. Ten years ago, we had no books about laws governing congregations and clergy, and the separation of church and state suggested we never would. That myth was put to rest when the variety of issues I have discussed here indicated a clear need for new resources and for experts who can define the evolving legal context in which congregations and their leaders live and who can provide guidance in an increasingly complicated, litigious society.

A Primary Resource

Richard Hammar (who holds J.D. and LL.M. degrees and is also a CPA) was the first to step forward, and he remains the preeminent expert in law relating to congregations and clergy in the United States. His book *Pastor, Church and Law* (now in its second edition, 1991) is comprehensive and thorough, with over a thousand pages of well-indexed discussion. *The Church Guide to Copyright Law* (also in its second edition, 1990a) is the most thorough book on the subject. It is marketed with an audiotape to be used in staff meetings and copies of a brochure that can quickly educate choir members about increasingly strict copyright law. Hammar's publisher, Christian Ministry Resources, is also responsible for Julie Bloss's *Church Guide to Employment Law* (1993), again the best book on the subject.

Richard Hammar's most important contribution is *Church Law and Tax Report*, a bimonthly publication specifically written for the religious community. It provides an ongoing discussion of legal and tax-related issues by reviewing church-related litigation throughout the nation. Leaders in large congregations and of denominations ignore this information at their peril.

In addition to its publications, Christian Ministry Resources offers seminars in law, tax, and administration for religious leaders, as well as access to a legal database that can keep your congregation's attorney apprised of new developments in the law that could affect your congregation and its leaders.

Hammar no longer has to be a one-man show now that Richard Couser has published *Ministry and the American Legal System* (1993), a book that deserves to stand next to Hammar's classic, *Pastor, Church and Law*. Couser's book covers at least as much territory, is more user-friendly with its rich indexes and bibliography, and does better at summarizing the applicable constitutional history and issues. Any attorney serving a congregation should have both Hammar's and Couser's works.

New Legal Specialities

Others are following in Hammar's and Couser's wake. Julie Bloss's book has been mentioned and will be reviewed in Chapter Six. Carl Lansing's *Legal Defense Handbook: For Christians in Ministry* (1992) is helpful regarding congregation-attorney relations and preventing and responding to lawsuits.

The legal realities of religious counseling raise a particularly complex web of issues. Two good books on the subject were published in 1993, *Legal Issues and Religious Counseling,* by Ronald Bullis and Cynthia Mazur, and *Law for the Christian Counselor,* by George Ohlschlager and Peter Mosgofian. The books have very different goals, but each team of authors brings to the task impressive professional credentials.

Bullis and Mazur focus on the threat of litigation to counselors working under the church's umbrella. For those uninitiated in the world of jurisprudence, the book offers a useful introduction before tackling specific issues. It is well written, full of good advice, and includes several comparative charts of relevant state law, reason enough to buy this inexpensive book. It does not pretend to be comprehensive.

Law for the Christian Counselor is much more ambitious. Three times as long, it sets out "to reveal current and developing law that impacts counseling practice, instructing you how to keep the law, prevent client harm, and avoid lawsuits" (Ohlschlager and Mosgofian, 1993, p. 4). The book is remarkably thorough. Where Bullis and Mazur give a page to working with suicidal counselees, Ohlschlager and Mosgofian devote a detailed chapter, all of it useful to a professional.

What also sets *Law for the Christian Counselor* apart from the rest of the legal library discussed here is its frankly theological point of view. The authors discuss their posture as evangelical Christians and the fact that they bring faith issues into the discussion. Readers to both the left and right will disagree on particular issues, but the authors' forthright self-critical point of view is refreshing. Their willingness to bring their faith perspectives to bear on legal professional issues offers the reader the same opportunity. And their genuine respect for and insight into the law serves to raise the interests of the counselee to the same importance as the interests of the counselor and church in being protected from litigation's ruins. Astute religious counselors will treat the book as a second bible.

Constitutional law has a long and distinguished bibliography, and important new books are published and reviewed in the religious press regularly. *The Journal of Church and State* and *Religious Freedom Reporter* are aimed primarily at lawyers, discuss church-state issues, and survey legislation and case law as it is made. *Church and State* is a publication of Americans United for Separation of Church and State. For background on religion and politics in America, read *Religion and Politics,* edited by James Wood Jr. of Baylor University's Dawson Institute for Church-State Studies.

The most thorough scholarly study of property taxes for the religious community is "Tax Exemption of Church Property: Historical Anomaly or Valid Constitutional Practice?" by John Witte Jr. (1991).

Throughout the religious community there is considerable debate about whether the Constitution has it right yet, whether we need more religiously inspired constitutional amendments, and whether we should modify the strange dance between the establishment and free exercise clauses out of which comes religious freedom as we know it today. Both liberal and conservative commentators have been highly critical of recent Supreme Court decisions, and a number of books are addressing the central issues in depth.

That Godless Court? Supreme Court Decisions on Church-State Relationship, by Ronald Flowers (1994), is a helpful primer in the history and developments of the First Amendment and its two clauses about religion. The book clarifies the historical relationship between religion and government in this nation. *Securing Religious Liberty: Principles for Judicial Interpretation of the Religion Clauses,* by Jesse Choper (1995), makes anew the case that the two clauses are both important and that without the intertwining claims they make we would lose what is important in our religious freedom.

Resources for Legal Requirements

Agencies

Christian Ministry Resources, P.O. Box 1098, Matthews, NC 28106;
(704) 841–8066.
Church-State Resource Center, Campbell University, P.O. Box 505, Buies Creek,
NC 27506; (910) 893–1804.
J. M. Dawson Institute of Church-State Studies, Baylor University, P.O. Box
97308, Waco, TX 76798–7308; (817) 755–1011.

Periodicals

Church and State, Americans United for Separation of Church and State, 1816
Jefferson Place, NW, Washington, DC 20036; (202) 466–3234.
Church Law and Tax Report, Christian Ministry Resources, P.O. Box 1098,
Matthews, NC 28106; (704) 841–8066.
The Journal of Church and State, J. M. Dawson Institute of Church-State
Studies, Baylor University, P.O. Box 97308, Waco, TX 76798–7308;
(817) 755–1011.

Religious Freedom Reporter, Church-State Resource Center, Campbell
  University, P.O. Box 505, Buies Creek, NC 27506; (910) 893–1804.

Books and Articles

Anderson, David E. "The 'Religious Freedom' Amendment More About Elections Than Eternity." *National Christian Reporter,* Aug. 16, 1996, p. 1.

Balmer, Randall. "Churches' Tax-Exempt Status Under Scrutiny." *National
  Christian Reporter,* Feb. 19, 1993, p. 2.

Bloss, Julie L. *The Church Guide to Employment Law.* Matthews, N.C.:
  Church Ministry Resources, 1993.

Bullis, Ronald K., and Mazur, Cynthia S. *Legal Issues and Religious Counseling.* Louisville, Ky.: Westminster/John Knox, 1993.

Buzzard, Lynn R., and Robinson, Sherra. *IRS Political Activity Restrictions on
  Churches and Charitable Ministries.* Buies Creek, N.C.: Church-State
  Resource Center, 1990.

Choper, Jesse H. *Securing Religious Liberty: Principles for Judicial Interpretation of the Religion Clauses.* Chicago: University of Chicago Press, 1995.

"Clergy Sex Abuse Widespread, Says Priest." *Christian Century,* Apr. 14, 1993,
  pp. 392–393.

Couser, Richard B. *Ministry and the American Legal System.* Minneapolis:
  Augsburg Fortress, 1993.

Flowers, Ronald B. *That Godless Court? Supreme Court Decisions on Church-
  State Relationship.* Louisville, Ky.: Westminster/John Knox, 1994.

Hammar, Richard. "The Legal Liability of Church Board Members." *Church
  Law and Tax Report,* Jan./Feb. 1988, pp. 6–8.

Hammar, Richard. *The Church Guide to Copyright Law.* (2nd ed.) Matthews,
  N.C.: Christian Ministry Resources, 1990a.

Hammar, Richard. "Three States Act to Limit Church Liability." *Church Law
  and Tax Report,* Jan./Feb. 1990b, pp. 1–5.

Hammar, Richard. *Pastor, Church and Law.* (2nd ed.) Matthews, N.C.: Christian Ministry Resources, 1991a.

Hammar, Richard. "The Personal Liability of the Members of an Unincorporated Church for the Church's Liabilities." *Church Law and Tax Report,*
  Sept./Oct. 1991b, pp. 1–4.

Hammar, Richard. "The Religious Freedom Restoration Act." *Church Law and
  Tax Report,* Sept./Oct. 1993, pp. 12–14.

Hammar, Richard. "Religious Freedom Restoration Act Declared Unconstitutional." *Church Law and Tax Report,* Sept./Oct. 1995, p. 24.

Hammar, Richard. "Freedom of Religion." *Church Law and Tax Report,*
  July/Aug. 1996a, pp. 24–25.

Hammar, Richard. "A Legal Profile of American Churches." *Church Law and Tax Report,* July/Aug. 1996b, p. 30.

Lansing, Carl F. *The Legal Defense Handbook: For Christians in Ministry.* Colorado Springs, Colo.: Navpress, 1992.

Ohlschlager, George, and Mosgofian, Peter. *Law for the Christian Counselor.* Irving, Tex.: Word, 1993.

Rabey, Steve. "Proposed Tax Amendment Targets Churches, Nonprofits." *Christianity Today,* Mar. 4, 1996, pp. 74–75.

"Ruled Constitutional." *National Christian Reporter,* Aug. 16, 1996, p. 1.

Schaefer, Arthur. "Divine Immunity: Should Clergy Be Subject to a Standard of Care?" *CPCU* Journal, Dec. 1987, pp. 217–218.

"Strikes Another Blow." *National Christian Reporter,* July 12, 1996, p. 1.

Witte, John, Jr. "Tax Exemption of Church Property: Historical Anomaly or Valid Constitutional Practice?" *South California Law Review,* Jan. 1991, 64(2), 363–415.

Wood, James E., Jr. (ed). *Religion and Politics.* Waco, Tex.: J. M. Dawson Institute for Church-State Studies, Baylor University, 1983.

3

THE ROLE OF THE
GOVERNING BOARD

THE GOVERNING BOARD of any religious institution plays a critical role in maintaining its health and effectiveness. The board is charged with the duty of directing the affairs of the congregation. Its members are its decision makers. Such groups come in many configurations labeled with different names—councils, vestries, sessions, trustees, and so on. Whatever the language used to describe it, the governing board represents the membership and makes decisions for it except when a vote from the "whole body" is needed or requested. Even in traditions where clergy have significantly more authority than the laity, such as the Roman Catholic Church, councils of priests and lay leaders may hold considerable influence and responsibility for the life of the community.

In thousands of congregations, the governing board is made up of committee chairs, one or two at-large members, specially elected board officers, and clergy, who may or not be authorized to vote when decisions are made. In the eyes of the law, this group is authorized to act on behalf of the congregation, following the institution's rules, between meetings of the full membership.

Because this group has the purse and the ultimate decision-making power in a congregation, the accountability that comes with the task is considerable. Poor relations between the board and the pastor (or, we might say, between the employer and the employed, or between the lay and the ordained) are a serious problem. When this critical relationship among leaders goes sour, the happiness and health of the membership is jeopardized. In contrast, a happy, engaged working relationship between clergy and board officers is a signal of good things to come.

The Scope of the Task

Every year hundreds of thousands of faithful worshipers are elected for the first time to the council or board that governs their house of worship and its membership. These new members may be handed a job description or invited to a retreat to prepare them for the work, but usually there is very little preparation or leadership training for the task at hand.

Two important responsibilities for the board or council members, the "officers" of the "corporation," are shaping policy and overseeing the daily operations of the congregation.

Learning to Shape Policy

Policy formation is a crucial role of the governing body, though often it is not used to advantage. Corporate law charges decision-making boards with writing and publishing policy for the corporate community, in this case the worshiping family. Like the constitution and bylaws that govern the long-term "rules of the game" for a congregation, statements of policy articulate the ongoing guidelines and agreements between the community and each member.

Successful policy and its implementation conform to the community's constitution and bylaws, support its purpose and goals, increase safety, and discourage negligence.

Most decisions made by governing bodies address single issues and fall short of the policy arena. A policy is a generalization about an agreed-upon way of behaving. Policy in this sense ranges from a government's decisions on how to treat international trade to the instructions posted inside the kitchen cabinet on how to make an urn of coffee.

Policy ranges from the general to the specific. In the broadest sense, policies reflect the basic values and goals of the community. An effective *general policy* is like a map that gives the community its direction. *Specific policies* clarify details. *Guidelines* call for certain kinds of behavior. *Norms* may define the programs and activities of the community, and *sanctions* offer special permissions ("the choir director keeps the key to the organ") as well as penalties ("drink at youth camp and you'll be driven home").

The interesting but difficult work of defining and implementing policy is learning how to deal with conflicting goals. Keeping the sanctuary in good shape and giving to mission projects may both be policies embraced by a congregation. But when resources are limited, leaders need to decide how to balance the different needs. The process of developing policy is often as important as the policy that is finally voted. The process can build consensus and educate people at the same time. Eventually, *procedures* emerge to implement specific policies.

A congregation's *employment policy* reflects how it screens, hires, pays, evaluates, disciplines, and terminates employees. *Personnel policy* defines the various responsibilities and benefits of employment. *Policies against sexual harassment* are being called for in many congregations, along with policies and standards regarding counseling, youth leadership, and child abuse reporting.

The quality of a congregation's *financial policies* helps make fiscal operations difficult or easy, careless or accountable. *Policy about outside users* can turn wasted space into a financial resource. *Safety policy,* when it is implemented, decreases accidents and saves lives, emotions, and budgets. Congregational leaders need considerable wisdom in discerning which issues are to be addressed by policy and which policies need publication.

The smaller the congregation, usually the more hands-on responsibility the governing board takes. The same individuals who recommend and vote a policy may be the only ones in a position to implement it. A small congregation caught between clergy assignments may call on board members temporarily to assume all the operational responsibilities of the community—preaching, praying, and paying the bills!

As congregations grow, boards do less policy implementation. The board focuses on governing (that is, steering the community through its decisions), and the staff focuses on program and management. Employees tend to have more prerogatives, including responsibilities for administrative policy and managing day-to-day operations. Clergy and other members of the staff need both support and freedom in developing the congregation's program.

Balanced against this, governing boards need to oversee and evaluate the work of all employees. Particularly in unaffiliated independent congregations, the board plays the critical role of ensuring that its employees are accountable for their work and regularly evaluated. In larger congregations, the board often evaluates the senior clergy, who in turn are sanctioned to evaluate others on the staff. A strong argument to evaluate any leader with significant power is made in *Organizing for Accountability: How to Avoid Crisis in Your Nonprofit Ministry* (Thompson and Thompson, 1991). However, this does not diminish the ongoing need to support and affirm good leadership.

Governing board policy appropriately addresses larger issues—those that affect the life of the whole community. Precisely because these issues matter to us all, policy is usually made slowly. A board may decide the congregation will give at least 20 percent of its budget each year to mission.

For such a policy to be effective, for it to be a genuine congregational commitment and goal, it will require considerable public discussion and a vote of the membership before becoming policy.

Articulating and publishing policy often begins with some kind of study group. Before the board votes and publishes rules regarding sexual harassment, for instance, all members of the congregation can be included in the learning process. Sermons and newsletter articles, a chance to discuss the issue with young and old, and input from expert resources all contribute to effective policy formulation on this issue. Policy then can emerge that is authentic, prudent, useful in building a safer community, and supported by all. (Sample policy language concerning harassment in the worshiping community is presented in Chapter Ten.)

The study and policy adoption process differs with each issue. A trustee study committee, for instance, may recommend a policy to rekey all locks and replace distributed keys following burglaries. The committee probably did its homework with law officers, a locksmith, and the congregation's insurance agent, not the membership at large.

Rather than burying policy language in meeting minutes, boards need to publish new policy, making it accessible to those affected by it. A sexual harassment policy, for instance, needs periodic notice and discussion. Every prospective employee needs to read the congregation's personnel policy. Every youth volunteer needs to be exposed to congregational policies relating to children.

Fortunately, policy is written and refined over the years, not reinvented with each new leadership election. Overseeing policy is an ongoing task. Policy can empower a congregation in numerous ways, or it can inhibit the group and make interaction more difficult. Discerning the difference and acting accordingly is one of the gifts of accountable leadership.

An important warning comes with policy formation. Policy that is passed and not implemented can become a thorn in the flesh and a financial liability. Imagine yourself in a witness chair answering a lawyer's questions about a convicted pedophile your congregation hired:

"Has First Church established policy about hiring new employees, specifically about requiring references and screening?"

"Yes."

"When Joe Doe was hired to drive the church bus, did you call any references or do any screening?"

"Well, not exactly. One of our members knows a cousin of his and vouched for him. He was such a nice guy . . ."

The mercy of the court tends to dry up after this kind of exchange.

In short, having no policy, a weak institutional posture to be sure, is better than passing policy that is ignored. Ignored policy does not help potential victims, and it can inspire significant financial judgments during litigation.

Overseeing Day-to-Day Operations

The governing board makes decisions, usually through proposing and voting specific motions, that provide the framework wherein day-to-day business is done. Keeping a permanent record of this business through regularly recording, correcting, and approving minutes is critical. Today's decisions always rest on yesterday's. Not having a record creates an organizational vacuum. Without a paper trail charting its course, the congregation loses its institutional memory and identity. So good record-keeping is the first step in being accountable.

Working within the framework of its constitution, bylaws, and any operational policy it writes for itself, the governing board needs to know and be in agreement about how it makes decisions. *Robert's Rules of Order* or a similar set of meeting rules is usually used, though *Robert's Rules* is justly criticized for being divisive and overly elaborate. The most important issue is not which system is used but that the method chosen be fair and effective in defining the common good, then acting in its behalf.

Institutional habit, ethnic background, and even theology will influence how any particular governing board does its work. An American missionary hired to teach on the faculty of a Japanese Christian university was surprised at the first faculty meeting she attended. After considerable discussion, no decisions were made, no motions passed. When this happened a second time, she went to a colleague who spoke English and asked what was going on. "When will we finally make some decisions?" With a smile, the Japanese professor explained that decisions had been made all along. "We talk until we know where everyone stands—but we would never embarrass the minority with a vote." The legal framework in the United States makes taking recorded votes a prudent, responsible way to do business. But the Japanese comparison reminds us of how many different ways groups of people can responsibly make decisions together.

New members on a governing board may be surprised at how much time is devoted to money (especially if they are used to their spouses managing their family finances). Money is less visible than land or buildings. Fluid, always moving, a congregation's dollars are pledged, budgeted, given, received, deposited, spent, loaned, and even grown. Being a trustworthy leader includes providing accountable oversight of financial processes. Typically, the board writes and raises budgets, oversees cash flow on a monthly basis, raises special funds, and manages assets, all issues that will be examined later in this book.

Much of the board's time is spent on the congregation's goals and the programs that implement those goals. But the business of a governing board also involves relationships with individuals and organizations outside the congregation. Vendors must be chosen, employees sought and hired, insurance secured, contractors selected, and a variety of reports regularly sent to ecclesiastical and governmental bodies. The board, often through specially designated individuals, acts as the responsible party in these outside relationships.

None of this may be as interesting as working on program and mission. But a strong program depends on a strong foundation, and these outside relationships provide an institutional foundation for the congregation, enabling and empowering its program.

Organizational Health Maintenance

Like it or not, we live in a fast-moving, complicated world, and congregational life is no oasis removed from these complications. On the plus side, today we know more about corporate accountability, practical peacemaking, and organizational dynamics than ever before. Plenty of churches are in trouble the same way plenty of families are in trouble. But good congregational leaders, lay and ordained, have an abundance of tools and resources to create thriving, fruitful congregations—even when acknowledging that "we were a basket-case last year!"

Recognizing Dysfunction and Responding

The suggestions about governance made earlier in this chapter are useful whether the congregation you serve is well or ill, troubled, dispirited, or thriving. A little experience on any board initiates us anew into the complex personal dynamics of groups. Like any other life-form, governing boards are subject to dysfunction, and most such ailments turn on character and personal relationships. A personality conflict between two people on a board of directors can create a nightmare for the rest of the group, and that inevitably reverberates through the membership, whether the issues and personalities are known or not.

It is tempting for people with little decision-making experience to overly relish the power of being on a governing board. In one of the first churches I served, one long-term board member used to say, without a smile, "I'm on the board to guarantee we'll always have someone to say no." This "leader" took his perceived responsibility very seriously and for years was a thorn in the flesh, claiming just enough votes at annual elections to stay in power.

An easy, ever-present temptation facing decision-making groups is to become polarized and political. Egos can run rampant, with internal cliques vying against each other instead of members pursuing the purpose that draws them into one body. Even groups gathered in prayer, focused on living authentically and faithfully, are vulnerable. Leaders who subconsciously work to manipulate rather than empower can set the community stumbling. Both clergy and laity are susceptible to the failing.

Knowing your congregation's constitution, policies, and rules is an invaluable tool when coping with a manipulator. But knowing the rules is not enough to understand, much less help transform, a community of faith. A set of unwritten informal decision-making agreements can be found in any corporate body. This silent protocol may be ethical and well intended, or it can be tyrannical, a disaster to the newcomer.

A retired pastor ruefully remembers a distinguished Boston church where appointments to the small board of trustees are for life. Entrance into this "club" is not easy. Before individuals are nominated, they are interviewed. Behind closed doors, they learn that when the church overspends its budget, the trustees dig into their pockets to make up the difference. This generosity invisibly purchases the decision-making power in the congregation. Whatever the trustees want, the trustees get, and a new pastor walking in unaware is due for a hard landing.

In fact, a wise leader begins his or her task by discerning the unspoken power configuration within the community. "A Guide for New Pastors" (Griffin, 1991) is a fascinating study of the unspoken power configurations in small towns and their effect on new pastors. Is the configuration healthy? How do you fit in, and does it feel comfortable? Occasionally, new leaders, unhappy with a governing board, arrive fighting the establishment. But the newcomer's reforming zeal is liable to be ineffective and destructive.

Encouraging rebellion is rarely helpful, but assuming the best from everyone is equally naive. Leaders in religious communities and nonprofits are made of mortal clay, like all of us! Without standards and accountability structures, the worshiping family is in danger. In 1987, religious pollster George Gallup reported, "Church attendance makes little difference in people's ethical views and behavior; religious people lie, cheat, and pilfer as much as the nonreligious." (Thompson and Thompson, 1991, p. 115) This grim assessment, a convenient sound bite for cynics, can better serve as a goad to integrity and an ethically articulate commitment to the community's ministry.

In your own faith journey, realize that churches and temples are capable of becoming abusive institutions. If you find yourself in such a dysfunctional situation, turn to those in charge and ask for accountability. Manipulative charismatic leaders can be conversational masters. Trust your instincts when events or issues raise red flags for you that are not sat-isfactorily addressed. Consider how personally powerful leaders some-times become, for either good or ill. Jim Jones built a huge enthusiastic congregation of well-meaning people in San Francisco, took it overseas, and convinced eight hundred to join him in a mass suicide. Everything leading up to this tragedy occurred without any effective calling to account within the congregation or from the denomination that ordained and gave him standing.

Your membership is freely conferred, and you always have the option to move it elsewhere.

Churches That Abuse, by Ronald Enroth (1992), is a superb study of the worshiping community gone bad. According to Enroth, traits of an abusive congregation include "control-oriented leadership, spiritual elit-ism, manipulation of members, perceived persecution, lifestyle rigidity, emphasis on experience, suppression of dissent, harsh discipline of mem-bers, denunciation of other churches, and the painful exit process." "Guilt, fear, and intimidation" are the tools of spiritual dictatorship. The book specifically examines a number of conservative independent churches on the fringes of the evangelical wing of the Protestant commu-nity. But Enroth's insights and guidance for victims of institutional abuse are germane wherever leaders are too hungry for power.

Enroth's book was well received, and he stayed with the subject, inter-viewing a number of survivors of abusive churches and publishing *Recov-ering from Churches That Abuse* (1994). This second book is full of good advice about the healing that has to follow the escape from an organiza-tion that has harmed you. Gaining independence and rebuilding relation-ships are major themes.

Independent congregations, accountable for their decisions to no larger body than themselves, are particularly vulnerable to institutional disease. They do not receive the support services and resources of trusted, connected institutions. Even more important, local leaders pri-marily attracted by access to power do not have to worry about anyone looking over their shoulders or asking "impertinent" questions.

Note, however, that labeling a congregation dysfunctional is dangerous because the label is imprecise by itself and can be misused as a sarcastic, vague judgment. Disease needs description. Abuse and conflict, for instance, can each bring a congregation to its knees, rendering it dys-functional. But abuse and conflict are two different problems, even when they appear at the same time. Systemically abusive institutions are dan-gerous and difficult to call to account without outside ecclesiastical help or the law. Congregant, beware.

Conflict Resolution: The Mandatory Skill

Conflicted congregations are as everyday as apple pie in a diner—and almost as tasty for congregations smart enough to make conflict safe. Differences and bad feelings become a problem when they are ignored and invisibly grow to dominate people's experience of the community. Preoccupation with internal difficulties means that care for the membership and ministry is corroding.

Alban Institute senior consultant Speed Leas has been called "one of the world's foremost authorities on church conflict" (Miller and Shelley, 1989, p. 13). He works with dozens of congregations where painfully broken relationships consume the membership. Conflicted congregations, according to this practical peacemaker, tend to make the pastor the focus of discontent, with or without good cause. Thus clergy without a strong relational aptitude or special training are extremely vulnerable.

The most important subject neglected by most seminaries is conflict resolution, beginning with the skills necessary for drawing out people and encouraging them to voice their feelings. In part, this is due to the "academic" rather than "clinical" environment of most seminary learning.

Successful clergy tend to be conflict resolution "naturals." Without such a gift or clinical training, clergy are extremely vulnerable as leaders. As described in Chapter One, over six thousand ministers are fired every year, a devastating experience for all involved. Usually, the conflict is red-hot by the time it surfaces. When members make public denunciations and start organizing their opposition to an ordained and "called" leader, 72 percent of the time the pastor will be terminated. Hiring a consultant can reduce risk, but only to about 50 percent, according to Leas.

Good training in resolving low-level conflict is any leader's best preventive medicine against the growth of unfocused, destructive conflict. Then the principles and the practice of peacemaking can be taught to everyone. Conflict resolution is a structured approach to telling the truth in safety. Without that sense of safety, the truth suffers. Members of worshiping communities share a cordiality that feels inviolable, for instance. Giving voice to complaints, particularly those accompanied by deep feelings, is silently, powerfully discouraged. Thus bad feelings easily remain hidden and fester. Breaking through the false cordiality is frightening, but the sooner it happens the better the prognosis.

Conflict resolution, properly used, is a valuable asset for healthy as well as troubled communities. It creates a safe environment by establishing ground rules for conflict, identifying common goals, and fostering clearer communication. Congregations that practice conflict resolution do a great service to all.

SUGGESTIONS FOR RESOLVING DISPUTES

○ Approach conflict as an opportunity instead of running from it. Begin by reading about the subject and, if possible, being trained.

○ Establish clear ground rules about the process.

○ Involve all sides in the argument and listen carefully enough that people's real interests become clear.

○ Lean on the issues instead of the people. Private animosity is usually different from simple conflict and is likely to call for counseling or therapy rather than conflict resolution. In conflicts, clarifying the issues should include unpacking personal agendas and setting them in context, so that the actual disagreement can be seen less emotionally and more realistically.

○ Support disputants in extricating themselves from a right-wrong mentality when they get stuck in blaming themselves or their opponents. Encourage them to feel good about making a serious commitment to create a collaborative resolution and agreement. Successful resolution reinforces this healthy self-esteem.

○ Foster commitment to principles instead of rigid positions.

○ Resist unexamined, unilateral solutions that might claim to make everything OK, and resist bargaining over the outcome. The goal is weaving a common bond, not making the best deal for yourself.

○ Always work to reduce fear, to communicate effectively, and to make decisions clear.

○ Include everyone influenced by a decision in the decision-making process.

A library of conflict-resolution material for congregations has been published since the mid-1980s. Speed Leas has written several books on the subject, including *Moving Your Church Through Conflict* (1985), a how-to manual written for church leaders. *Resolving Conflict with Justice and Peace,* by Charles McCollough (1990), is excellent both theoretically and practically. The bibliographical essay at the end is particularly helpful in identifying additional resources exploring the many aspects of conflict resolution in worshiping communities.

The winter 1992 issue of *Leadership* is devoted to conflict. Twenty different articles unpack the issue, ranging from "Caring for the Confused" to "A Wounded Pastor's Rescue." The issue is particularly helpful regarding clerical terminations and resignations. A more recent resource is *Church Conflict: The Hidden Systems Behind the Fights,* by Charles Cosgrove and Dennis Hatfield (1994). It compares conflict in congregations to family quarrels and seeks to identify who is assuming which roles and how the conflict can be remedied.

When leaders, committees, boards, or whole congregations become dysfunctional, they need spiritual nurture, outside help (often resisted), clear talking, appropriate ways to address problems with a measure of fairness, and "safe" time and space established so people can find respite from the burdens of the group.

Personnel and pastoral relations committees frequently help. They can offer a confidential environment where problems can be safely addressed.

Congregations that can afford to do so sometimes call in *organizational healers.* Once upon a time, such local difficulties meant calling in the bishop or a similar ecclesiastical authority. Today, they may mean contacting a specialized consultant like Speed Leas, someone trained in the dynamics of organizational development and the principals of conflict resolution.

One resource in obtaining perspective on a congregation's health is *The Life Cycle of a Congregation,* by Martin Saarinen (1986). This popular book about institutional dynamics analyzes the "stage of life" your congregation is experiencing. It points to appropriate opportunities and warns about predictable pitfalls for each stage of life an organization encounters along its way.

Ultimately, whether a congregation is healthy or ailing, growing or failing, each leader shares a responsibility to see and nurture the good of the whole community, in all its complexity. Until this sense of commonalty transcends the differences people bring to their decisions and voting, the congregation is vulnerable to divisiveness and unmet goals. An aligned leadership team, in touch with its membership, inspired by the community's mission, and focused on being caring and effective can do more in two hours than polarized leadership can accomplish in a year.

Coping with the Troublesome Person

Some personality problems defy mediation. Conflict resolution offers little help with people who can "function" in public but not without troubling everyone around them. For them, conflict is not something to be solved but enjoyed, and the rest of your members have little choice but to put up with it. Troublesome individuals are not a new problem. But they are being taken more seriously as we rediscover how fragile the worshiping family can be and how vulnerable to truly troubled people.

Problem personalities come in every shape and size: the long-term board member whose "compliments" are sexually offensive to women; the person who insists on being the center of attention and takes offense at being called on that trait; the "control freak" who has good ideas but condemns anyone else's contribution. We want these and other people with problem personalities to change their behavior. We sense the problem has spiritual roots but lack the tools to help. And everyone gets tied up emotionally in the process.

Help is available. Getting it often means turning to professional counselors for advice and references, a process discussed later in these pages. Sometimes, with great reluctance, congregations turn to the law to do what cannot otherwise be done. In one congregation, two women insisted on shouting their prayers throughout their church's worship service each Sunday. After the women refused all pleas and prayers to desist from shouting during worship, the congregation finally sought a court-ordered injunction, which was successfully enforced.

Was that a wise strategy? Whether you agree or disagree, it was milder than some of the ploys congregations have used over the years with particularly irksome individuals. Disrupters, malcontents, egotists, "heretics," and the mentally ill have been threatened, condemned from the pulpit, and ostracized when more pastoral approaches failed. In contrast, the congregation with the shouting sisters sought an alternative to coercive, hateful tactics. They decided that the legal solution was the least mean-spirited option at their disposal, and their hijacked worship service was finally returned to them (Bowman, 1996).

When mental illness is involved, it is important to bring in professional therapeutic help. Often, though, the toughest cases are not pathological. The retired pastor who will not leave, the chronic antagonist, connoisseurs of blame, and persistent bullies—what do you do with them? An entire issue of *The Christian Ministry* (May/June 1996) was devoted to the congregation's "least wanted" members, and it is full of useful suggestions.

A short but well-received book by Wayne Oates, *The Care of Troublesome People* (1994), identifies five problem-personality types—the backbiter, the authoritarian, the competitor, the dependent person, and the star performer. Rather than judge them or see them as prodigals, Oates suggests that behind the trouble in each case there is a gift, some "runaway creativity" that can be identified and freed for the good of the community.

Going the Next Step

Every few years, a crop of new books reexamines what it takes to make a governing board successful. A recent version is *The Effective Church Board: A Handbook for Mentoring and Training Servant Leaders*, by Michael Anthony (1995). Particularly helpful for the new pastor, it is full of good ideas for building a strong bond between clergy and decision makers.

A newer approach, based on research funded by Lilly Endowment, seeks to identify the source of vitality in governing boards. The results of the study, which was led by Charles Olsen, are detailed in the two-part article "Research: What Makes Church Boards Work" (Olsen, 1993a, 1993b). The study interviewed over two hundred leaders from six denominations, lay and ordained, local and denominational, including academicians and consultants.

The study uncovered a "high level of disillusionment" among those who actually serve on boards. Many did not like the work. They criticized the traditional board-clergy structure as too dependent on a business model, wondered why "something is missing" from the experience, and not infrequently dropped out of the congregation after finishing the task. The research found that seminaries spend little time on congregational governance, and denominational offices, with reduced budgets and staff, have given it low priority.

Olsen concludes that the important missing element has been "spiritual vitality." His book based on the research, *Transforming Church Boards into Communities of Spiritual Leaders* (1995), explores ways to reintegrate a sense of spirituality into the congregation's decision making. Olsen envisions a new kind of board, more occupied with its task, less preoccupied with its rights, privileges, and procedures. Olsen seeks a board in which "the individual board member is no longer seen as a political representative but as a spiritual leader. The board or council is no longer seen as a group of corporate managers, but as the people of God in community. The meeting is no longer seen as a litany of reports and decisions held together by 'book-end' prayers but as 'worshipful work.'"

To inspire and guide this new kind of leadership group, Olsen suggests all sorts of exercises that introduce the congregation's history, biblical stories, and theological reflection into the work of the governing body. Spirituality ceases being "out there" and disconnected from the daily activities of the congregation, and what is "ordinary" starts to assume an extraordinary vitality.

Alban Institute publications, including Olsen's, remain the best starting place to get practical help when building a strong board, regardless of your theology. And the periodicals listed at the end of Chapter One remain the most likely place to find new resources for board enrichment.

Resources for the Governing Board

Agencies

Alban Institute, Suite 433 North, 4550 Montgomery Avenue, Bethesda, MD 20814; (800) 486–1318.

Periodicals

Please refer to the list in Chapter One.

Books and Articles

Anthony, Michael J. *The Effective Church Board: A Handbook for Mentoring and Training Servant Leaders.* Grand Rapids, Mich.: Baker, 1995.

Bowman, Gail. "Mixing Law and Religion in Church Disputes." *Christian Ministry,* Mar./Apr. 1996, pp. 11–14.

Christian Ministry, May/June 1996 (special issue: "The Congregation's Least Wanted," six articles on troublesome people).

Cosgrove, Charles E., and Hatfield, Dennis D. *Church Conflict: The Hidden Systems Behind the Fights.* Nashville, Tenn.: Abingdon Press, 1994.

Enroth, Ronald M. *Churches That Abuse.* Grand Rapids, Mich.: Zondervan, 1992.

Enroth, Ronald M. *Recovering from Churches That Abuse.* Grand Rapids, Mich.: Zondervan, 1994.

Griffin, Richard. "A Guide for New Pastors." *Action Information,* Jan./Feb. 1991, pp. 19–22. (*Action Information* is now called *Congregations.*)

Leadership, Winter 1992 (special issue on conflict).

Leas, Speed. *Moving Your Church Through Conflict.* Bethesda, Md.: Alban Institute, 1985.

McCollough, Charles R. *Resolving Conflict with Justice and Peace.* Cleveland, Ohio: Pilgrim Press, 1990.

Miller, Kevin, and Shelley, Marshall. "Inside Church Fights: An Interview with Speed Leas." *Leadership,* Winter 1989, p. 13.

Oates, Wayne E. *The Care of Troublesome People.* Bethesda, Md.: Alban Institute, 1994.

Olsen, Charles M. "Research: What Makes Church Boards Work? 1. Why Do Church Board Members Burn Out?" *Congregations,* May/June 1993a, pp. 11–12.

Olsen, Charles M. "Research: What Makes Church Boards Work? 2. Church Boards as Spiritual Leaders." *Congregations,* July/Aug. 1993b, pp. 16–18.

Olsen, Charles M. *Transforming Church Boards into Communities of Spiritual Leaders.* Bethesda, Md.: Alban Institute, 1995.

Saarinen, Martin F. *The Life Cycle of a Congregation.* Bethesda, Md.: Alban Institute, 1986.

Thompson, Robert R., and Thompson, Gerald R. *Organizing for Accountability: How to Avoid Crisis in Your Nonprofit Ministry.* Wheaton, Ill.: Shaw, 1991.

PART TWO

ACCOUNTABILITY, ADMINISTRATION, AND THE SHARED LIFE OF THE CONGREGATION

THE ABILITY TO DEAL with people is as purchasable a commodity as sugar or coffee. And I pay more for that ability than for any other under the sun.

—John D. Rockefeller

4

DEVELOPING LIFE-SUPPORT SYSTEMS FOR THE CORPORATE BODY

WHEN THE ALBAN INSTITUTE celebrated its twentieth birthday, founder and retiring president Loren Mead recalled that when the institute began in 1974, "no one" in theological higher education was interested in local congregations. Focusing on "the Church" was appropriate, but not on "the congregation" (Mead, 1994a). Happily, this is no longer the case, though many seminary professors still go pale at the notion of requiring future pastors to take a course in administration. Congregational administration, like leadership development, remains a second-class citizen on most campuses, and forerunners like Mead and Lyle Schaller continue to be welcomed more in clergy convocations than on seminary campuses.

As we shall see though, these pioneers and those who followed have already had an enormous impact on theological academia. Congregational studies is finally a legitimate field of inquiry, and significant research has begun in all sorts of related areas. In countless ways, congregations from every tradition have begun benefiting from this development.

Finding the Heartbeat

Any seasoned pastor or teacher knows that each congregation and each class has its own distinct personality. The corporate body is a living, breathing life-form. Each one is as valuable, complex, and unpredictable as a human being, or more so, because each corporate body is made up of all sorts of specific human beings. As a member of a living species, each congregation is like hundreds of thousands of other similar congregations; at the same time, it is particular, unique, with its own fingerprint, flavor, and history.

Congregations, in other words, are full of complex systems, but they are not machines. They are alive, so mechanistic ways of looking at them tend to be inadequate and misleading. A generation of writers who understand this distinction has come of age, and a richly creative discussion about the dynamics of congregational life is going on throughout the nation. This book is an attempt to footnote some of that discussion and make clear how yeasty it is, coming from brothers and sisters everywhere who want to make the world work better, beginning in their own backyards.

So even as the religious community goes through radical change, down-sizing, future-shock, steady shrinking, or phenomenal growth, at this very time the opportunities for participating in a blessed faith community are better than ever. Examples of congregational birth, death, and rebirth stretch across the horizon; check out your own neighborhood. You will hear dozens of stories about birth, death, and rebirth. When you feel brittle, the stories all feel fairly frightening. But after brittleness comes breaking, or melting, or molting, and with it the possibilities of new life. Your worshiping family may not feel like the heaven you hope for. Yet never have the opportunities or resources for bringing new life into that family been greater.

Vision-Driven, Team-Empowered Administration

We look in vain for a model of the perfect congregational administration, but we can find plenty of congregations with administrations that serve them more than adequately. Some administrations are brilliant. The adage about not fixing what is working is true enough to make observing, listening, and discerning the "make-it-or-break-it" homework for new leaders. Poorly administered programs can seem to cry out for immediate improvement. But the worst-run program may be the pride and joy of an older leader; you do not have to be in this work long before identifying some leaders whose self-esteem depends on sustaining a failing program. First, work with the person, establishing friendship one hopes, then work together reforming the program. Good relationships are the hallmark of effective administrations; sour relations are poison.

When you find yourself at the helm of a congregation living up to its goals, enjoying goodwill inside and outside the community, relating well to the neighborhood, slow down and enjoy it for a while. It is particularly important to listen before acting or charting a new direction for a thriving congregation. If your membership, by contrast, is depressed, conflicted, beset with anger, or otherwise wounded, a strategy for a healing process needs to be explored as soon as possible, a complex effort we will explore in the final chapter.

Most of us live between success and missing the mark, of course, individually and corporately. Many congregations feel "in between"—that they are treading water and lack vitality. From a survey of the literature on congregational leadership and health, some common elements for revitalizing a congregation emerge.

Worshiping communities, like other life-forms, thrive when they have a vision and pursue it. Administration empowers the pursuit. It puts the rubber to the road and makes things happen. First, though, comes the vision. A thousand ways await creative leaders for identifying and promoting vision. In some congregations, a sense of vision is firm and established, the ground the members walk on. Other congregations disagree about vision and values or feel they are wandering blindly. They need to wake up; or to use a religious word, they need to be reborn.

Focusing the community on its unique vision is a powerful wake-up call. Periodically and regularly, congregations can profitably rearticulate their reason for being and commit it to paper. That vision needs a mission statement—and a motto if the mission statement is not short. That vision needs goals, and those goals need strategies that call forth the participation of everyone in the community. Congregations with a strong, easy-to-remember mission statement use it to stay on purpose.

In creating a mission statement, a community can find help in the statement of purpose in its 501(c)3 tax status application, language from its constitution, its history, and of course, theological study. This *reason for being* should be discussed with staff, volunteers, and officers—and regularly with the entire membership.

The vision is only a beginning, but it is a beginning to live with. The idea is to have a common purpose owned by all, beginning with leaders and decision makers and extending to every member. The metaphor of a team with a mission is appropriate. When you build a team where everyone feels ownership and commitment and is given an opportunity to contribute meaningfully, administration will follow.

SUGGESTIONS FOR EFFECTIVE TEAM BUILDING

o Through prayer and sharing experiences, build a sense of solidarity whenever people work together for the worshiping community.

o Spend time setting goals, making plans, and evaluating as you go along.

o Keep plans as clear and simple as possible and relate them to time lines.

o Talk with the team about trust, how it is grown, how lost, how modeled.

○ Define staff and officer responsibilities carefully with job descriptions so that matters of accountability are clear. This keeps false expectations from brewing and discourages political sniping.

○ Clarify specific assignments at the end of each meeting with individuals taking responsibility for particular tasks.

○ Document the responsibilities of specific volunteer roles so that newcomers understand what is expected when asked to serve.

○ Without being enslaved to them, work at perfecting operational systems and procedures so that people can consistently depend on them.

○ Use consistent, attractive publication and administrative formats, allowing people to recognize information easily.

○ Keep the distribution of minutes and congregational publications as timely and attractive as possible. Communication that is regular, clear, and repeated in different formats is a strong resource in any leader's toolbox.

○ Stay away from writing or endorsing employee handbooks, especially those that wax poetic about employer and employee. Employee handbooks can be construed in a court of law to confer benefits that the congregation as an employer may not be able to offer. Depend instead on published personnel policy and procedure manuals that focus on appropriate behavior and performance expectations and detail administrative rules and systems.

Leadership is a gift and a discipline. Both the gift and the discipline influence how your congregation operates, how it is fed, and how it can be fruitful in nurturing gifts and discipline in others. Over a dozen resources designed to help you grow as a leader are reviewed at the end of this chapter, and they are excellent. But if I had a dear friend just entering parish ministry, I would first give that person a copy of *Church Leadership,* by Lovett Weems Jr. (1993) (reviewed in Chapter One). With passion and clarity, Weems has scoured leadership literature and created an administration and management model that centers on vision, team, integrity, and transformation.

Embracing this model, or any other, is the easy part. The hard work is bringing the vision to bear in your particular community. Most congregations have a board, and board members often chair committees, and meetings move from committee reports to old business to new business, according to *Robert's Rules of Order.* This way of doing congregational business, however comfortable, is not very enlivening, is often a constraint on enthusiasm and anything new, and as described in Chapter Three, sometimes facilitates leader burnout.

Think in terms of evolution, not revolution. The temptation is to create an ad hoc group for every exciting project and bypass the board. But this is a recipe for disaster. When your rules of the game (your bylaws) do not serve you well relationally and organizationally, reform them as a part of your new development.

Some small but significant part of eternity separates a good idea from its implementation, and if you quit playing by the rules, that separation becomes infinitely larger. Implementing something valuable is like giving birth, a process where everything is important. Capturing the vision and creating a team; preparing, educating, and engaging the members of the community; honoring your history and bylaws; and enjoying the outcome— this is an organic process in which every player and every step in the journey is important for its own sake.

In all of this, bringing a spiritual point of view to bear on a congregation's business is like putting down the keel on a sailing boat. Charles Olsen's *Transforming Church Boards into Communities of Spiritual Leaders* (1995), reviewed in the last chapter, is particularly good on this crucial factor in developing a healthy congregation.

When Is Bigger Better?

In the late 1980s, seminary faculties, always buffeted to add courses to already busy traditional curricula, realized that no one understood congregations very well and that some serious study was in order. The message from the pew indicated considerable pain and brokenness at the local level. Continually shrinking memberships had become a problem for thousands of older, more established congregations. Dying churches tend to be very unhappy places, and seminaries started taking note.

The results are instructive. For instance, researchers discovered that the size of a congregation is a critical factor when evaluating leadership and administrative needs. Congregations with memberships of 50, 250, 500, and 5,000 represent very different types of communities. Large congregations from different traditions usually share more characteristics with each other than with small congregations in their own traditions, and vice versa. Not understanding this dynamic can mean trouble: if a congregation has grown to 200 and seeks to retain the sense of "one big family" it enjoyed in the past, it should not be surprised if it plateaus and loses membership.

Today, numerous resources can be found focusing on congregations of a particular size, though small congregations get more than their share.

Church consultant Lyle Schaller was one of the first to focus systematically on different sized congregations, from the smallest to the largest. Today, most religious publishers have at least one book about *small* congregations and one about *multiple staff* congregations, a code term for larger institutions.

Smaller congregations receive special attention in several periodical publications focused on their unique concerns, including *The Five Stones* and *The Small Church Newsletter.* Conservative seminaries paid attention to small faith families earlier than their liberal counterparts, but by now almost everyone assumes the need to be "contextual," the context being the local congregation. Bangor Theological Seminary in Maine is a interesting example of a seminary unapologetically embracing the small church as an ideal congregation for vital ministry.

Two excellent books that share this attitude are *Small Churches Are Beautiful,* edited by Jackson Carroll (1977), and more recently, *The Big Small Church Book,* by David Ray (1992), a superb combination of reflection and how-to ideas used in conservative and liberal institutions alike. *Making It Work: Effective Administration in the Small Church,* by Douglas Walrath (1994), puts to rest the idea that small congregations can get by without considering administration; Walrath focuses on the difficulty most small-church members have with any kind of change.

A number of church growth and fundraising consultants, along with numerous denominational executives across the theological spectrum, predict the demise of most small congregations in the next decade or two. But do not send out funeral notices yet. Large-church apologists simply may be making an unproved bigger-means-better assumption. Small churches are discovering all sorts of ways to thrive and to define success beyond the size of their membership. Ron Crandall, who must be an institutional doctor at heart, surveyed one hundred clergy who have brought "dead" churches back to life. He has published his results in *Turnaround Strategies for the Small Church* (1995). His stories demonstrate that banishing boredom and revitalizing a worshiping community is difficult but joyful and rewarding work.

Fewer resources have been created for large congregations because there are fewer of them and their leaders depend more on informal networks than on national publications. Leadership Network is an organization that supports congregations of one thousand members or more. Its electronic newsletter, *NetFax,* a quarterly called *Next,* a newsletter called *Into Action* about team building and lay ministry, a series of conferences or "forums," and an ongoing series of reports provide resources and connections for those serving larger congregations.

Congregations unhappy with their size can take advantage of the cottage industry encouraging institutional growth with consultants, publications, tapes, and workshops. Before jumping on the growth bandwagon, however, congregations, or at least their leaders, can benefit from examining recent *typological* research that compares congregational sizes. For example, three short articles published by the Alban Institute discuss the serious differences in clergy roles when congregations move from one size to another (Oswald, 1991; Burt, 1992; Finney, 1992). They provide an excellent backdrop to any congregational leaders' discussion of "what kind of congregation we'd like to have here" and the implications of getting what one wants.

When congregations lose members, the resulting blame game often is far off the mark. Research suggests that neither the sociopolitical actions of a congregation nor the theological views of a pastor are significant in driving people away. Rather, failed expectations, activity burnout, not being accepted, failing to find significant relationships, inadequate pastoral support after major transitions and loss, and such neutral factors as "I work Sunday mornings" are to blame (Jeambey, 1993). In other words, caring better for each individual and providing a context where people can build strong personal relationships are the actions many fading congregations need from their leaders.

The Rebirth of the Local Congregation

Although adding new members is a top priority in many congregations, discerning the future and seeking a rebirth to empower the community's role in that future is as important to thousands of others. Religious institutions mirror the cultural "future shock" generated by the enormous changes going on in society. Trends are topsy-turvy, and it is hard to see what is happening. Ordained leadership in the Roman Catholic Church has plummeted, as has the membership of mainline Protestant congregations. Huge, largely independent congregations are attracting an increasing percentage of Christian worshipers as thousands of small congregations are having difficulty supporting a full-time pastor.

In short, the religious community as a whole is going through major transformations in which congregational size is one of dozens of issues. Getting an overview is tough because almost everyone is too close to the trees to see the forest. *Progressions: A Lilly Endowment Occasional Report* helps you see the forest by surveying current research. Regarding long-term membership loss, for instance, a good place to start is "Rough Waters for Mainstream Protestant Churches" (Jan. 1990) and "American Catholicism:

Tradition and Transition" (June 1989). Each issue of *Progressions* lists new research and resources about institutional religious life. It is sent for free to anyone who asks (its address is listed in the Chapter One resources).

Plenty of good news accompanies the changes we are witnessing. Growing congregations outnumber shrinking ones two to one (LaRue, 1994). Imaginative local ecumenical and interfaith partnerships are being forged in communities with scarce resources, and high technology offers congregations extraordinary new tools to extend their work. For instance, two dozen congregations from one tradition that are engaged in local television ministries reach an audience larger than the combined membership of the other 6,400 congregations in that denomination (Schaller, 1992).

Riding this cultural, institutional roller coaster, we hear from precious few voices who can see across the horizon and say anything meaningful. In 1991, Loren Mead proved that founding the Alban Institute had not been a stroke of luck, that he has his finger on something important, something he shared in a short book titled *The Once and Future Church* (1991). It is not difficult to find those who disagree about this or that with Mead. But he was among the first to open the door to the future of the worshiping community, and the issues he raised are topics everyone agrees are important.

Mead suggests that Christianity is experiencing its most important transition since the underground church 1,700 years ago became the "Church Universal," an institution dominating Western culture ever since. Mead sees the old institution crumbling and a new religious community emerging. For Christians, at least, the local congregation clearly will continue going through radical change. In particular, Mead observes old organization models crumbling from lack of support, observes mission evolving from an "overseas" to a backyard issue, and observes leadership and community being redefined. Rather than make many flat predictions about the long-term consequences of these changes, Mead invites the reader to contemplate all sorts of transformative possibilities as the religious community is reinvented.

The Once and Future Church, the Alban Institute's best-seller, became the most discussed book about congregations since people started studying the worshiping communities we attend each week. The institute saw that a raw nerve had been touched and created the Once and Future Church Series. The list includes a dozen books, initial explorations into the future of the worshiping community. A number of books in the series are reviewed in these pages, and you can survey them all in the Alban catalog.

Three of the series' first contributions came from Mead. *Transforming Congregations for the Future* (1994) is about learning how to change. *More Than Numbers: The Ways Churches Grow* (1993) distinguishes between numeric, maturational, organic, and incarnational growth. Most growth consultants, including Lyle Schaller, tend to use numerical growth as the most important benchmark. Mead refuses to treat size as an automatic asset. Offering a small group of people a much deeper spiritual life; streamlining the way a church does business and therefore the effectiveness of its mission; designing activities to take advantage of a smaller group—in such ways Mead suggests that growth can be about more than getting bigger. His analysis, incidentally, is valuable whatever the size of your congregation.

Loren Mead's third contribution to the series is *Five Challenges for the Once and Future Church* (1996), an interim agenda for the coming years, spurred on with a series of questions: Who owns the church? In a world of communities, what is the place of the congregation? How can our institutional structures be changed to work? How do we rediscover a passionate faith? How do we move from a mission of personal, passive nurture to an apostolic mission?

One of Mead's students, Davida Foy Crabtree, examines several of these questions in a book predating *The Once and Future Church*. *The Empowering Church: How One Congregation Supports Lay People's Ministries in the World "Outside" the Church* (1989) offers a fascinating new approach to congregational management. Crabtree began her ministry at Colchester Federated Church in Connecticut with a startling observation: "There is a disjuncture between the stated purpose of the Christian church and the way it is organized locally. Form does not follow function. The church exists for mission, for the sake of the world. Yet it is organized to build itself up as an institution. It draws people to itself, but fails to send them back out. It blesses the work its members do within the institution, but pays no attention to the work they do 'outside' the church" (p. xii).

Crabtree's book is the intriguing study of a community reorganizing itself so that its structure and administration support the ministry of the laity in their day-to-day lives—without taking too much away from the reasons for which members have attended Colchester Federated over the years. Crabtree became a conference minister in the United Church of Christ before the new approach was fully implemented, but the congregation's continuing progress is being reported in *Congregations* (Avena, 1996).

It is particularly heartening eight years after *The Empowering Church*'s publication to find a new crop of resources about taking faith generated in the sanctuary out into the workplace. *Faith Goes to Work: Reflections from the Marketplace*, edited by Robert Banks (1993), is an anthology of first-person accounts representing a wide range of vocations. *Where in the World Are You? Connecting Faith and Daily Life*, by Norma Cook Everist and Nelvin Vos (1996), explores various ways for nurturing support within the congregation for what its members do in the world.

The two-volume study *American Congregations* (Wind and Lewis, 1994), published by the University of Chicago, marks "a major milestone in professional recognition and new resources for congregational studies," says Carl Dudley (1995, p. 41), himself a pioneer in this arena. Twenty scholars participated in writing *American Congregations,* twelve congregations from different faiths were put under the microscope, and some of the nation's most distinguished academics in religious studies contributed to the analysis of congregations over the last four hundred years.

James Wind, one of the two editors of this milestone study, was responsible for Lilly Endowment funding for congregational studies until his selection in 1995 to succeed Loren Mead and become the second president of the Alban Institute. Then early in 1996, Alban completed the academic-practitioner loop; its journal *Congregations* published an article called "Understanding a Congregation's History: Can It Make a Difference?" (Carroll, Richey, and Wacker, 1996). The article allows the reader to apply the *American Congregations* story-telling approach to his or her own congregation.

Most of the books surveyed in this chapter come from the Alban Institute, pointing to its historical role in turning the attention of the religious community to the life and dynamics of the local worshiping community. Along with Lyle Schaller, Alban deserves the thanks of everyone in love with where we worship and who we are when we do.

The Bigger Picture for Your Congregation

Being a congregational leader is an education in the complex corporate personality of a worshiping community. Congregations are idiosyncratic, fond of peculiar traditions and habits. Within this unique culture, systems that work quietly and efficiently, keep people informed, move business forward, and forge common purpose can contribute enormously to the effectiveness of any ministry.

Improving old systems and inventing new ones can be highly creative and need to be done with sensitivity. The well-intentioned reformer can do damage by walking roughshod over people and systems "that have served us very well, thank you, for the past twenty years."

A much better approach is to take advantage of the new movement in congregational studies in your own congregation. One way to start is by researching its "story." *Congregation: Stories and Structures* (1987) was written by the late James Hopewell, a theologian who taught at Atlanta's Candler Theological Seminary. Hopewell's work, funded by

Lilly Endowment, suggests that every congregation weaves its own unique story from the personalities, history, values, habits, and stories that develop over the years.

Inspired by Hopewell's work, Lilly funded eighteen scholars to study individual congregations from a variety of perspectives in order to discern their particular stories. The result was *Building Effective Ministry: Theory and Practice in the Local Church*, edited by Carl Dudley (1983). Hearing and understanding your congregation's story places you in a much better position to be a positive influence for change.

Dudley was joined by congregational specialists Jackson Carroll and William McKinney in editing the classic resource for institutional self-study, *Handbook for Congregational Studies* (Carroll, Dudley, and McKinney, 1986). Published nearly a decade before the more academic *American Congregations,* it leads congregations through careful research about who they are and wish to be. An anthology with a number of contributors, it shows how to assess a worshiping community's values, resources, strengths, weaknesses, and demographics. The book includes an "inventory," like the evaluation exercise in Exhibit 4.1 but more extensive and detailed, along with a number of other tools that can shed light on a congregation's identity. An enlarged and revised edition is scheduled for publication in 1998.

Hartford Seminary in Connecticut may have been the first theological school to pay close attention to congregational life. In the late 1970s, it began doing *parish inventory profiles* for congregations that want to know more about themselves. Over five hundred churches have gone through the exercise, some evaluating the results themselves, some asking the school for tabulation and an analysis.

Statistics can be as important in understanding your worshiping family as stories. A good way to stay in touch with the real needs and feelings of the larger congregation is to make evaluation an everyday part of community life. Evaluation is associated with judgment and fear in many minds. Turning around this prejudice is worth the trouble, because *the conscious act of valuing* is a critically important tool in a community. Without ongoing affirmations and regular self-criticism, healing, growth, and development are extremely difficult, often impossible.

The valuation in Exhibit 4.1, based on one published by the United Church of Christ, is a tool around which a council or membership retreat can organize membership assessment of congregational life. Essentially, it asks people about their satisfaction with the life and mission of the community.

Once the valuations have been completed, they can be analyzed to discover what most members think is working well and where they think more attention is needed. The exercise is not specifically aimed at administrative

Instructions. Circle the appropriate number for each item.

1 = strongly agree; 5 = strongly disagree.

A. Understanding our goals

1. Our mission is understood and
accepted by our members.   1   2   3   4   5
2. Our goals are consistent with our mission
and purpose.   1   2   3   4   5
3. Our congregation helps members
grow spiritually and personally.   1   2   3   4   5
4. Our congregation encourages and equips
members for ministry and service to other
members and the larger community.   1   2   3   4   5
5. Overall, our clergy is doing a good job.   1   2   3   4   5
6. Overall, our lay leaders are doing a good job.   1   2   3   4   5
7. Overall, our congregation is doing well.   1   2   3   4   5
8. Our membership actively supports the life and
ministry of related and/or ecumenical bodies.   1   2   3   4   5
9. Our members actively support and participate
in social justice concerns of our city, region,
state, nation, and world.   1   2   3   4   5

B. Clarifying roles and relationships

1. The decision-making process in our
congregation is clear, fair, and helpful
for working together effectively.   1   2   3   4   5
2. Our members, clergy, and staff agree on
what the clergy is supposed to do.   1   2   3   4   5
3. Our clergy and staff meet the needs of
our congregation.   1   2   3   4   5
4. Our members, clergy, and staff agree on
what lay leaders are supposed to do.   1   2   3   4   5
5. Members know, trust, respect, and enjoy
working together.   1   2   3   4   5
6. Members know and accept what is expected
of them.   1   2   3   4   5
7. Our congregation is aware of the needs of
members and finds ways to help address
these needs.   1   2   3   4   5
8. Our congregation has ways of reaching beyond
the differences people bring to our community.   1   2   3   45
9. Our congregation is sensitive to people with
various kinds of handicaps.   1   2   3   4   5

C. Creating effective systems

1. Our worshiping community acts on the basis
that God is present in our lives and is at work
in the world today.   1   2   3   4   5
2. Our congregation acknowledges and grows
from conflict.   1   2   3   4   5

Exhibit 4.1. An Exercise in Valuing the Life of the Congregation.

3. Our congregation has adequate resources to maintain our facilities.	1	2	3	4	5
4. Corporate worship is well planned and nurtures members in faith and service.	1	2	3	4	5
5. Meetings are well planned and nurture members in faith and service.	1	2	3	4	5
6. Children and youth are welcomed, included, and guided to grow in faith.	1	2	3	4	5
7. Visitors are greeted and welcomed warmly.	1	2	3	4	5
8. We are intentional and effective in inviting new people into membership.	1	2	3	4	5
9. We are effective in integrating new members into the life of our community.	1	2	3	4	5
10. Our members study, pray with, and use scripture.	1	2	3	4	5
11. Our members study, pray with, and use contemporary theological and devotional resources.	1	2	3	4	5
12. Our clergy and staff are appropriately compensated with salary and benefits.	1	2	3	4	5
13. The life of our congregation is regularly and adequately evaluated so that improvements can be made.	1	2	3	4	5

Exhibit 4.1. Continued.

Source: *Based on United Church of Christ*, 1988.

responsibilities. But good administrative systems can empower congregations as they move from vision to action regarding any of their goals. Wherever serious concerns are shared, analyze the administrative work needed to create change.

Discussions can be scheduled once the results of the valuation are in hand. Choosing two or three ways to improve the life of the congregation is a way to focus decision making once the research is complete. Even after consensus has been built, be ready to talk to self-appointed critics. Change usually invites resistance. Being able to meet resistance creatively is a useful skill. A book that continues to sell well nearly fifteen years after publication is *Leading Churches Through Change*, by Douglas Walrath (1979).

As the benefits of evaluation became clearer, the subject received new attention, beginning with *Evaluating Ministry*, by Jill Hudson (1992). This book compares four different evaluation models and explores how to take advantage of what is learned in the evaluation process. Jeff Woods takes the discussion the next step in *User Friendly Evaluation: Improving the Work of Pastors, Programs, and Laity* (1995). Woods builds on Hudson's work to discuss how to deemphasize anxiety and maximize what can be achieved through reflection on the life and mission of a congregation.

Going the Next Step

Church administration may sound like a dull subject, but the resources available prove otherwise, and more are published every day. The Alban Institute dominates the field, but dozens of religious publishing houses are taking a new look at how congregations succeed or fail and sharing what they learn.

Resources for Congregational Management

"Everyone wants to become a manager except the pastor," observes eminent church historian Martin Marty (Luecke and Southard, 1986, p. 7). Interested or not, clergy and lay leaders have numerous management and administration resources at their disposal.

At the turn of the twentieth century, congregational leaders in training depended on books of stories about congregational life to explain the vocation. In 1931, *Church Administration,* the first book of its kind in the United States, was written by William Leach. Leach's original contribution placed "emphasis on a holistic approach," focusing the congregation's program and support systems around worship and education (Schaller and Tidwell, 1975, p. 11).

Since then, numerous books have been devoted to administrative issues facing congregations, with considerable attention to finance, planning, staffing, record keeping, risk management, working with volunteers, building maintenance, growth, communications, and conflict resolution. The following resources are a few of the best among many available. Most of them were written prior to the extraordinary new work from the 1990s that I surveyed earlier. No doubt a generation of new books is gestating in ecclesiastical computers across the country. Meantime, these books, each with a specific focus, remain extremely valuable for various reasons.

The most academic and theological study of "ecclesiastical administration" is *Ministry and Management,* by Peter Rudge (1968). It is recommended for serious students of the subject.

Ethical problems faced by professional managers are examined by Michael Rion in *The Responsible Manager: Practical Strategies for Ethical Decision Making* (1990). Following a case-study approach to various problems, Rion offers ethical guidelines.

Creative Church Administration, by Lyle Schaller and Charles Tidwell (1975), is an excellent one-volume text for creatively revitalizing administration and, thereby, the life of the worshiping community.

The Church Organization Manual, written and compiled by Robert Welch (1992), a professor of administration at Southwestern Baptist Theological Seminary in Fort Worth, offers a do-it-yourself kit for comprehensively defining organizational policies and accountability structures to guide the congregation. It helps identify administrative tasks and responsibilities, and it also provides sample job descriptions, committee policy, salary plans, use and benevolence policies, and forms that can be copied.

The *Clergy Desk Book,* by Manfred Holck Jr. (1990), may be the best of these resources for new clergy, administrators, and governing board leaders. It is a compendium of information for nearly every conceivable day-to-day situation a Christian congregation faces. In spite of its massive amount of information, the book is not designed to be comprehensive. It is a detailed sampler, not an encyclopedia. Interested in strengthening congregational communications? You will find sixteen large, densely packed pages with ideas about your newsletter, worship bulletin, bulletin boards, direct mail, the many faces of advertising, brochures, sermon publication, directories, attendance records, and letterheads!

Mastering Church Management, by Leith Anderson, Don Cousins, and Arthur DeKruyter (1992), is easy to read, offers on-the-job insights, and champions ethical concerns along the way. DeKruyter's essay on the stewardship of power may leave you disagreeing with a decision he makes while appreciating his clarity and honesty. The book makes management interesting, provides useful guidelines about a number of practical subjects, and takes accountability issues in stride. The study is part of a twelve-book series called *Mastering Ministry.* Each volume is written by a group of local church leaders recognized "for their experience and expertise." In addition to management, the series addresses preaching, outreach and evangelism, worship, pastoral care, transitions, teaching, counseling, conflict and controversy, finances, and personal growth. The books come out of the local church but are not connected with any single tradition or denomination. They are mostly by pastors for pastors. This is Christian evangelical territory, largely to the right of liberalism and the left of fundamentalism, but the theology does not show much here. Faithful, accountable leadership is the goal, and the material is stimulating.

How Your Church Family Works: Understanding Congregations as Emotional Systems, by Peter Steinke (1993), turns to the family as an apt metaphor for congregational life, just as Cosgrove and Hatfield use family systems to understand congregational conflict resolution. Steinke uses family systems as a familiar context in which to examine anxiety and reactivity, separateness and closeness, stability and change, and clarity and compassion.

Numerous parachurch agencies offer congregations and their leadership advice and support. Within the Christian community, two of the best are the Center for Parish Development in Chicago and Stephen Ministries in St. Louis. The former provides support in the kind of development described in the first half of this chapter. Stephen Ministries, in contrast, is well known across the country for its assistance in developing small groups and lay care within congregations.

Learning from Secular Nonprofits

Excellent new resources can be found in the nonprofit community, a sector of U.S. society with annual revenues of $500 billion and eight million paid staff members. The best-known text in nonprofit management is *Managing the Nonprofit Organization: Principles and Practices*, by Peter Drucker (1990), a pioneer of modern management theory. Larger congregations in particular have much to learn from those who have developed Drucker's work. Articles and books about endowment management, fundraising, board revitalization, and administrative effectiveness proliferate in nonprofit publication catalogues.

The secular nonprofit community frequently addresses issues important to the religious community even without making reference to religious institutions. Occasionally, congregations and religious agencies do become the focus. The Institute for Nonprofit Organization Management, for example, part of the College of Professional Studies at the University of San Francisco, offers a program called Advanced Management Training for Religious Professionals.

Perhaps the most useful book for religious congregations to emerge from the secular nonprofit community is *Governing Boards: Their Nature and Nurture*, by Cyril Houle (1989). Long respected in the field, Houle's book, full of practical advice, is particularly useful for its focus on leadership liability and accountability.

Three resources that can thoroughly acquaint you with the diversity of publications available from and about the nonprofit community are *Nonprofit World*, a journal published eight times a year by the Society for Nonprofit Organizations that includes a useful bibliography of the society's publications; the *NonProfit Times*, a monthly publication covering nonprofit news, marketing, and management; and Jossey-Bass Inc., Publishers, a highly respected publisher of professional texts concerning the full spectrum of nonprofit concerns.

Great attention in recent years is being paid to nonprofit entrepreneurs seeking ways to expand their income base to support their organizations' goals and operation. An anthology and annotated bibliography of this material is found in *The Nonprofit Entrepreneur*, edited by Edward Skloot (1988) and published by the Foundation Center. The Foundation Center itself is an important resource, with a catalogue of publications and services. Its *Managing for Profit in the Nonprofit World* (Firstenberg, 1986) is a hefty text surveying the legal and economic challenges in the nonprofit world. It explores financing growth, planning change, professionalizing management, and managing from an entrepreneurial point of view.

Doing business as a congregation is not a safe arena for the uneducated, however. Attorneys expert in nonprofit tax law and certified public accountants need to be included in any marketing plans. Income from business unrelated to your congregation's religious purposes can be taxed and may even jeopardize your IRS nonprofit designation. *Organizing for Accountability* (Thompson and Thompson, 1991, pp. 127–155) recommends against *any* unrelated business income, including income from ads from the business community in your newsletter. Not everyone's recommendations go that far, but good legal counsel is important if your congregation "goes into business." *Render unto Caesar: Unrelated Business Income Tax: Liabilities of Churches and Ministries,* by Robert Buzzard and Lynn Buzzard (1990), is a monograph focused on congregational liability for unrelated business income.

Resources for Congregational Administration

Agencies

Center for Parish Development, 5407 South University Avenue, Chicago, IL 60615; (312) 752–1596.

Church Administration and Religious Institutions Study Center, 1325 North College Avenue, Claremont, CA 91711; (909) 626–3521.

Graduate Theological Foundation, P.O. Box 5, Donaldson, IN 46513; (800) 423–5983.

Hartford Seminary, 77 Sherman Street, Hartford, CT 06105; (860) 509–9500. (Contact Professor David Roozen concerning "parish inventory profiles.")

Institute of Church Administration and Management, 700 Martin Luther King Drive, SW, Atlanta, GA 30314; (404) 688–5960.

Institute for Nonprofit Organization Management, College of Professional Studies, University of San Francisco, 4306 Geary Boulevard, Suite 201, San Francisco, CA 94118; (415) 750–5180.

Jossey-Bass Inc., Publishers, 350 Sansome Street, San Francisco, CA 94104; (415) 433–1740.

Leadership Network, P.O. Box 9100, Tyler, TX 75711; (800) 765–5323.

Lilly Endowment, 2801 North Meridian Street, P.O. Box 88068, Indianapolis, IN 46208–0068; (317) 924–5471.

National Association of Church Business Administration (NACBA), 7001 Grapevine Highway, Suite 324, Fort Worth, TX 76180; (817) 284–1732.

National Center for Nonprofit Law, 2001 S Street, NW, Suite 410, Washington,
DC 20009–1125; (202) 462–1000.
Society for Nonprofit Organizations, 6314 Odana Road, Madison, WI 53719;
(608) 274–9777.
Stephen Ministries, 8016 Dale Street, St. Louis, MO 63117–1449;
(314) 645–5511.

Periodicals

The most important periodicals regarding administration are listed at the
end of Chapter One. Those that follow are focused on one or several
aspects of congregational management.

The Five Stones, P.O. Box D2, Block Island, RI 02807.
Into Action, NetFax, and *Next,* Leadership Network, P.O. Box 9100, Tyler, TX
75711; (800) 765–5323. (For larger congregations.)
NonProfit Times, 190 Tamarack Circle, Skillman, NY 08558; (609) 921–1251.
Nonprofit World, 6314 Odana Road, Madison, WI 53719; (608) 274–9777.
The Small Church Newsletter, P.O. Box 104685, Jefferson City, MO
65110–4685; (573) 635–1187.

Books and Articles

Anderson, Leith, Cousins, Don, and DeKruyter, Arthur. *Mastering Church Man-
agement.* Portland, Ore./Carol Stream, Ill.: Multnomah Press/
Christianity Today, 1992.
Avena, Erica W. "The Empowering Church Experiment: A Progress Report."
Congregations, Jan./Feb. 1996, pp. 14–17.
Banks, Robert (ed.). *Faith Goes to Work: Reflections from the Marketplace.*
Bethesda, Md.: Alban Institute, 1993.
Burt, Stephen E. "Does Size Make a Difference?" *Congregations,* Nov./Dec.
1992, pp. 19–20.
Buzzard, Robert, and Buzzard, Lynn. *Render unto Caesar: Unrelated Business
Income Tax: Liabilities of Churches and Ministries.* Buies Creek, N.C.:
Church-State Resource Center, 1990.
Carroll, Jackson W. (ed.). *Small Churches Are Beautiful.* San Francisco: Harper
San Francisco, 1977.
Carroll, Jackson W., Dudley, Carl S., and McKinney, William (eds.).
Handbook for Congregational Studies. Nashville, Tenn.: Abingdon
Press, 1986.
Carroll, Jackson W., Richey, Russell B., and Wacker, Grant. "Understanding a
Congregation's History: Can It Make a Difference?" *Congregations,*
Jan./Feb. 1996, pp. 3–7.

Crabtree, Davida Foy. *The Empowering Church: How One Congregation Supports Lay People's Ministries in the World "Outside" the Church.* Bethesda, Md.: Alban Institute, 1989.

Crandall, Ron. *Turnaround Strategies for the Small Church.* Nashville, Tenn.: Abingdon Press, 1995.

Drucker, Peter F. *Managing the Nonprofit Organization: Principles and Practices.* San Francisco: Harper San Francisco, 1990.

Dudley, Carl S. (ed.). *Building Effective Ministry: Theory and Practice in the Local Church.* San Francisco: Harper San Francisco, 1983.

Dudley, Carl S. "Congregational Journeys." Review of *American Congregations,* by James P. Wind and James W. Lewis (eds.). *Christian Ministry,* July/Aug. 1995, pp. 41–43.

Everist, Norma Cook, and Vos, Nelvin. *Where in the World Are You? Connecting Faith and Daily Life.* Bethesda, Md.: Alban Institute, 1996.

Finney, John. "Big Church? Little Church? What's the Pastor's Job?" *Congregations,* Nov./Dec. 1992, pp. 20–21.

Firstenberg, Paul B. *Managing for Profit in the Nonprofit World.* New York: Foundation Center, 1986.

Holck, Manfred, Jr. *Clergy Desk Book.* Nashville, Tenn.: Abingdon Press, 1990.

Hopewell, James. *Congregation: Stories and Structures.* Minneapolis: Augsburg Fortress, 1987.

Houle, Cyril O. *Governing Boards: Their Nature and Nurture.* San Francisco: Jossey-Bass, 1989.

Hudson, Jill M. *Evaluating Ministry: Principles and Processes for Clergy and Congregation.* Bethesda, Md.: Alban Institute, 1992.

Jeambey, Robert W. "'Why I Left My Church?' Research on the Rupture of Church Relationships." *Congregations,* July/Aug. 1993, pp. 11–15.

Jordon, Ronald R., and Quynn, Katelyn L. "Tax Consequences of Charitable Giving." *Nonprofit World,* Mar./Apr. 1991, pp. 13–16.

LaRue, John C., Jr., "Characteristics of Growing Churches." *Your Church,* May/June 1994, p. 48.

Luecke, David S., and Southard, Samuel. *Pastoral Administration: Integrating Ministry and Management in the Church.* Irving, Tex.: Word, 1986.

Mead, Loren. *The Once and Future Church.* Bethesda, Md.: Alban Institute, 1991.

Mead, Loren. *More Than Numbers: The Ways Churches Grow.* Bethesda, Md.: Alban Institute, 1993.

Mead, Loren. "Learning Points: An Interview with Loren Mead." *Christian Century,* Mar. 23, 1994a, pp. 310–312.

Mead, Loren. *Transforming Congregations for the Future.* Bethesda, Md.: Alban Institute, 1994b.

Mead, Loren. *Five Challenges for the Once and Future Church.* Bethesda, Md.: Alban Institute, 1996.

Miller, Herb. *Turnaround Strategies for the Small Church*. Nashville, Tenn.: Abingdon Press, 1995.

Olsen, Charles M. *Transforming Church Boards into Communities of Spiritual Leaders*. Bethesda, Md.: Alban Institute, 1995.

Oswald, Roy M. "How to Minister Effectively in Family, Pastoral, Program, and Corporate Sized Churches" *Congregations,* Mar./Apr. 1991, pp. 1–7.

Progressions: A Lilly Endowment Occasional Report. June 1989 (entire issue: "American Catholicism: Tradition and Transition").

Progressions: A Lilly Endowment Occasional Report. Jan. 1990 (entire issue: "Rough Waters for Mainstream Protestant Churches").

Ray, David. *The Big Small Church Book*. Cleveland, Ohio: Pilgrim Press, 1992.

Rion, Michael. *The Responsible Manager: Practical Strategies for Ethical Decision Making*. San Francisco: Harper San Francisco, 1990.

Rudge, Peter F. *Ministry and Management*. London: Tavistock, 1968.

Rueter, Alvin C. *Personnel Management in the Church*. Minneapolis: Augsburg Fortress, 1984.

Schaller, Lyle E., and Tidwell, Charles A. *Creative Church Administration*. Nashville, Tenn.: Abingdon Press, 1975.

Skloot, Edward (ed.). *The Nonprofit Entrepreneur*. New York: Foundation Center, 1988. (Available from Foundation Center, 79 Fifth Avenue, New York, NY 10003.)

Steinke, Peter L. *How Your Church Family Works: Understanding Congregations as Emotional Systems*. Bethesda, Md.: Alban Institute, 1993.

Thompson, Robert R., and Thompson, Gerald R. *Organizing for Accountability: How to Avoid Crisis in Your Nonprofit Ministry*. Wheaton, Ill.: Shaw, 1991.

United Church of Christ. *Local Church Evaluation*. Cleveland, Ohio: Office of Church Life and Leadership, United Church of Christ, 1988.

Walrath, Douglas. *Leading Churches Through Change*. Nashville, Tenn.: Abingdon Press, 1979.

Walrath, Douglas. *Making It Work: Effective Administration in the Small Church*. Valley Forge, Pa.: Judson Press, 1994.

Weems, Lovett H., Jr. *Church Leadership: Vision, Team, Culture, and Integrity*. Nashville, Tenn.: Abingdon Press, 1993.

Welch, Robert H. *The Church Organization Manual*. Fort Worth, Tex.: National Association of Church Business Administration, 1992.

Wind, James P., and Lewis, James W. (eds.). *American Congregations*. Vol. 1: *Portraits of 12 Religious Communities*. Vol 2: *Perspectives in the Study of Congregations*. Chicago: University of Chicago Press, 1994.

Woods, C. Jeff. *User Friendly Evaluation: Improving the Work of Pastors, Programs, and Laity*. Bethesda, Md.: Alban Institute, 1995.

5

RESPONSIBLE
FINANCIAL MANAGEMENT

A CURSE, A BLESSING, or both—coming to terms with money is an issue every congregation, like every individual, has to face each day. In congregations throughout the land, clergy are uncomfortable about money, and too often lay people check their financial acumen at the door. Occasionally, someone bright and imaginative about money shows up in a leadership position, and extraordinary things happen, but it does not happen nearly as much as it might.

Like almost every other clergyperson, I have had to work through resentments concerning money and wealth. Unhappily, we have precious few resources helping us to think clearly about all of this, though several should be in the works. Loren Mead has a touching short article, "Caught in the Financial Bind" (1996), designed to assist clergy in talking to each other about financial feelings. Mead lists fourteen instances where he himself has felt upset and confused about money and the clerical profession. The first, for instance, goes, "I understood my job as 'pastor' to include being in a servant role, not 'lording' it over others, and I often got in an emotional bind because I also wanted to have a salary based on my training and professional skill" (p. 3). Most clergy will score high on their identification with the fourteen situations, so it proves an effective discussion stimulant.

This discussion is exceedingly important for leaders, especially in light of the fact that most are receiving less advice and financial support these days from regional and national bodies. The issue has come home. As long as we remain neurotic about money, and until we share our financial stories and plumb the extraordinary passages about money throughout scripture, we will remain largely clueless about the stuff so vital to paying the sanctuary's gas and electric bill, to say nothing of next year's mission goals.

If that is not reason enough to take on the subject, it is worth remembering that nowhere in the life of the worshiping community is the state more likely to intrude than in financial and tax matters. Novice pastors and treasurers who lack professional experience in the financial community may feel overwhelmed when first confronted with the law's demands. Special information is needed to understand leadership responsibilities in these areas, among others:

- o Nonprofit, tax-exempt status
- o Acceptable accounting practices
- o Employee and independent contractor compensation law, including requirements to submit payroll taxes and make timely reports
- o Commercial property
- o Liability insurance
- o Charitable contributions

In a worst-case scenario, not knowing this information may jeopardize a congregation's corporate status, make leaders personally liable for the congregation's inappropriate loans or unpaid payroll taxes, give rise to litigation, and even lead to charges of fraud. It is not necessary that every member of a governing board know all this information in great detail. But it is critical that responsible parties, such as treasurers, trustees, or clergy, know the territory.

Legal standards of accountability in tax-exempt organizations are particularly high when money is involved. One of the most valuable benefits of nonprofit incorporation is that it allows donors to receive certain tax benefits for their gifts to the nonprofit, claimed in the tax year they are made. There are rules, however, and when you do not play by them, the process is abused and the benefit may be lost.

Honesty is the foundation of financial integrity for institutions as for individuals. The policy and practice of *full disclosure to members and whoever else gives money or property to a congregation* is a criterion of responsible financial management, both ethically and legally. This is true in annual pledging and the operating budget as well as in planned giving programs and capital campaigns (discussed later in this chapter).

Governing boards can be tempted to hide their financial mistakes, out of embarrassment or as a way to protect people from bad news. But leaders who conceal financial problems risk acting in bad faith. Financial reporting needs to be regular, accurate, and complete.

Numerous handbooks are available that summarize the law's requirements regarding accounting practices, payroll taxes, governmental reporting requirements, tax-exempt status, charitable donations, employer responsibilities, and fiscal management. Two of the best are reviewed at the end of the chapter. In addition, *Church Finances for People Who Count,* by Mack Tennyson (1990), is an excellent overview of congregational finances. It is aimed at pastors and administrators rather than bookkeepers and accountants. The book reads easily and covers the variety of financial issues important to congregations.

An attitude of trusting vigilance is important with the congregation's finances. Trusting vigilance allows you to trust the other person's good faith, and it seeks clarity without nit-picking. At the same time, it means keeping your eyes open and supporting the congregation's best interests.

As was noted in Chapter One, worshiping people, on average, are not appreciably more ethical than others. Plenty of anecdotal evidence underlines the point. Church scandal, preoccupied with sexuality in the early 1990s, more recently has turned to the misuse of money. Ellen Cooke has claimed the biggest headlines. As treasurer of the Episcopal Church in the United States, she embezzled $2.2 million over a period of five years and received a five-year prison sentence for the betrayal.

Even as Cooke began her sentence in mid-1996, a pension manager for the Roman Catholic Diocese of Brooklyn was being accused of stealing $1.1 million over a six-year period. Insurance files record plenty of cases with smaller figures. Understanding this sad reality makes you vigilant, but it does not have to make you cynical or strip you of the trust you extend to people as a matter of course. Suspicion is the last thing you want in your leadership group. So trust everyone, and be as vigilant in your oversight of the congregation's money as if your child's life depended on it.

Playing by the Rules

When a congregation puts its trust in leaders, asking them to handle its finances and property, in the eyes of the law the entrusted leaders become *fiduciaries.* A fiduciary is legally required to meet particularly high standards of honesty and fair dealing.

SUGGESTED STANDARDS FOR FIDUCIARIES

○ Any financial transaction between a congregational officer and the congregation needs to be fully disclosed. A vote can be taken with the interested party voting a recorded abstention. The agreement must be fair to the congregation. Undisclosed interest on anyone's part must be avoided. Secretly buying land from a church trustee, for example, is prohibited.

- Governing bodies should not make loans to directors or officers. In some states, such loans are specifically forbidden. If a loan is made, those who vote for it may become personally liable if it is found impermissible and not repaid. For loans to ministers, priests, and rabbis (such as a down payment for a home), consult an attorney about applicable state laws.

- When a donor designates a gift for a particular purpose, it must not be used for any other purpose. Ignoring this rule can constitute fraud and lead to civil suits and legal indictments.

- Learn the law about tax-deductible giving and an institution's responsibilities when it solicits and receives gifts.

- Leaders have a responsibility not to exceed the scope of their authority. For instance, amending bylaws without an approving vote by the congregation is always inappropriate unless the constitution specifically sanctions such amendment.

Record-Keeping

Recording and accounting for income and expenses is absolutely basic to living within the law as a nonprofit corporation. Many congregations depend on a readily available software program like QuickBooks or Excel to help with the day-to-day tedious but essential record-keeping (particularly because such programs create reports and accounting information). The mistake to avoid is putting the whole responsibility into the hands of a single skilled volunteer who knows the computer program and is willing to do all the work. Such a Lone Ranger arrangement tempts the vulnerable and burns out the best-intentioned.

Finance is every leader's responsibility. Every board member should know what is happening with cash flow and have a hand in defining and implementing the kinds of policies and procedures that protect both treasurers and congregations. A good introduction summarizing important financial policy and procedure can be found in "Honest Financial Church Policies," by David Pollock (1996). In fewer than four pages, he identifies several dozen policies and procedures you can use to protect congregational finances.

Your treasurer, prompted by someone like Pollock, should be the one who suggests ways to improve financial accountability. Doing so establishes the officer's credibility, keeps suggestions from sounding like criticism, and gives the treasurer ways to share the burden.

An Annual Audit

Formally auditing the congregation's finances is an annual event for large congregations and a frequent first step whenever serious financial problems exist in any congregation. Do not use the services of a board member or a friend willing to do the job inexpensively. It is safest to rely on well-recommended certified public accountants who are not connected with the congregation. Remembering the principle of "conflict of interest" and behaving appropriately can save you a heap of trouble. Accountability is the underlying issue, and doing "favors" for either the congregation or one of its members in this matter is inappropriate. For more detail about what an audit does and does not do, see "The Independent Audit: A Wise Investment?" by Gregory Capin (1995), which makes the distinctions in a few short pages; and yes, Capin thinks all churches should have an audit each year.

Plenty of small congregations simply lack the wherewithal to retain a CPA to do an annual audit. If your budget keeps you from the formal route, you can appoint an internal audit committee (again, not a single individual) that can follow a specified series of procedures to make sure congregational finances were administered legally and appropriately. Dan Busby's annual volume on church finance and taxes (*The Zondervan Church and Nonprofit Organization Tax and Financial Guide*) now includes a list of forty-eight guidelines that a committee can follow to reproduce what a CPA would do with a nonprofit's financial records in an audit. You can also see Todd Zastrow's "How to Self-Audit Church Books" (1994). Smart do-it-yourself folks know that their work will not be professional. But with the right tools, a high commitment level, and someone looking over your shoulder, you may save the congregation some money and still do what is needed to be financially accountable.

In the same spirit, a church treasurer I worked with asked a different member of the board to make the financial report each month, a exercise requiring each of them to look carefully at the whole financial picture periodically.

Part of the benefit of careful, shared financial management is that it will probably scare away that occasional person seriously tempted to steal the congregation's money. Even better though—a polished, well-implemented financial administration is like a car you can trust to run reliably. Handled well in a healthy congregation, money ceases to be a problem and serves as a support structure, with joyful givers receiving more satisfaction than they ever expected.

Pointing the word *audit* in a different direction, it is worth noting that taxation law for clergy is a complex ever-evolving set of rules and strictures. It is important for all ordained clergy to understand their special financial relationship with the government and receive advice at tax preparation time from a specialist. The resources by Daniel Busby and Richard Hammar listed at the end of this chapter can educate you. A particularly helpful recent clergy tax article by Hammar is "Avoiding an Audit" (1995). The 5,000 clergy (out of 500,000) who will be audited by the IRS this year probably missed this article! Most clergy wisely seek help with their taxes; Busby and Hammar are your leverage with the expert you use, a way to let that person know you are on top of the issues.

Meeting the Annual Budget

Designing and meeting a goal budget is the financial backbone of thousands of congregations. Specialists in fundraising for religious organizations, however, ask that congregations focus on the *act of giving* rather than on *budgetary need,* or "what we think we can raise." The practicality of goal budgets can be irresistible to a congregation that believes it has many more needs than available resources. But professionals have discovered that *worshiping communities invariably have more resources than they know.*

Attending primarily to a dollar goal not only sets aside the spiritual value of giving, but it also puts an unnecessary psychological limit on the amount the membership is willing to think about giving. I recall one consultant making the point by saying, "A budget is not a fundraising device. It is a fund-spending list."

Plumbing the depths of what it means to give transforms giving from a duty to a highly satisfying opportunity, particularly when good givers witness to the personal value of giving to other members. Focusing on the goals of the operating budget, by contrast, tends to keep the institution living on the edge, defining success as paying the bills, with pocket change left over at the end of the year.

Driven by need or inspired by the precious impulse to give, annual fundraising goes to support the budget. As in other corporate enterprises, the budgets—financial maps of the past, present, and future—direct the life and mission of the worshiping community. Being responsible for the budget through the year means continually monitoring the congregation's cash flow. Treasurers, bookkeepers, clergy, and administrators create various systems to give order to the community's daily finances.

Income from pledges, gifts, loose offerings, investments, rent, grants, and fees is balanced against expenditures each month to see what the financial picture is. One of the most common of all institutional problems is spending more than you raise. Facing up to a projected or actual deficit is never pleasant. People become emotional and call for draconian measures.

Happily, considerable help can be found in the area of congregational finance, ranging from books and articles you can study to consultants and programs you can import. Receiving less income than planned, for instance, is addressed specifically in "Five Ways to Counter a Budget Shortfall," by Lyle Schaller (1992a). "Cutting the budget isn't the only option when trustees want to get the red out" (p. 70), writes Schaller. The article offers procedures for understanding the cause of a shortfall and alternatives for responding.

Spending money is often necessary to stem the tide of debt, contradictory as it seems. QUILL is a program marketed by Church Fund-Raising Services for pledge improvement. It involves members' handwriting letters to each other. Created by a respected church fundraising firm, it is available as a manual and costs $1,000. This may sound expensive, but it could turn out to be cost effective. New leaders quickly learn that asking for money costs money and that going the cheapest route (such as a single letter mimeographed and mailed to members) guarantees poor results. Half a dozen pledge program products can be found, ranging in cost from $50 to $1,000 and more if a consultant comes on-site to work with you.

These products will come with testimonials—but testimonials can be rigged. Always check them out when considering a product. More important than testimonials is the accountability a consultant or resource creator offers. QUILL has been around for a number of years and has many happy customers—good measures when checking out a product. Faced with an ad in a magazine such as *Your Church,* how do you find out more about the product than the advertisement tells you? Call up the publisher with a dozen questions, including how its product compares with others on the market. After two or three calls, you start to get educated.

Very few money-back guarantees are to be found, of course. A good fundraising consultant can only point to his or her record and make a case that his or her guidance will work with your congregation. In a capital campaign, a promise to raise a specific amount of money is impractical, foolish, and unethical. Your studied evaluation of a product, particularly in light of some comparisons, is your best guarantee.

Examine a firm's literature and "pitch" to see whether and how accountability is addressed. Solicit confirmation in writing that the consultant or firm you hire adheres to the American Association of Fund-Raising Counsel code of ethics (reprinted near the end of this chapter; see Exhibit 5.1). Ask a representative of the firm about the firm's competitors—and check them out. Good businesspeople may be taken aback at the question, but most recognize that honest competition is healthy for everyone.

Institutional finance is often fairly technical, but it is more than systems and numbers. For instance, a good pledge program is usually evidence of fiscal health and more. When givers withhold pledges as a covert criticism of the clergy, when good programs are lost due to inadequate funds, when the atmosphere becomes suffused with an unending "give, give, give," when salaries become a source of grumbling—in such difficulties, the emotional and financial safety of the community is at risk. Prayer, conflict resolution, and theological reflection are all in order. Congregations trapped in a mentality of scarcity can fruitfully study the theme of abundance in the scripture.

At the same time, a little more learning about finance and the worshiping community is in order for clergy, treasurers, trustees, and administrators.

Research indicates that only about 5 percent of all church members actually tithe a tenth of their incomes; the average member contributes 2.2 percent, according to one study. Leaders attempting to raise pledge income should realize that low-income members give an average of 3.4 percent of their income, as opposed to the average 1.6 percent given by the most affluent members (Gotwals, 1991).   .

Growing Your Money

Funding the operating budget and staying out of debt each year, by themselves, are not enough. Good stewards learn how congregations can enjoy *two* methods of generating income. First, money is received in the form of offerings, pledges, dues, rent, grants, or fees. Strong congregations also depend on a second source of income: money owned can become money grown.

Paying attention to *both* support strategies invariably strengthens a community's life and mission. At the simplest level, this means maintaining an interest-bearing savings account at the local bank. A much better alternative is investing funds not needed for immediate cash flow purposes in a portfolio of financial investments. Such funds are treated as a capital asset, left alone to grow and develop. A prudent mixture of conservative and more aggressive investment strategies results in a small steady income flow. In an important sense, capital is alive and has a generative quality. As Benjamin Franklin put it a letter to a friend, "Money is of a prolific generating nature. Money can beget money, and its offspring can beget more." The congregation that develops an investment program for itself benefits enormously.

Some leaders object to accumulating any capital until *all* human needs have been met, an attitude that is no friend to the needy human race. Imagine operating your congregation's ministry without its buildings! Congregations with endowments or foundations similarly value the usefulness of a financial asset.

About half of the churches in America are in debt, usually in the form of mortgages or bank loans. The other half have combined financial assets of approximately $10.3 billion, held primarily in real estate, savings accounts, certificates of deposit, and mutual funds. Nearly half of this investment ($4 billion) is held in low-paying savings accounts. If this were invested in other ways so as to increase the interest received by a *single* percentage point, the religious community would have an additional $40 million, or an average of $350 per congregation, for ministry every year.

Choosing a good financial adviser may help raise the rate of return on a congregation's investments. The proliferation of different investment products means advice is important. Unfortunately, every banker, stock broker, insurance agent, investment consultant, and tax attorney in the land is interested in your account. As a lightly regulated industry, financial planning is "fraught with abuse," according to *Business Week*. "By some estimates, fifty percent to ninety percent of most financial planners' income is derived from undisclosed commissions on products sold to clients" (Dunkin, 1992, p. 112).

So many people want to offer expert financial advice that the industry has created a variety of certifications, all accompanied by fancy capital letters. The most professional have the right to put CPA after their name. Here is a rundown of who does what with financial counsel.

CPA: certified public accountant. Highly trained, works for hourly fees. Drawback: tends to be very conservative.

PFA: Personal Financial Advisor. Offers fee-only services (no commission income). Contact through referrals from National Association of Personal Financial Advisors. Drawback: fairly expensive service.

CFP: Certified Financial Planner. Certified through Institute of Certified Financial Planners following course work and qualifying exams. Drawback: CFPs can accept commissions and referrals in addition to fees, and ICFP's code of ethics has been criticized as inadequate.

RIA: Registered Investment Advisor. Most CFPs become RIAs by voluntarily registering with the Securities and Exchange Commission, which regulates and thereby gives a level of accountability to their work.

CLU: Chartered Life Underwriter. Sells life insurance products, regulated by state insurance commissions.

CFC: Chartered Financial Consultant. Trained in the insurance industry, parallels certification of a CLU.

Unfortunately, the professional certification of financial planners does not guarantee either competence or honesty. Nevertheless, having credentials attests to an adviser's good intentions; disdain for professional certification and affiliation is a red flag. Having the letters after the name, however, is no guarantee that your congregation will get good advice.

The best way to find good advice, given these circumstances, is the strong recommendation of a banker, lawyer, or accountant you trust. Fee-only advisers do not make commissions, but they will ask for 2 to 3 percent of your portfolio for their advice. Fee-based advisers receive a smaller fee but also receive some commission income from products purchased. Insurance products, real estate partnerships, securities, and mutual funds are also sold with hefty commissions. Financial advice and financial products have costs, some of which may be hidden unless you insist on full disclosure.

In advisers, a good sense of humility is also an asset. Anyone who thinks he or she has mastered finance is not worth trusting, and no one is immune to disaster. In early 1994, the National Council of Churches suspended two executive staff members, for example, one from human resources, the other from finance and administration. Apparently $8 million, a substantial part of the portfolio paying health premiums for retired NCC staff, had been lost in an investment made through a Czechoslovak bank. Suits and countersuits flew as police from several countries and the Czechoslovak government tried to untangle the loss. The case turned on conflicting definitions of "guarantees"; in this instance, eventually much of the money was returned.

SUGGESTIONS FOR SELECTING INVESTMENT ADVISERS

○ Interview three to five potential advisers, talk to current clients (ask for their names and numbers), and check out credentials.

○ Make sure potential advisers serve congregations or other nonprofit corporations and are well acquainted with the legal and financial realities governing these institutions. (Most financial planners serve individuals.)

○ Consider whether prospective advisers are acquainted with your congregation, its finances, and its decision-making procedures or with similar congregations in the same tradition. On the one hand, not knowing your congregation and tradition is a strike against any financial adviser. On the other hand, having an adviser who is a member brings up conflict-of-interest concerns. Ultimately, congregational leaders must select an adviser based on their best-educated choice as to who is most trustworthy and competent.

o Ask potential advisers about their ethical understanding of the work they do. Their own ethical standards as advice givers should be considered in relation to the congregation's ethical standards as an institutional investor.

o Know how conservative or how willing to take risks the congregation is about its savings and look for an adviser with an appropriate perspective.

o Have those participating in financial decisions get to know a potential adviser personally. Talk about long- and short-range goals and strategies before going forward with anyone. Do not retain an adviser if members do not feel a high comfort level with the person.

o Ask each potential adviser if his or her service is fee-only or includes commissions. If commissions are involved, ask for written disclosure statements describing the commission agreement in detail for each kind of financial product purchased.

o Be particularly rigorous in evaluating any financial product sold *by* your adviser. This is legitimate business, but an outside evaluation of the product is prudent, and the congregation's representatives need to know exactly how the adviser is benefiting financially through the transaction.

A final factor that seems at first to complicate finding financial advice actually helps focus and simplify the task. *Socially responsible investing,* or SRI, as this arena is known, means taking an ethical stance when making investment decisions. Money has a life and power of its own, and investors can make a ministry of that power. The concept of SRI became generally known in the late 1970s, when a group of Quakers and Methodists opposed to war industries founded the Pax World mutual fund.

Apartheid in the Union of South Africa put SRI in the spotlight. Investors across the United States joined in an boycott of industries participating in the South African economy. Investor ventures representing $500 billion in assets took a stand against apartheid. Starting in the late 1980s, over one hundred companies withdrew from South Africa until it outlawed the racist law.

Many other moral and ethical issues have been raised as criteria for investing or not in a given enterprise. Tobacco, alcohol, and gambling interests are avoided by a number of funds. Companies with poor employee relations or irresponsible environmental records or those involved with nuclear power, animal research, or junk bonds are also screened out of certain portfolios—each cause is called a *screen* in the investment industry. In some funds, you can design your own strategy, selecting the screens most important to you.

Plenty of skeptics were ready to criticize socially responsible investing at first. Cynicism subsided when screened funds demonstrated that they can perform better than the regular market. The Domini Social Index (DSI), for instance, follows four hundred "clean" companies and compares their financial growth with Standard & Poor's 500 stock index, and a number of SRI funds often outperform the S&P. Others do not, but the funds have become a serious segment of the market. Being socially responsive *and* making more money is a powerful mix, accounting for the phenomenal growth of SRI funds. The $65 billion invested in SRI ventures grew to $625 billion by 1991. When apartheid came to an end in the Union of South Africa, many thought these funds would significantly decrease. They have not, generally staying above the $600 billion mark for the past five years, and showing $640 billion at the end of 1995. This is because new issues—such as the tobacco industry—have the attention South Africa had a few years ago.

Because money brings its own clout, gathering large sums together is a way for it to work more efficiently. The larger the pool, the greater the earning potential. Religious traditions have an excellent resource for sharing information and cooperating with like-minded investors in the Interfaith Center on Corporate Responsibility. Ten times a year it publishes the *Corporate Examiner.* Under its sponsorship, shareholder resolutions are put together on numerous issues. Institutional members investing large amounts receive financial advice. An important service for investors large or small is the center's series of short publications about investing and particular social justice issues.

Securing financial advisers well versed in SRI is enormously facilitated by the Social Investment Forum. It is a membership organization of financial planners. The organization also invites "associates" and "friends" to subscribe to its newsletter, *The Forum,* and to purchase its *Guide,* an annual directory. Indexed by geographical region, it introduces readers to Forum's professional members, along with addresses and phone numbers, and provides a treasury of information about financial institutions, investment opportunities, and socially responsible perspectives. Co-op America is a related nonprofit committed to serving individual investors and is a good place for congregations as well as individuals to start learning how to invest with a happy conscience.

A highly regarded publication, *The Clean Yield* publishes specific recommendations on individual stocks and also serves as a money manager.

How much money should a congregation be able to invest before consulting with financial planners and considering a socially responsible investment portfolio? If $5,000 is waiting to be invested, you may not find many advisers lining up for your business. However, you are likely to find two or three willing to visit for an evening to talk about the issues raised in this chapter. If, however, a $5,000 bequest represents the first step in establishing a planned giving program, one of these meetings could develop into a solid relationship with a trusted financial adviser.

With $50,000, $100,000, or more in congregational funds to invest, make haste to find a good planner! By doing this through the Social Investment Forum, you enhance the potential financial return while using your assets in an ethically beneficial manner.

A good approach with smaller sums of money is to invest in mutual funds rather than individual stocks. These funds pool large sums of money, and their managers make the actual investment decisions. Socially responsible mutual funds require anywhere from $250 to $2,500 minimum investments. Fund representatives will send you literature about their offerings, the "screens" they use when investing, and records of how well they have done.

Some advisers will push no-load investments because you pay less for the privilege of buying them. The basis of any fund's success, however, is not the load it carries but the quality of the fund manager's investment decisions. Any given year for a mutual fund may be a goldmine or a disaster, so look to funds that do well over a five-year period. If you have enough money, invest in more than one. Popular authors like Jane Bryant Quinn and magazines like *Money* offer background material about investing in specific funds. The Social Investment Forum remains particularly helpful for anyone responsible for making recommendations to a congregation about wisely investing its funds.

The Challenge of an Endowment

Creating an *endowment* through a planned giving program is often a favored strategy when a congregation decides to benefit through income earned from capital. Establishing an endowment is like constructing a building. Extensive planning, education, and elbow grease is required. Once they are created, assets go to work and continue providing benefits year after year. Like any other asset, well-structured endowments represent a continuing source of blessing and support.

However, creating an endowment is a complex process, takes considerable work, and presents a number of potential pitfalls. Is it worth the trouble? Let us imagine that First Church has a membership of two hundred and a whittled-back annual budget of $96,000. It is barely enough to pay the denominational dues, the electric bill, a full-time clergyperson, a half-time secretary, and a quarter-time custodian, with a few thousand left over for mission. By the end of the year, all the projected income arrives. For various reasons, spending exceeded the budget by $3,000. The congregation has a $10,000 savings account for just such emergencies. In a sense, the congregation is doing well, running a tight ship, paying its bills. But members are unhappy to be spending so little for mission, with little chance of increasing it.

Now, superimpose this scenario: the difference it would have made if a decade earlier the congregation had initiated a planned giving program. Over a period of several years, the church's bylaws were amended appropriately, a qualified committee to oversee the funds was formed, endowment policy was established, and a special giving program inaugurated. First Church received one bequest for $200,000, a piece of property valued at $125,000, several gifts of over $25,000, and nearly two dozen others between $1,000 and $10,000. Over one hundred donors gave much smaller gifts through the memorial fund program. Ten years later, the endowment stands at $485,000. The integrity of the fund is based on a firm policy never to use any of it for the church's operating budget.

A 7.5 percent return the previous year generated $36,375 in interest income. Two-thirds of the income will be added to the principal, putting it at $509,250 for the coming year. No large capital expenses came up this year, but next year First Church will use $30,000 of the income to paint the sanctuary.

The remaining $12,125 from interest last year will be given to ministries and programs beyond the scope of the church's operating budget. Half goes to international mission, the other half to local ecumenical efforts.

To be sure, interest rates are always fluctuating, and every time they do, all the numbers change. Since the start of the 1970s, interest rates have bounced between 2 and 22 percent. When inflation is hard on a church budget, it is kind to endowments. Because of the mercurial habits of interest rates, endowments can be nurtured for their long-term support, not their short-term profits.

The following list outlines how an endowment works.

○ Capital raised is set aside permanently (although it might be used for emergencies). Dipping into the principal essentially kills the goose laying the golden eggs. Borrowing against the principal is an option but is ill advised except in emergency situations. Adding to the principal means enriching the benefits accruing year after year.

- Only interest earned is spent. The interest income is primarily designated for large, one-time capital expenses that an operating budget is not equipped to handle—a new roof, a computer, a van, repainting the sanctuary, and so on.
- Allowing the income to roll over and grow keeps up with inflation and replenishes the fund after major disbursements.
- In some endowments, special ministries beyond the scope of the operating budget sometimes receive grants from the fund's pool of wealth.

Careful planning and congregational education are needed for endowment development. Such development is different from the one-time capital campaign, which sets a specific goal to reach and focuses its energies within, usually, a thirty-six-month time line. By contrast, endowment generation is slower paced and lower keyed.

Taking Advantage of Planned Giving

Denominations, nonprofits, and independent companies have honed planned giving to a fine art. Using their expertise is critical. Reinventing the wheel and insisting on local talent are both mistaken approaches. A good way to become educated in the subject is to contact a local college, seminary, hospital, or similar nonprofit. Ask to be sent their package of planned giving material. Most nonprofit development officers will be happy to explain their programs and share their literature.

Wills, bequests, charitable remainder trusts, and a number of other financial instruments make it increasingly easy for individuals to give significant donations without compromising their cash flow or the inheritance they hope to leave their children. Financial managers and insurance agents often market planned giving instruments. Because such advisers have a financial interest in the instruments they promote, these plans need particularly close scrutiny and comparison with similar plans. Reject any programs that do not go out of their way to protect the donor from hardship or incomplete disclosure.

SUGGESTIONS FOR PLANNED GIVING PROGRAMS

- When establishing an endowment, take steps to appropriately amend the congregation's constitution, articles of incorporation, and bylaws to institute and provide guidance for the asset and its management.
- Craft the goals in any long-term fundraising effort and the policy governing the use of endowment income with great care and detail, in dialogue with a professional financial planner.

○ Use a committee of carefully chosen leaders in dialogue with one or more professional investment counselors to oversee the congregation's endowment management. Consider having at least one or two committee members who are not members of the congregation but are invited to serve for their financial expertise.

Ashley Hale, a distinguished church fundraiser, offers a serious warning regarding endowments. "For every dollar of the annual operating budget that comes from any other source than the living, resident members, the congregation will give about one dollar less" (1991b, p. 16). In other words, using endowment dollars to compensate for operating debt compromises the whole system and means less giving.

Properly used, capital assets, in the form of endowments or foundations, empower congregations to pay any unusually big bills *and* to enlarge their giving capacity. On both ethical and practical grounds, Hale suggests that any congregation committed to raising large funds become a big institutional giver in the process. Theologically and organizationally, learning to give is an important step in being able to receive.

A longer study of the benefits of and problems with congregational endowments is *Endowed Congregations: Pros and Cons,* by Loren Mead (1992).

Organizing Capital Campaigns

Living on the financial edge is a daily fact of life in thousands of congregations. Paying bills may be difficult, meeting the budget an annual struggle. Program and personnel support can be threatened, particularly in smaller worshiping communities. Schaller reports: "Long-established smaller congregations averaging fewer than a hundred at worship are experiencing increasing difficulty in being able to attract, challenge, provide an adequate compensation package, and keep a competent full-time resident pastor who can help that congregation attract new generations of younger members" (1992b, p. 165). During tough financial circumstances, it is difficult to imagine having the resources to bounce out of debt, much less raise significant new funds.

This unhappy scenario, though, needs to be set next to another slice of reality. At a large fundraising firm exclusively serving the religious community, an executive vice president confided to me, "There is enough money in the church to bring in the Kingdom—believe me, all the money we need. People simply don't realize it and don't understand how to get access to it." Ashley Hale has said, "I have never known a pastor who did not seriously underestimate the income of members" (1992, p. 32).

Moving from the financial doldrums to financial health is difficult, first of all emotionally. The wake-up call for fundraising often arrives when a congregation experiences a serious loss. Thousands of worshiping communities suffer major fires each year, for example. If they are underinsured, congregations need to raise substantial funds to rebuild.

The Problems with Mortgages

A large mortgage was the traditional solution for raising large amounts of money. Today worshiping communities have difficulty attracting loans. Benjamin Franklin wrote, "If you would know the value of money, go and try to borrow some." Your local lending institution may be owned by a financial corporation far away, removing loan decisions from your neighborhood. Using congregational property as collateral is a problem because the market for sanctuaries is very small. Bank officers usually do not feel free to pursue financially delinquent religious institutions, so offering loans in the first place may seem an imprudent risk. Who wants to risk foreclosing on a community congregation?

Compounding the problem once a loan is secured is that you and the future members are saddled with the debt. In effect, a mortgage commits the congregation to "growing" money for a financial institution on a long-term basis.

In light of these difficulties, some congregations sell bonds to their members, financing the building expenses from within. But debt to your membership is not much different from debt to the savings and loan. It represents an extended drag on the community's budget and program, today and in the future. Some church finance experts advise against ever taking loans from members, not because they are illegal but because they pose dangers if you have less than expert advice and good judgment. We all know that fights over money can get nasty, so many suggest minimizing the opportunities for them. In the right context, however, a member's loan may be appropriate and empowering.

In contrast, Eugene Rudnicki (1994) argues the benefits of *bond financing*, calling it "an affordable way to refinance, remodel, or expand your church." A number of finance companies have emerged in recent years that specialize in church bonds, and periodically you can find their advertisements in *Your Church*. Depend on experts who are certified to sell securities and financial institutions you know you can trust. Ask mortgage, banking, and bond firms if they are a member of NACIFO, the National Association of Church and Institutional Financing Organizations, a group seeking to improve industry standards and attuned to the special circumstances surrounding congregational finances.

If your congregation goes after financing, you will have to do the same kinds of things you would as a private individual looking for a loan. The details of how the community plans to spend the money, the last three years of financial records, the success of its pledge program, the names and addresses of board members, and so on have to be produced in the application.

The same issues pertain when you consider refinancing a congregation's debt. Professional expertise you can trust remains critical. "In the Best Interest," by Peary Perry (1996), provides a good background discussion about corporate refinancing.

Different Approaches to Fundraising

Successful fundraising is usually a sophisticated, complex, and difficult task. An unannounced general appeal for funds during worship, for instance, will likely raise more resentment than money. Carefully conceived and implemented efforts, ranging from one-day "miracle Sundays" to three-year capital pledge programs (quite different from annual budget pledging or planned giving), can empower a congregation.

Capital campaigns represent a happy alternative to borrowing. Sometimes a congregation borrows as much as it can, then mounts a campaign seeking the balance of what it needs for the task at hand. Reversing the process makes much more sense. Borrow the least amount possible, *after* a campaign is concluded. Borrowing first inevitably means the campaign will be perceived as a debt-retirement campaign, always more difficult to succeed at than a building campaign.

Temples and churches approach these campaigns in a number of ways. For small congregations (under seventy-five families) and those that refuse to hire a fundraising firm, gathering appropriate literature and becoming self-educated is an alternative to hiring a consultant. Partners for Sacred Places, an ecumenical nonprofit in Philadelphia, publishes *The Complete Guide to Capital Campaigns for Historic Churches and Synagogues,* by Peggy Powell Dean and Suzanna Jones (1991). The guide is a systematic approach to capital campaigns. Partners for Sacred Places does not do consulting itself, but it will advise you when your congregation is preparing to make such a choice. Unfortunately, a campaign can be botched in all sorts of ways, particularly when it is home grown.

A leader in the congregation, perhaps someone with business and fundraising experience, may be tapped to lead the task. Nine of out ten times this is a mistake. Serious fundraising is too complex an effort to be designed in-house and implemented without access to expert resources.

Even large nonprofits with full-time financial development offices turn to outside firms for guidance and management during special campaigns.

Another popular approach should be avoided at all costs—employing a fundraising expert "someone knows" who will do all the solicitation for a percentage of what is raised. This is a red-flag alert. First, individuals, by themselves, probably lack resources necessary to do the job. Second, the fact that the acquaintance is "local" means little in terms of qualifications to do a good job. Third, asking for a percentage of what is raised means less money will be raised. And fourth, asking for a percentage also violates the codes of ethics of the American Association of Fund-Raising Counsel and of the National Society of Fund Raising Executives. Large donors shy away from anyone's receiving a commission from the gifts they make. And the temptation to abuse the solicitation process always exists when percentages are involved.

Denominationally affiliated congregations will wish to check with their national leadership about fundraising assistance, but the track record here is not encouraging. Fundraising is just one of *many* areas where denominational leaders are asked to provide assistance, and they usually cannot give adequate attention to the subject.

By far the best approach to a capital campaign is to employ a professional firm offering management guidance and resources exclusively to religious congregations and related agencies. Whether you have a goal of $10,000 or mount a million-dollar campaign, experts in this business are ready and able to talk extensively about fundraising, including providing very specific services for a fee.

Church Fund-Raising Services will send you its free thirty-one-page *Standard Guidance for Church Capital or Building Fund-Raising*, full of commonsense suggestions and warnings for the congregation seeking professional help. The booklet also details particular services offered by the firm, providing a good comparison if you are talking to a number of firms.

The primary difficulty with consultants is a congregation's distrust of inviting any outsider into the financial dynamic of the community. Enough nightmare stories are recited, indeed, to justify considerable study before any consultant or firm is recommended and retained. One or two such tales can scare congregations away from this approach, cutting them off from the best resources available. Adequate research and preparation is the best safeguard as you proceed.

Good preparation includes refusing to set goals or assign roles before it is appropriate. Resist the temptation to short circuit the integrity of each step in organizing a campaign. When a building has burned down, for example, leaders may feel tremendous pressure to make quick decisions and move forward. Withstanding the pressure and honoring the process is a boon to the community's treasury and will later bring the gratitude of the congregation. For instance, before implementing any fundraising plan, conduct a thorough feasibility study, preferably guided by a professional. Without the study, a capital fundraising project will be flying blind.

Whomever they work with in fundraising efforts, leaders need to be aware that the responsibilities rest on both the giver and the receiver. Some specific rules accompany the special privilege congregations have of receiving gifts that are tax deductible to the donor.

SUGGESTIONS FOR ASKING FOR MONEY

- When a fundraising strategy is planned, *clearly distinguish that effort from the offerings and annual pledging that support the operating budget.* Capital formation, in contrast to annual pledging, comes from bequests, special gifts, large fundraisers, memorials, and gifts to capital campaigns. These large gifts often are received from special trusts set up by members and friends. Many are noncash assets, such as real estate.

- Full, honest disclosure to donors is mandatory when soliciting gifts and in reporting the results of the giving program.

- Congregations must always honor the intention of the donor when receiving *restricted gifts,* that is, gifts given for a specific purpose. Any claims and promises you make in your solicitation must be kept. If your promotional literature says the money will be spent on a children's playground, do not decide later to spend it on hymnals! Doing so may constitute fraud. The key—wait until the whole project is planned before publishing your literature or soliciting potential donors.

- Donors must not be manipulated or tricked in any way. To the contrary, they should have time to consider their giving and be encouraged to talk the matter over with their families and financial advisers. Do not accept gifts that place a significant hardship on the giver.

- In order to receive tax benefits, donors can be given a receipt they will use for the IRS. The congregation is legally bound to make this receipt accurate.

- Gifts other than money should always be assigned a financial value by the donor, not the congregation.

- Gifts, other than money or publicly traded securities, that are valued at $5,000 or more require that the donor have an appraisal. The donor is also expected to file IRS Form 8283 (Noncash Charitable Contributions) with the IRS after obtaining a confirming signature from an appropriate officer of the congregation. If such property is sold by the congregation within two years, the congregation is required to file Form 8282 and give the donor a copy. (Noncash gifts between $500 and $5,000 require the first page of Form 8283, but a confirming signature from the congregation is not necessary.)

o Beware of noncash donations that may arrive with hidden problems. If donated land once was secretly used as a chemical dump, a new owner (that is, the congregation) may have a financial monster by the tail in the form of legal responsibilities. Encourage donors to sell their property then make a financial gift of the proceeds. If this fails, secure a legal analysis of potential liability before accepting any large noncash gift.

o If you develop your own capital campaign, ask a tax attorney to review it for you, including any literature to be used in solicitation. (Attorneys whose clientele include members of the congregation should be avoided for this particular task. Attorneys administering trust funds for members may have financial incentive for limiting any charitable donation from their clients to the congregation. Taking these attorneys out of the running for this assignment saves them from a potential conflict of interest.)

o Rewarding donors with a book or some other tangible thank-you gift may reduce the amount of tax deduction available to donors.

Along with considering these suggestions, review updates in the law about charitable gifts at the outset of any large fundraising project. The easiest way to do this is to purchase the most recent of the annual guides by Daniel Busby and Richard Hammar. Similar books exist, but no one else has the track record these two authors have established.

Working with Professional Fundraising Consultants

A semantic point here is important. On the one hand, a professional *fundraiser* essentially offers to do the job for you, including the actual solicitation. On the other hand, a professional *fundraising consultant* is a trainer and a manager, educated in fundraising, equipped with a variety of specific fundraising systems, and ready with resources that empower the congregation's particular campaign. As I mentioned earlier, beware of Lone Ranger fundraisers who depend on personal charisma to sell their services. Clergy status and friendliness are not good measures of competence in this arena. Rely on professional consulting companies with good track records who involve the entire congregation as they facilitate an integrated, theologically sound, and demonstrably effective feasibility study and campaign.

The *AT&T Toll-Free Directory* lists over two hundred fundraising firms with toll-free numbers. The largest ones in the nation, old and venerable, usually have a small, dependable department for religious congregations. In the late forties, Lewis G. Wells founded the Wells Organization, Inc., devoted exclusively to fundraising for congregations. The company no longer exists, but over a hundred campaign managers were trained by the Wells group, and some are still in business. Firms working exclusively for worshiping communities tend to be the most experienced with what congregations need.

You can find firms locally, others have offices around the country, and still others depend on airplanes and the telephone. Close does not mean better—the quality of its services is much more important than whether a firm is near or far. One way to begin your search is to contact the American Association of Fund-Raising Counsel and ask for a membership list and the association's booklet about fund-raising consultants.

Companies primarily serving religious congregations arrive on your doorstep with their own theology of stewardship, explicit or implicit. Typically, it is biblically focused and full of promise. But do not let an enthusiastic "politically correct" firm sign you up before you can evaluate its attitude toward giving. *Giving is an important, valuable experience for the faithful member.* Look for companies that focus on the *meaning* of giving before you raise the subject; steer clear of those who only emphasize the bundle you will make with them. Make sure the religious language and perspective of any firm you work with is appropriate in your worshiping community.

Be skeptical of the outside professional who wants to help with preaching and teaching. In these areas, a congregation's own leadership, informed but not supplanted by the consultant, is more likely to be effective than an outsider's. Turn to professional firms for the expert management services and experience the congregation lacks. The influence required to persuade givers to give ultimately develops from a congregation's own leaders, trained but not replaced by the outside expert.

SUGGESTIONS FOR SELECTING A FUNDRAISING FIRM
- Ask about the range of services offered and how much time the company spends with groups similar to yours in size and need.

○ Ask for recent references and check them out.

○ Ask about percentages of money raised in comparison to goals set. Remember, though—receiving a lower percentage of a very high goal is usually preferable to meeting 100 percent of a low goal. Therefore, ask how each prospective consultant sets goals and favor the firms that aim high.

○ Avoid fundraisers who do the actual soliciting themselves. Good consultants, instead, are managers and trainers who teach your best givers to do the soliciting.

○ Ask if the firm's consultants receive commissions for contracting the campaigns they manage. If they do, they may spend more time finding future clients than managing your campaign. Commission-driven firms may be the largest, but bigger does not necessarily mean better in this business.

○ Avoid companies that charge a percentage of what they raise. Reputable companies charge fees for services. Ask for specific fee schedules and compare what different firms offer and charge. Do not ask for guarantees that a specific financial goal will be met. A reputable firm will make no such promise. Fees should range from three to ten cents out of each dollar raised. They should be estimated on the basis of (1) basic fees for specific services and (2) the number of families in the congregation. Fees for completing good work range widely, so research can save your congregation money. Be forewarned that companies do not make comparisons easy, so perseverance is important.

○ Ask about the firm's theological point of view and any religious affiliations it may have.

○ Compare the literature companies provide in your search for the best professionals. Read slick four-color promotional pieces very carefully. Are the materials furnished completely self-serving? Or can you find other information, warnings, suggestions, and ideas that will be useful whether or not you retain this specific firm? Trust those who teach (rather than impress) you as they get to know you. Good references are not enough.

○ Ask for specific information about the actual venture you contemplate sharing with the firm. What kind of leadership training is provided? How is the pre-fundraising study designed, and what will it accomplish? What kind of manuals and publications are used? How-to information is more important than posters and balloons. What kind of record-keeping materials and analysis does a firm offer? Will it provide toll-free telephone contact for you when the consultant is not on-site? What kind of ongoing services are built into the program? All this information should be detailed, and costs should be specified.

○ Campaigns typically begin with a feasibility study, and signing separate contracts for the study and the campaign is advantageous to the congregation. Do not be seduced by a "free" feasibility study. By separately contracting these two steps in the process, you strengthen the value and trustworthiness of the study. A feasibility study examines the type of gifts anticipated, which members to ask for fundraising leadership, a survey of planning to be done, and goal formation and defines the professional services needed. Without the study in hand, you are inadequately prepared to define the campaign and agree to a fair fee.

○ Both operating and endowment income come directly from the membership, through annual pledging or fundraising. But some congregations, particularly in older urban areas, may find financial partners for special projects such as improving facilities that serve the community at large as well as the congregation. Ask if the firm provides any guidance for raising funds through relationships with the larger community, local foundations, and outside user groups.

○ Ask if the firm is affiliated with the American Association of Fund-Raising Counsel (AAFRC) or the National Society of Fund Raising Executives. If not, ask for any published code of ethics the firm uses. Stay away from firms that do no more than claim to be good honest people.

○ Perhaps the most important suggestion is this last one. Standards of accountability are critically important when a congregation opens up its financial planning process to outside experts. If you are contemplating working with a firm that is not affiliated with a professional association, ask if they will endorse in writing the AAFRC code of ethics (see Exhibit 5.1).

A final warning: do not trust conventional wisdom about good fundraising. It is an evolving discipline, and yesteryear's orthodoxy may be folly. Instead, find a firm that the congregation's leaders and officers can trust and feel comfortable with. Learn what it has to offer, and follow its advice. Delay defining your goals, making plans, or even choosing your campaign chair until you have established your relationship with this expert advice. Similarly, do not make premature solicitations—you will raise less money.

- Initial meetings with prospective clients should not be construed as services for which payment is expected.
- No payments or special consideration should be made to an officer, director, trustee, employee, or advisor of a not-for-profit organization as compensation for influencing the selection of fund-raising counsel.
- Fees should be mutually agreed upon in advance of services.
- A flat, fixed fee is charged based on the level and extent of professional services provided. Fees are not based on the amount of charitable income raised or expected to be raised.
- Contracts providing for a contingent fee, commission, or percentage of funds raised, are prohibited. Such contracts are harmful to the relationship between the donor and the institution and detrimental to the financial health of the client organization.
- Fundraising expenditures are within the authority and control of the not-for-profit organization.
- It is in the best interest of clients that solicitation of gifts is undertaken by board members, staff, and other volunteers.
- Member firms do not engage in methods that mislead the public or harm the client, such as exaggerating past achievements, guaranteeing results, or promising unrealistic goals.
- Subsequent to analysis or study, a member should engage a client only when the probability for fundraising success exists.
- Member firms should not profit directly or indirectly from materials provided by others, but billed to the member firms, without disclosure to the client.
- Any potential conflict of interest should be disclosed by the firm to clients and prospective clients.
- Member firms will not acquire or maintain custody of funds or gifts directed to the client organization.

Exhibit 5.1. The AAFRC Code of Ethics.
Source: *American Association of Fund-Raising Counsel.*

By far the largest portion of the work in a good campaign happens in preparation. Hurrying the process compromises the results. And remember that an important factor in retaining a good firm is your ability to educate your membership about the wisdom of contracting expert help.

Trouble in Paradise

The various resources and opportunities surveyed in this chapter are important tools in the congregational leader's kit. They help but cannot prepare the first-time board officer or a new pastor for the grim financial realities sometimes facing religious institutions. The long-term decrease in giving in evangelical as well as mainline churches points to a fiscal crisis in the Christian community that will escalate until we learn more about money and its use.

Two groups have taken the lead in studying the troubled finances of the Christian church in the United States. John Ronsvalle and Sylvia Ronsvalle founded empty tomb, inc., which studies long-term congregational giving patterns and publishes *The State of Church Giving*, the most recent volume released in late 1996. Their research cuts across most of the twentieth century, tracking dozens of denominations. Their prognosis: if long-established patterns of decreasing giving are not better understood and turned around, congregations will run out of funds before the middle of the next century.

When empty tomb claimed that evangelical congregations also face declining giving, the report was disbelieved, perhaps because evangelicals tend to give more than their liberal counterparts. But the *Christianity Today* article "Churches Struggle with New Factors in the Giving Equation" (1995) confirms empty tomb's report. Since 1968, the decline has been greater in a set of National Association of Evangelicals denominations than in a set of National Council of Churches denominations.

Research by the Ronsvalles going back to the thirties shows that per-member giving, measured as a percentage of income, was less in 1993 than in 1933, the height of the Great Depression. It is hard to miss the irony of doing better in poor times than in the richest economy the planet has ever known. The Ronsvalles' 1996 book *Behind Stained Glass Windows: Money Dynamics in the Church,* confronts this financial distress head-on and begins exploring a theology that accounts for faithful giving in an affluent culture like our own.

Alert readers of the religious press may notice occasional stories about benevolent giving increasing, with religious organizations enjoying a growing bonanza each year. These prognostications probably come from the AAFRC, whose code of ethics we examined previously or from the organization INDEPENDENT SECTOR. The Ronsvalles point out that AAFRC's analysis does not take into account population growth, and that INDEPENDENT SECTOR asks people what they give, rather than using statistics gathered from congregations or denominations recording what they actually receive, which is the empty tomb approach.

The complexity intensifies when the Ronsvalles' methodology is also questioned. William McKinney, president of Pacific School of Religion and a congregational studies specialist, suggests that the Ronsvalle straight-line analysis (which supposes that today's decreases will never vary), does not make sense. Lyle Schaller agrees with McKinney and points out that religious organizations receive income in various ways that never make it into statistical reports ("Incredible Shrinking Church?" 1994). These points are well taken, but the Ronsvalles continue to be the only serious economic scholars studying congregational giving. It would be foolish to ignore their wake-up call about the attitude of congregational leaders toward giving and receiving money. Contact empty tomb, inc., for a methodological discussion of their work and the actual data.

Lilly Endowment is the nation's largest independent donor to religious institutions. So it was one of the first to recognize the financial doldrums being recorded by the Ronsvalles. Lilly commissioned a survey of eleven thousand members and clergy from 625 congregations in five denominations, as part of its Initiative on the Financing of American Religion. In addition, thirty projects have been funded that study financial practices, membership attitude, and the uses of money in the religious community. An article in the endowment's *Initiative in Religion* newsletter, "Financing American Religion Means More Than Dollars" (1995), reviews this activity and the handful of books already published.

As this book goes to press, the journals that keep cropping up in these pages are planning new articles about money, the discussions ranging from statistical analysis to the pain of downsizing to the experience and theology of giving. More books will follow, and the library of religious stewardship will bulge with new resources.

In the midst of this extended discussion, remember the point at the beginning of this chapter—good stewardship is more about the individual than the group, more about the art of giving than fundraising. So claims Kennon Callahan in *Giving and Stewardship in an Effective Church: A Guide for Every Member* (1992), a good resource to begin with when you want to enhance your congregation's experience of giving.

To conclude this discussion of finances, two dramatic stories juxtapose the serious dangers and extraordinary possibilities money sets before the religious community.

In the early 1990s, the Foundation for New Era Philanthropy was the darling of nonprofits and foundations for its ability to double an investment through a "matching grant" program. Apparently, it was a Ponzi scheme: today's investments paid yesterday's investors. This gradually accelerating process inevitably collapses when it cannot keep up with itself. New Era went bankrupt in May 1995, and several months later the court-appointed bankruptcy trustee asked over one thousand charitable organizations to return the $174 million they had received unfairly as the early

investors. Evangelical researcher George Barna says that Christian evangelical groups alone lost "tens of millions" through New Era ("Financial
Scam Makes Little Impression," 1995). So much for the devil at the door
commanding our vigilance.

Conversely, when goodwill, imagination, and financial acumen mix it up,
money can empower the religious community in ways no one imagined
before. The 2.5 million member Progressive National Baptist Convention,
a predominately African American denomination, has used its institutional
clout to start a number of cooperative financial projects to improve badly
suffering neighborhoods. In one program, it has joined hands with
NationsBank to build a senior-housing model project in Washington, D.C.
It is not just a financial partnership; the bank is offering workshops to
members on cash management, personal investments, retirement planning,
and stewardship of assets.

In a much larger project, the Progressive Baptists have joined with four
other large black denominations to create Revelation Corporation of America. The denominations will own 70 percent of the company. Members will
receive large discounts on consumer goods and services; congregations will
receive significant rebates generated through the sales; and most of the
income will be used to generate housing construction and underwrite mortgages. Twenty percent of the rebates are funneled back to local congregational operating budgets, with 10 percent going to a clergy retirement fund.

There are dozens of reasons the Revelation Corporation of America
could never happen, yet it has. No doubt it will attract critics within and
outside the religious community. What Revelation aims to achieve is new
and fairly complex; but because everyone involved ends up a beneficiary,
it will have powerful forces moving it forward. If it succeeds, it will serve
millions of people, members of faith families and their neighborhoods.
The strategy comes from religious leaders whose imagination was not
stopped by cynicism or a sense of scarcity, people who were smart enough
and cared enough to figure out better ways to serve people.

Going the Next Step

The most thorough financial handbook for clergy and congregational
treasurers is the *Church and Clergy Tax Guide* by Richard Hammar.
Revised and reissued each January, it is packed full of information
(including useful summaries in each section) about both institutional and
clergy responsibilities.

Religious leaders with financial responsibilities can also find an
excellent overall survey of their legal obligations in *The Zondervan*

Church and Nonprofit Organization Tax and Financial Guide, by Daniel D. Busby, a well-respected CPA and author. In contrast to the Hammar book, which is devoted equally to clergy and congregational concerns, Busby focuses primarily on institutional responsibilities. Like Hammar though, Busby revises and updates his book each year to include legal news from the prior year. Section two in Busby, about congregational leaders and clergy being accountable to the governing board itself, to donors, and to the government, is particularly good. Special sections later in the book address employer standards and fiscal management, including accounting practices. This information changes every single year, so do yourself a favor and buy Busby one year, Hammar the next. It is the same story with their respective newsletters. Busby writes *Pastor's Tax and Money* while Hammar writes *Church Treasurer's Alert!* They are both good. Ask for samples and make up your own mind.

In addition to Busby and Hammar, one can find all sorts of helpful resources. A large library of denominational and independent resources addresses the many different aspects of stewardship, including the administrative and management systems that support a congregation's local economy. One useful book is a guide for new congregational bookkeepers, complete with sample worksheets. *Demystifying the Congregational Budget* (1988) by H. H. Morris provides an easy way to do your bookkeeping and an easy way to report regularly to the congregation. A number of similar publications are available.

Daniel Busby published helpful guidelines in "Embezzlement: It Could Happen to Your Church" (1995). He suggests strict procedures for offerings, timely financial reports on a monthly basis, good internal auditing systems, controls on negotiable instruments, donation reports, and insurance for theft.

Basic Accounting for Churches (1994) and *Basic Budgeting for Churches* (1995), by Jack Henry, have both received high praise as technically competent and well communicated. *Mastering Church Finances* (Bergstrom, Fenton, and Pohl, 1992) offers twelve essays, ranging in topic from the relationship between spiritual and financial values to protection against embezzlement. Written by Richard L. Bergstrom, Gary Fenton, and Wayne Pohl, the essays are refreshing, useful, and concerned with financial integrity.

Catalogs from Abingdon Press in Nashville, Tennessee, and Zondervan in Grand Rapids, Michigan, feature books about the financial administration of local congregations, and your own denominational resource list probably also offers helpful materials in this area.

Resources for Financial Management

Agencies

American Association of Fund-Raising Counsel, 25 West 43rd Street, New
York, NY 10036; (212) 354–5799.

Christian Ministry Resources, P.O. Box 1098, Matthews, NC 28106;
(704) 841–8066.

Church Fund-Raising Services, 825 Collyer Street, Longmont, CO 80501;
(800) 826–2048.

Co-op America, 1612 K Street, NW, Suite 600, Washington, DC 20006;
(800) 584–7336.

empty tomb, inc., P.O. Box 2404, Champaign, IL 61825–2344;
(217) 356–2262.

Foundation Center, 79 Fifth Avenue, New York, NY 10003; (212) 620–4230.

INDEPENDENT SECTOR, 1828 L Street, NW, Washington, DC 20036;
(202) 223–8100.

Institute of Certified Financial Planners, 7600 East Eastman Avenue, Suite 301,
Denver, CO 80231; (800) 282–7526.

Interfaith Center on Corporate Responsibility, 475 Riverside Drive, Room 550,
New York, NY 10115; (212) 870–2295.

Jossey-Bass Inc., Publishers, 350 Sansome Street, San Francisco, CA 94104;
(415) 433–1740.

National Association of Church Business Administration (NACBA),
7001 Grapevine Highway, Suite 324, Fort Worth, TX 76180;
(817) 284–1732.

National Association of Personal Financial Advisors, 355 West Dundee Road,
Suite 107, Buffalo Grove, IL 60089; (800) 366–2732.

Partners for Sacred Places, 1616 Walnut Street, Suite 2310, Philadelphia, PA
19103; (215) 546–1288.

Social Investment Forum, P.O. Box 57216, Washington, DC 20037;
(202) 872–5319.

Society for Nonprofit Organizations, 6314 Odana Road, Madison, WI 53719;
(608) 274–9777.

Periodicals

Church Treasurer's Alert! P.O. Box 1098, Matthews, NC 28106;
(704) 841–8066.

The Clean Yield, P.O. Box 117, Greensboro, VT 05841; (802) 533–7178.

Corporate Examiner, Interfaith Center on Corporate Responsibility,
475 Riverside Drive, Room 550, New York, NY 10115;
(212) 870–2295.

The Forum, Social Investment Forum, P.O. Box 57216, Washington, DC 20037; (202) 872–5319.

NonProfit Times, 190 Tamarack Circle, Skillman, NY 08558.

Nonprofit World, Society for Nonprofit Organizations, 6314 Odana Road, Madison, WI 53719; (608) 274–9777.

Pastor's Tax and Money, P.O. Box 50188, Indianapolis, IN 46205; (800) 877–3158.

Books and Articles

"Analysis of Church-Giving Patterns Shows a Steady Decline Since 1960s." *Initiatives in Religion,* Fall 1993, pp. 8,10.

Anderson, Leith, Cousins, Don, and DeKruyter, Arthur. *Mastering Church Management.* Portland, Ore./Carol Stream, Ill.: Multnomah Press/Christianity Today, 1992.

Ashton, Debra. "How to Start a Planned-Giving Program," *Nonprofit World,* May/June 1991, pp. 10–13.

"Baptists and Bank Form Partnership." *Christian Century,* Mar. 13, 1996, p. 288.

Bergstrom, Richard L., Fenton, Gary, and Pohl, Wayne. *Mastering Church Finances.* Portland, Ore./Carol Stream, Ill.: Multnomah Press/ Christianity Today, 1992.

"Black Churches Form Economic Partnership." *National Christian Reporter,* Jan. 26, 1996, p. 2.

Bruyns, Noel. "Church Treasurer Jailed for Stealing $2.2 Million." *National Christian Reporter,* July 26, 1996, p. 1.

Building Relationships: A Guide for Institutions on How to Work with an Architect. New York: American Institute of Architects, Public Affairs Department. (Available from American Institute of Architects, Public Affairs Department, 1735 New York Avenue, NW, Washington, DC 20006; (202) 626–7461.)

Busby, Daniel D. "Embezzlement: It Could Happen to Your Church." *Pastor's Tax and Money,* Mar. 1995, pp. 3–4.

Busby, Daniel D. "Internal Control and Audit." *Clergy Journal,* Jan. 1996, p. 14.

Busby, Daniel D. *The Zondervan Church and Nonprofit Organization Tax and Financial Guide.* Grand Rapids, Mich.: Zondervan, published annually.

Callahan, Kennon L. *Giving and Stewardship in an Effective Church: A Guide for Every Member.* San Francisco: Harper San Francisco, 1992.

Capin, Gregory B. "The Independent Audit: A Wise Investment?" *Clergy Journal,* Sept. 1995, pp. 42–45.

Carroll, Jackson W., Dudley, Carl S., and McKinney, William (eds.). *Handbook for Congregational Studies.* Nashville, Tenn.: Abingdon Press, 1986.

"Churches Struggle with New Factors in the Giving Equation." *Christianity Today*, Apr. 24, 1995, pp. 48–49.

Dean, Peggy Powell, and Jones, Suzanna A. *The Complete Guide to Capital Campaigns for Historic Churches and Synagogues*. Philadelphia: Partners for Sacred Places, 1991.

"Diocesan Treasurer Accused of Embezzling." *Christian Century*, June 5, 1996, pp. 610–611.

Dunkin, Amy. "The Perils in Picking a Planner." *Business Week*, Dec. 14, 1992, pp. 112–113.

Ethics and the Nation's Voluntary and Philanthropic Community. Washington, D.C.: INDEPENDENT SECTOR, 1991.

"Financial Scam Makes Little Impression." *Christian Century*, Oct. 11, 1995, p. 919.

"Financing American Religion Means More Than Dollars." *Initiatives in Religion*, Summer 1995, pp. 5–8.

Firstenberg, Paul B. *Managing for Profit in the Nonprofit World*. New York: Foundation Center, 1986.

Gallup, George, Jr. "Confidence in Clergy Found Slipping Steadily." *National Christian Reporter*, Nov. 12, 1993, p. 3.

Gotwals, Martha. "New Study on Giving to Churches Reveals Striking Patterns." *EcuLink*, Feb./Apr. 1991, p. 5.

Hale, Ashley. "Denominational Fund-Raising Services." *Clergy Journal*, Oct. 1991a, p. 4.

Hale, Ashley. "The Endowed Church." *Clergy Journal*, May/June 1991b, p. 16.

Hale, Ashley. "How to Start a Planned-Giving Program." *Nonprofit World*, May/June 1991c, pp. 10–13.

Hale, Ashley. "Recent Advances in Fund Raising." *Clergy Journal*, Mar. 1992, p. 32.

Hammar, Richard. "Fund-Raising Practices Come Under IRS Scrutiny." *Church Law and Tax Report*, Nov./Dec. 1988, pp. 7–8.

Hammar, Richard. "Tips on Completing 1991 W-2 and 1099 Forms." *Church Law and Tax Report*, Jan./Feb. 1992, pp. 7–12.

Hammar, Richard. "Avoiding an Audit." *Leadership*, Winter 1995, pp. 99–102.

Hammar, Richard. *Church and Clergy Tax Guide*. Matthews, N.C.: Christian Ministry Resources, published annually.

Henry, Jack A. *Basic Accounting for Churches: A Turnkey Manual*. Nashville, Tenn.: Boardman & Holman, 1994.

Henry, Jack A. *Basic Budgeting for Churches: A Complete Guide*. Nashville, Tenn.: Boardman & Holman, 1995.

Holck, Manfred, Jr. *Clergy Desk Book*. Nashville, Tenn.: Abingdon Press, 1990.

"Incredible Shrinking Church?" *Christian Century,* Jan. 5–12, 1994, p. 7.

Jordan, Ronald R., and Quynn, Katelyn L. "Tax Consequences of Charitable Giving." *Nonprofit World,* Mar./Apr. 1991, pp. 13–16.

LaRue, John C., Jr., "The Money Churches Borrow and Save." *Your Church,* Nov./Dec. 1992, p. 48.

Lowry, Ritchie. *Good Money: A Guide to Profitable Social Investing in the Nineties.* New York: Norton, 1991.

Mead, Loren. *Endowed Congregations: Pros and Cons.* Bethesda, Md.: Alban Institute, 1992.

Mead, Loren. "Caught in the Financial Bind: Reflections on Clergy and Money." *Congregations,* July/Aug. 1996, pp. 3–4.

Morris, H. H. *Demystifying the Congregational Budget.* Bethesda, Md.: Alban Institute, 1988.

"New Era Founder to Sell Assets." *Christian Century,* Feb. 7, 1996, p. 125.

Perry, Peary. "In the Best Interest." *Your Church,* May/June 1996, pp. 29–34.

Pollock, David R. "Honest Financial Church Policies." *Clergy Journal,* July 1996, pp. 29–32.

Ronsvalle, John L., and Ronsvalle, Sylvia. *Behind Stained Glass Windows: Money Dynamics in the Church.* Grand Rapids, Mich.: Baker, 1996a.

Ronsvalle, John L., and Ronsvalle, Sylvia. "The End of Benevolence? Alarming Trends in Church Giving." *Christian Century,* Oct. 23, 1996b, pp. 1010–1014.

Ronsvalle, John L., and Ronsvalle, Sylvia. *The State of Church Giving.* Champaign, Ill.: empty tomb, published periodically.

Rudnicki, Eugene H. "Bond Financing: An Affordable Way to Refinance, Remodel, or Expand Your Church." *NACBA-Ledger,* Jan./Mar. 1994, pp. 4–6.

Schaller, Lyle E. "Five Ways to Counter a Budget Shortfall." *Leadership,* Winter 1992a, pp. 70–73.

Schaller, Lyle E. *The Seven-Day-a-Week Church.* Nashville, Tenn.: Abingdon Press, 1992b.

Skloot, Edward (ed.). *The Nonprofit Entrepreneur.* New York: Foundation Center, 1988.

Standard Guidance for Church Capital or Building Fund-Raising. Longmont, Colo.: Church Fund-Raising Services, n.d.

Tennyson, Mack. *Church Finances for People Who Count.* Grand Rapids, Mich.: Zondervan, 1990.

Zastrow, Todd. "How to Self-Audit Church Books." *Your Church,* Mar./Apr. 1994, pp. 18–20.

6

EMPLOYMENT PRACTICES THAT SAFEGUARD COMMUNAL VALUES

A HAPPY, UNIFIED STAFF is a powerful instrument for any congregation's life and ministry. Employed leaders need to be nurtured, their work held up and honored. Good musicians, secretaries, administrators, custodians, and clergy deserve respect and special attention from their governing boards. Receiving such support inspires them to continuing improvement and minimizes burnout. The results benefit everyone and can lead a community to new achievements.

The legal thicket grown up around employment law is complicated, and we will see how securing expert advice periodically is appropriate. But once you understand the basic issues, obeying the law is relatively easy. The more important tasks have to do with building trust levels and an ability to get good things done well. The leadership of any congregation is a web of relationships, none more important than those the employees and volunteers (the unpaid staff) have with everyone else.

Before Hiring Anyone

Most religions call their members to serve. They claim that doing good and being good are basic to faithful life. It is particularly sad, then, that those who specialize in serving our congregations—and make it their livelihood—sometimes suffer unfair expectations, disrespect, and mistreatment.

Quality of the Employment Relationship

Nowhere is the gift of human kindness more important than in and around a congregation, beginning with its staff and volunteers. Good leaders model respect. The law, in an attempt to be fair, makes everyone jump through hoops; we try to appreciate the goal as we jump. Inside the community, we hope for more than fairness, for graciousness perhaps.

Even graciousness needs education, and we have considerably more information about employees of the religious community than ever before. The *Compensation Handbook for Church Staff* (Cobble and Hammar), for instance, is updated and published annually. It tracks salaries for nine types of congregational employee, ranging from senior pastor to custodian. It is fascinating reading, particularly for search committees, personnel committees, and prospective employees. Hundreds of thousands of musicians serve congregations as volunteers or employees, for example. The *Handbook*'s statistics suggest that nationally about two-thirds of all full-time choir directors make between $25,000 and $53,000 in total annual compensation. The best indicator of a congregation's ability to secure a professional musician is the size of its budget. Despite laws forbidding wage discrimination, women are paid about a third less than men for their musical gifts and leadership. Salaries tend to increase for the first ten years of a musician's employment, after which they taper off. In this handbook and others like it, you can find similar data for most of those employed in the religious community.

Considering Support Structures

Clearly, most congregations expect a certain amount of administrative work from their clergy, and most clergy like administrative work least of all they do. If you ask your rabbi to address spiritual and liturgical needs, build a strong community, and attract new members and then say that the job includes staffing multiple committees, leading the pledge program, producing bulletins, newsletters, and directories, and even paying bills, you may be guaranteeing burnout.

Overbooking employee responsibilities is nothing new in nonprofits, religious or otherwise, so you have to use your imagination to bolster whatever support structures you have. Volunteers are critical in worshiping communities and need to be treated with the same care extended to employees. In small congregations, volunteers often keep the doors open and the hearth warm, and clergy pick up a significant part—but not all—of the administrative tasks, just as they do in large congregations. But volunteers can burn out just like employees.

Tens of thousands of small to moderate-sized congregations depend on the ministry of a secretary. Often underpaid, a church or temple secretary tends to hear all the rumors, catch all the criticism, and do considerable grunt work at the copying machine and on the telephone. Typically, secretaries are responsible for entering computer data, composing correspondence, making purchase decisions, producing the newsletter, supervising volunteers, and doing desktop publishing.

Those who succeed at the task are often thick-skinned, good listeners, and excellent at systems and details. They deserve the same benefits any other staff member receives, along with every penny they are paid. Average secretarial wages range from $7.35 to $10.20 an hour depending on the size of the church, whether the work is full-time or half-time, the denomination, and the region. Most receive some paid vacation. But only 47 percent receive medical insurance and 37 percent a retirement plan, figures that fall to 7 and 12 percent for part-timers (Hilligoss, 1995).

In recent years, more resources have become available for church secretaries. *The Church Secretary Communique* and *Profile: The Church Office Professional's Information Source* are newsletters that pass along helpful information and offer some solidarity with others in what is sometimes lonely work. The *Calendar and Workbook for Church Secretaries*, published annually by Abingdon Press, like a number of similar resources, is full of useful information to make the work easier and more effective.

A full-fledged secretary doing a good job may already be functioning as an administrator. As congregations become larger, however, the need increases for a professionally trained administrator. Administrators usually offer special skills in directing support services, operational finances, personnel and training, administrative systems, program coordination, facilities maintenance, risk management, community relations, and plenty of computing.

Often a secretary can study business administration and assume professional administrative responsibilities. The National Association of Church Business Administration (NACBA) is a good resource for its members. It features meetings at sixty-six local chapters, national conferences, and a four-week certification program offered at six different seminary sites. Founded in 1956, it has approximately 1,550 members serving congregations across the nation today, making it the largest network of ecumenical business administrators in the nation. Local chapters sponsor secretary workshops.

NACBA's publications are available to all at economical prices. The subject matter includes financial oversight and risk management, purchasing, plant maintenance, safety and security, new technology, and clergy compensation. These are areas the Alban Institute leaves aside, so NACBA has had a corner on research and resources about these administrative nuts-and-bolts issues.

Today others have begun to catch up. A number of enterprising seminaries and universities are sponsoring nonprofit administration programs where religious leaders are welcomed. An eighteen-month MBA in church management is available from the Graduate Theological Foundation in Chicago, and a similar program can be found at the Institute of Church Administration and Management in Atlanta.

As you consider support structures, it is worth noticing that in the past quarter century the personal computer has utterly changed how most congregations operate. This new machine waltzed into America's offices in 1981 and, in the process, offered congregations, large and small, powerful new tools. The temple, mosque, or church that lacks at least one PC today is either brand-new or dying. Data from 1994 reported one or more computers owned by 66 percent of all congregations, and starting in 1991, the figure was growing at over 10 percent a year (LaRue, 1994).

The easiest way to keep up with new software applications for congregations is *Your Church,* which periodically reviews new products. Dozens of integrated program packages are available for the various administrative needs of congregations (membership, payroll, donations, and so on), along with schedule planners, scripture translations, and numerous specialty items. Congregations receive millions of direct mail promotional pieces each week, and these days often the product is software. For the computer aficionado, *Church Bytes* is a good way to learn more and connect with the technologically advantaged in the religious community.

Knowing the Difference Between Employees and Independent Contractors

Who is an employee? Congregations are frequently tempted to designate workers as independent contractors in order to save payroll taxes and avoid paying for employee benefits. What begins with saving money and cutting red tape can result in civil suits for thousands of dollars. Worshiping communities are extremely vulnerable, in other words, when they inaccurately characterize a worker who is being financially compensated. These few guidelines help clarify a person's work status. A worker is usually an employee when he or she

- Is an integrated part of a congregation's operation (the person's name in the bulletin each Sunday generally means employee status, for instance)
- Works hours set by the congregation
- Works under supervision of congregational officials, performing tasks in a particular way

○ Works exclusively (or nearly so) for the congregation, using its tools and supplies

○ Receives training provided by congregational leaders and performs all duties personally

○ Is paid by time periods: hourly, weekly, or monthly

○ Is covered by workers' compensation insurance from the congregation

A worker is usually a contractor when he or she

○ Is not integrated into a congregation's operation

○ Sets his or her own hours and secures his or her own insurance

○ Enjoys flexibility in the way tasks are performed

○ Operates a business beyond the congregation, such as catering, plumbing, landscaping, or bookkeeping

○ Uses his or her own tools and supplies

○ Has been trained for a craft or profession and often has special licenses to perform a trade

○ Can arrange to have work done by others and may use assistants or replacement workers in performing tasks

○ Is paid by task: audit, speech, architectural plan, hedge trimming, furnace maintenance, and so on

Even when contractors are paid by the task, if they have no insurance, cause injury, and are sued, the court may consider them employees and the hiring congregation liable.

Worshiping communities, like other institutions, are required by law to file IRS Form 1099 whenever a contractor has been paid more than $600 in a single year.

Contractor-employee confusion is particularly complex regarding clergy, notably for those who decide to file their taxes as self-employed persons. Expert tax and legal advice best informs such decisions. The issue continues to be the subject of court judgments, and contractor status is becoming more narrowly defined, particularly for groups where there is ascending decision-making authority. The Internal Revenue Service recently prevailed in a long, complex case that effectively revoked the "self-employed" status of thirty thousand United Methodist ministers. The IRS convinced the court that the denomination and its clergy enjoy an employer-employee relationship. Richard Hammar (1994) details that decision in "Tax Court Rules That a Methodist Minister Is an Employee for Income Tax Reporting Purposes" and discusses a further decision in

"Tax Court Rules That a Pentecostal Holiness Minister Is Self-Employed for Income Tax Reporting Purposes" (1995b). The message held in these article titles is clear: talk to an expert before filing taxes as a clergyperson.

Screening Employee Applicants and Volunteers

Failure to screen an applicant's past significantly increases a congregation's vulnerability to lawsuits if and when employee misconduct is alleged or established in a court of law. Courts are not reluctant to address employer negligence in hiring employees or assigning volunteers. For instance, if a child is abused at camp by a volunteer, a lawyer is apt to ask what kind of screening was done in selecting the volunteer. If the answer is none, there is precedent for imposing liability on the congregation.

The law does not object to trust, except when the trust is extended negligently. Negligence here means conduct that creates an unreasonable risk of foreseeable harm to others.

Screening employees and volunteers is a confidential process governed by community policy. Screening may sound dismaying, particularly when longtime members are involved. The tragedy of abuse by an employee or volunteer is infinitely more dismaying.

If a screening policy applies to all employees, including clergy, and to all volunteers working with children and young people, a climate of safety can be created. Molesters are known to shy away from congregations that have established such policies. Congregations that do no screening statistically face the greatest risk in asking an adult, especially a male, to be in charge of an otherwise unsupervised overnight trip for children.

Once guidelines are established as policy, be particularly careful that they are followed. In a courtroom, evidence that guidelines have been broken may be worse than evidence that there were none in the first place.

SUGGESTIONS FOR SCREENING PROSPECTIVE EMPLOYEES AND VOLUNTEERS IN POSITIONS OF SPECIAL TRUST

○ Prudent congregations use *screening applications* for all employees or volunteers, particularly those who work with children and youths and those who are new to a community.

○ A screening application should ask for

Name, current address, and phone

Preferred kind of work with children/youths

Date available and level of commitment

Any physical limitations for this kind of work

Any allegation of abuse or attempted abuse

Religious affiliation for past five years, including any youth work

Special gifts or training to prepare for this kind of work

Two or three references (not relatives or friends), including most recent employer, with addresses and phone numbers

Authorization to call references (see waiver language later in this list)

An affirmation that the information is correct

An affirmation to follow the constitution and bylaws of the congregation.

○ Review the published guidelines used by the Boy Scouts, Girl Scouts, Big Brothers, and similar organizations using screening processes. They usually are willing to share their materials with congregations that are establishing policy.

○ Any information supplied on these applications or gathered through references should be kept confidential. Those involved with the screening process should be kept to a minimum, as established by the congregation's decision-making body.

○ When leaders are satisfied with a proposed application form, they should consult an attorney to put it in final order. This step is important in protecting everyone. When someone under eighteen fills out the form, a parent or guardian should also sign.

○ A *reference response form* can be created for every reference contacted, recording whether the contact was by telephone or in writing and summarizing the communication. Keeping such a record is critical for the screening process to work.

○ Before asking for references, ask prospective employees to sign a *waiver* giving appropriate people permission to share job-related information (see Exhibit 6.1 for a sample waiver).

○ When obtaining references, ask factual questions that are job related; when you do this over the telephone, have your questions written down before the conversation and document the answers on your reference response form.

○ Courts encourage "background checks" for prospective employees but have not clarified exactly what a background check includes. It is advisable to ask local law enforcement officials to do a criminal record check. They may ask for a consent form signed by the

I authorize all previous employers and supervisors, including all persons with and for whom I have worked, to give the representatives of _____ Church any and all information regarding me and my previous employment. I release _____ Church and all previous employers and supervisors from liability for any damages that may result from furnishing this information to _____ Church.

Exhibit 6.1. Sample Waiver for Permission to Give a Reference.
Source: *Hammar,* 1995a, p. 22.

applicant before doing the check or may even require the applicant to be the one to secure it.

○ When they have a record of abuse, volunteers must be asked to take assignments other than those involving children and youth, even if they have experienced a conversion or change of heart. Prospective employees with a record of abuse present a particularly complex set of issues (discussed in Chapters Nine and Ten).

○ Communities might emulate those congregations that add to their margin of safety by asking all volunteers for youth activities to first conclude six months or a year of membership and training in the worshiping community.

○ Newcomers who are screened need to be asked to provide a photo identification, such as a driver's license, because molesters often use pseudonyms.

○ When asking the attorney to review your screening application, inquire about your state's laws regarding reporting abuse of minors. Post the law so staff and volunteers know local reporting requirements.

Screening is a tough issue for us all, and "tough" only begins to convey the size of the problem if we do screening carelessly. But learning to do it with care and an educated approach takes most of the sting away and actually serves to build trust. And more than trust is involved. In recent years, thousands of churches have been taken to court for negligently hiring employees who abused children. Richard Hammar's "Sexual Abuse in the Church Nursery" (1992b) (built around a case in Alaska), brings home the need for screening and is an excellent primer when creating your congregation's policy.

Of even more use is the inexpensive screening kit called *The National Church Safety Program,* produced by James Cobble Jr. and Richard Hammer in 1996. It is accompanied by a short book titled *Selecting and*

Screening Church Workers. The package has three parts, designed for clergy, other employees, and volunteers, respectively, and it was initially offered for $100 if you secured all three. Each part includes instructions, both written and telephone reference response forms, and a review of applicable law. The novel element in this kit is that it connects you to the Pinkerton Employment Verification Services. For nominal fees, Pinkerton will verify that the person you get to know on paper is the person behind the handshake.

Employer Responsibilities

Like all other employers, congregations must be aware of their responsibilities in regard to the Fair Labor Standards Act, payroll taxes, and workers' compensation.

The Fair Labor Standards Act

The preceding discussion of independent contractors versus employees is particularly important because many congregations mistakenly call their employees contractors, thinking that doing so makes them exempt from minimum wage and overtime provisions in the Fair Labor Standards Act (FLSA). Certain employees are indeed exempt—pastors, for instance, and some executives. Typically, custodians, choir directors, and secretaries are not exempt, and issues such as minimum wage and equal pay for men and women apply. The U.S. Department of Labor is particularly interested in making sure schools, including those sponsored and administered by congregations, live up to the provisions of labor law.

Officers of any congregation that employs more than a pastor are well advised to check with a CPA or attorney to make sure they are abiding by the law. This is another fairness issue, and the law is willing to defend an employee's legal rights regardless of the congregation's perceived ability to meet fair labor standards. An excellent discussion of FLSA requirements can be found in the two-part article by Julie Bloss (1995a, 1995b) titled "Wage and Hour Laws." A shorter summary is "Paying by the Rules" by Daniel Busby (1994).

Payroll Taxes

Congregations are under a legal obligation to withhold federal payroll taxes and submit them to the Internal Revenue Service. Failure to submit payroll taxes to the government, under certain circumstances, is one of the rare instances when a leader in a nonprofit corporation may become personally liable. This vulnerability is carefully analyzed by Richard Hammar (1992a) in "The Personal Liability of Church Officers for Uncollected or Unpaid Payroll Taxes." Chapter Ten of Hammar's *Pastor, Church and Law* (1991) makes the withholding tax process relatively simple and is reason enough to buy this excellent resource.

Follow these steps when submitting payroll taxes:

- Obtain an employer identification number from the IRS.
- Know which workers are independent contractors and which are employees.
- Keep the social security number and a W-4 tax form for each employee.
- Withhold income tax and social security taxes for all employees except clergy (if clergy have so requested).
- Deposit the withholding tax and file a quarterly Form 941 with the IRS.
- Fill out and distribute W-2 forms for employees and 1099 forms for contracted workers who have been paid $600 or more in the past year.

If you are ordained or plan to be, the fourth bullet point may have caught your attention. Clergy are given a number of special tax benefits, including an opportunity to bow out of the social security system and to enjoy tax-free housing allowances. The popular, annually updated clergy tax guides mentioned in these pages are testimony to how the details of these benefits keep changing.

Workers' Compensation

Maintaining workers' compensation insurance is another requirement all congregations shoulder, as they are financially liable (as institutions) for all work-related injuries, whether at or away from congregational facilities. State law makes coverage mandatory for church and temple employees in most states.

Unfortunately, many congregational leaders fail to comply with the workers' compensation obligations and tax procedures detailed in law, putting their congregations and officers, beginning with themselves, at serious financial risk. Do not let a bad record in the past deter you from cleaning up an inadequate system. Accountable leadership means acting to correct a problem once you understand it.

Even though you do not pay your volunteers, it is important to ask an attorney to check workers' compensation law in your state to see whether volunteers are required to be covered by workers' compensation insurance when they start providing services with any risk attached. On the face of it, this may at first seem outlandish, unnecessary, more busy work, and an unacceptable cost. But all these arguments are turned on their head when you understand that such coverage, particularly where legally required, is a moral, legal, and financial way of taking care of those who occasionally put themselves at great risk for the congregation. Then when there is a bad accident or injury involving a volunteer, his or her needs will be taken care of, and the congregation will not risk picking up a twenty-year intensive-care medical bill.

The Rudiments of Employee Relations

Building a healthy, fruitful relationship between a congregation and its employees is like an art form—whatever you do, there are no guaranteed outcomes. Common sense, clarity, and a few guidelines, however, can protect a congregation from some of the typical pitfalls.

Hiring Employees

Congregations usually have very specific needs when they hire any kind of employee and understand the need for a precise job description. Regardless of who is being employed, a prudent employer takes considerable care with the entire process. Much of the mushrooming litigation against places of worship during the 1980s came in the form of suits for wrongful discharge.

Consider including in all employee contracts a binding arbitration clause regarding disputes. Although it involves giving up one's constitutional rights to a jury trial and appeal, arbitration is much less expensive than litigation. Secure legal advice, however, when writing such a policy.

Keep anything *contractual* by nature or implication out of employee handbooks. A handbook that says, "We seek dedicated Christians who wish to make the church their vocation," can be construed in a court of law as a long-term employment commitment. As suggested earlier, instead of having a handbook to introduce employees to the community, depend on application forms, job descriptions, careful evaluations, and published personnel policy.

SUGGESTIONS FOR HIRING EMPLOYEES
- Hire and evaluate employees on the basis of aptitude, skills, training, and past record, *not* on the basis of sex, age, race, marital status, or handicaps, unless they hinder ability to do the job.

- Use carefully written job descriptions and employee contracts. Spoken agreements are notoriously difficult to enforce if problems arise.
- The same prohibitions that apply to the hiring process apply to compensation. Adjust compensation based on the quality and quantity of work done.
- Provide employees with thorough training and good equipment.
- Establish a policy stipulating screening, including thorough reference checks, for all employees and also all volunteers working with children.
- Establish written rules of conduct, including a policy prohibiting sexual harassment and establishing a complaint procedure. Ask new employees to read these documents and then to sign off on their understanding of what they have read.

"Hiring and Firing," a chapter by Arthur DeKruyter in *Mastering Church Management* (1992), is a useful essay surveying issues related to hiring and firing employees from a pastor's point of view.

Disciplining Employees

Most employees thrive in an atmosphere where expectations are understood and met, where correction happens quickly and easily, and where commitment and achievement is acknowledged and appreciated. In a less-than-perfect world, disciplinary action sometimes is needed to indicate the seriousness of a situation that requires change. The right approach to discipline can make the difference between a successful transformation and a failure.

SUGGESTIONS FOR DISCIPLINING EMPLOYEES

- Before problems arise, set employee policy regarding discipline, publish the policy, ask new employees to read and sign off on it, and be sure that guidelines are followed conscientiously and fairly.
- Know the facts of a situation before moving to discipline.
- Maintain consistency and fairness in all disciplinary activity.
- For most employee problems, warnings and second chances should precede discipline. Talk problems through, but also put warnings in writing.
- Frequently, disciplinary problems revolve around unhappy relationships between two or more individuals. Sometimes there is no solution but to remove at least one of them. Use of conflict resolution, however, can often turn a problem into an opportunity to strengthen community.

Dismissing Employees

Anyone hired for an indefinite term can be terminated by the employer or decide to leave the job "at will," without cause or notice, though a number of states have begun to qualify the at-will rule. Even if at-will legislation prevails in your state, it is prudent to list carefully the causes for a dismissal before going forward. Use probationary terms prior to termination.

Prudence also suggests creating an at-will employee policy that all prospective employees read. It can clearly assert that both employer and employee have the freedom to conclude the relationship simply by deciding to do so (often with a stipulated period of advance notice).

Be aware that the following are grounds for wrongful termination lawsuits brought by employees:

○ Being fired for refusing to break a law, such as backdating a check

○ Being fired in a manner that fails to take into account any established disciplinary procedures

○ Having a history of excellent employee evaluations

Nowhere is a leader's maturity so tested as in the arena of employee relations. The spirit of these relations contributes to staff and volunteer morale, satisfaction, and effectiveness. Those without experience as employers best approach the task with care, respect, and humility.

Playing It Safe

Respect, trust, mutual support, and accountability are the hallmarks of a good employment relationship. The work it takes to build that relationship is as important as any a leader does. Sometimes relationships go sour. When that happens with an employee, the financial and legal responsibilities and liabilities of an employer are complex and not to be taken lightly. Even as you build a trustworthy team of leaders, take the kinds of precautions that *keep* them safe and happy and offer you damage control if unresolvable conflict is generated.

In terms of liability, congregations face at least three important kinds of employment-related exposure: causing injury, treating a employee unfairly, and giving false, ill-willed references about former employees. (A fourth, sexual abuse of or by an employee, is discussed later in this book.) The courts have nudged the religious community into responding to these risks, and the community is safer and more just as a result.

On-the-Job Injury

On-the-job employees sometimes harm people, others or themselves, usually by accident. Whenever employees are doing the work of the congregation, *the congregation itself is financially liable* for any damage or injury. If a child is hurt in a day-care center through inadequate care, the congregation as well as the employee is responsible. Safety is a high priority in any healthy congregational program or facility. When religious decision makers neglect safety and serious injury occurs, courts have been happy to provide a financially based learning experience never to be forgotten. A number of states now require congregations, like businesses, to have an ongoing safety program. California, as a result, has platoons of consultants providing congregations and nonprofits with such a program.

Disgruntled Employees

Congregations live with the reality that unhappy former employees may sue their onetime employer, particularly if they feel discriminated against or fired unfairly. One cheers the fact that discrimination and unfairness can be countered by the little guy. At the same time, trustees might remind themselves that a former employee can pursue a civil suit for next to nothing, while accused congregations, even when they are vindicated, may need to pay many tens or hundreds of thousands of dollars to establish their innocence. If the congregation is found guilty of mistreating an employee, a financial settlement or judgment can be added to the bill.

The sting of discrimination has generated more than one lawsuit. We hope that worshiping families will not discriminate against potential employees on the basis of age, race, gender, ethnic background, national origin, or disabilities. Many that have discriminated have been sued.

The one area where congregations and their educational institutions are legally allowed to discriminate is on the basis of people's faith, their religion. If you want to hire someone from within your faith family, that is legal. This freedom comes with an important caution. If you are always going to say no to the religious outsider, make it a policy to inform potential employees that religious affiliation is a requirement for the job at hand.

The issue of disabilities is more complex. The Americans with Disabilities Act (ADA), which Congress passed in 1990, was inspired by clergyman Harold Wilke. But its employment language does not require compliance from congregations with less than fifteen people on staff. Because this exempts most congregations, some will end up less hospitable to potential employees with disabilities than the local library or grocery store.

Julie Bloss, the preeminent expert on the church as employer, makes a passionate plea for being fair whether or not government regulations apply to your congregation: "Your church has everything to gain and nothing to lose by trying to comply with the law voluntarily" (1996a, p. 37), she observes. Being fair includes making reasonable accommodations that allow a person with a disability to do as good a job as anyone else.

Those congregations with fifteen or more on the staff need to seek legal counsel about complying with ADA provisions, which are lengthy and complex. In another of Bloss's fine articles ("Interview Update: What You Can and Can't Ask," 1996b), she summarizes how the government construes "fairness" regarding employment opportunities for persons with disabilities.

Being fair is the most important guideline in congregation-employee relations, but it is not enough by itself to protect an institution from claims of discrimination.

Refrain from making any more promises to employees than you have to. Grandiose heartfelt pledges (for example, "For all you have done, be assured that you've got a job here as long as you like!") can turn into a bitter memory and a monster lawsuit, particularly if conveyed in writing.

Another excellent rule, a favorite with lawyers, is to document everything in employee relations: promotions, injuries, discipline, special requests, and everything else that details an employee relationship. Documenting the relationship is good for both employer and employee. If ever a problem emerges, a record of the relationship helps clarify most disagreements.

Negative References

As we have seen, it is important for congregations to seek references about prospective employees. *Giving* references, however, can come with its own liability, and some employers simply refuse to say anything about former employees, protecting themselves but effectively shutting down the whole accountability process.

Rather than being fearful, if you are an appropriate person (someone who supervised the former employee) and policy does not otherwise govern your decision, be willing to give references. But do so wisely:

SUGGESTIONS FOR GIVING REFERENCES

- Before giving a reference, ask if the applicant has signed a waiver authorizing references. If not, ask why not.
- Be sure you are talking to someone who is authorized to ask the questions.
- Limit your comments to job-related information.

○ Be honest and factual and avoid any mean-spirited comment.

○ Document the conversation and file your note, whether the reference is given on the telephone or written.

Going the Next Step

Congregational employee relations has a short bibliography. The best single resource for maintaining fair employment practices and living within the law is *Church Guide to Employment Law,* by Julie Bloss (1993). All it is missing is her commentary on developments since 1993. You can catch up by looking at the last few years of *Clergy Journal* for the articles she has published since then (Bloss, 1995a, 1995b, 1996a, 1996b, 1996c).

Bloss does not have the field all to herself, of course. Leading clergy journals often run helpful employment-related articles. For instance, a detailed discussion of the employer-contractor distinction for congregations can be found in "Employee or Independent Contractor?" by Charles Watkins (1996), like Bloss, an attorney.

Keeping up with employment law is an impossible task unless you have someone who thrives on that kind of information, such as a small business personnel officer. If you lack this congregational resource, securing professional advice, the subject of the next chapter, is important. Unless clergy are your only payroll responsibility, find someone who can be trusted to help get the details right. For anyone so inclined and willing to spend the time, Julie Bloss's writings can provide the education. The best approach may be to secure a trustworthy professional and make sure he or she has read Bloss's work.

A subset of congregation-as-employer issues is legal liability, an arcane subject, which justifies multimillion-dollar legal judgments. If you want a course in the subject, go through the Richard Hammar articles listed in the resources for this chapter. For a good summary of employee-related liability, read "Church Liability for Staff Conduct" by Bullis and Mazur (1996).

Several times, I have mentioned that the tax status and social security laws pertaining to clergy are idiosyncratic. Again, turn to the experts. A good background discussion on clergy tax status can be found in the latest edition of Richard Hammar's *Church and Clergy Tax Guide* or Daniel Busby's comparable guide.

Hats off to those who specialize in this arena. The exemplar has been Christian Ministry Resources (CMR). Its founder is a quiet dynamo who is one of the best-kept secrets in the country's religious community. James F. Cobble Jr. is not a familiar name to most theologians, pastors, and laypeople, but tens of thousands of clergy and lay leaders regularly read his publications, listen to his audiotapes, watch the videotapes he produces, use his software, and attend the seminars he organizes around the country each year. Among regional and denominational leaders, Cobble is becoming well known; he and colleague Richard Hammar have been consultants to dozens of them.

Cobble earned doctoral degrees at Princeton Theological Seminary and the University of Illinois, and in recent years CMR has published more of his work. His most important, ongoing achievement is to publish the work of both Richard Hammar and Julie Bloss. These two have provided expertise for a religious community in shell shock from a barrage of litigation. Bloss and Hammar have clarified issues, offered appropriate warnings, and been legal partisans for the whole religious community. In all, CMR's work helps congregations do a good job at creating safe sanctuaries and programs. CMR publishes three periodicals, for treasurers, secretaries, and anyone concerned with how government and the courts influence the life of the local congregation. CMR also maintains an online legal database to keep leaders (or at least their attorneys) up to date on appropriate case law and legislation.

Of all congregational systems, the legal responsibilities of the employer may be the most frustrating. The underlying employment law, though, is our nation's best attempt to be fair with and offer a safe workplace to those who serve us for their living. If the spirit of this fairness can be captured, your congregation will be a happier place.

Resources for Employment Practices

Agencies

Christian Ministry Resources, P.O. Box 1098, Matthews, NC 28106; (704) 841–8066.
Graduate Theological Foundation, P.O. Box 5, Donaldson, IN 46513; (800) 423–5983.
Institute of Church Administration and Management, 700 Martin Luther King Drive, SW, Atlanta, GA 30314; (404) 688–5960.
National Association of Church Business Administration (NACBA), 7001 Grapevine Highway, Suite 324, Fort Worth, TX 76180; (817) 284–1732.

Periodicals

Church Bytes, 304-C Crossfield Drive, Versailles, KY 40383–1470; (606) 873–0550.

Church Law and Tax Report, Christian Ministry Resources, P.O. Box 2301, Matthews, NC 28106; (800) 222–1840.

The Church Secretary Communique, Christian Ministry Resources, P.O. Box 2301, Matthews, NC 28106; (800) 222–1840.

Clergy Journal, Logos Productions, Inc., 6160 Carmen Avenue East, Inver Grove Heights, MN 55076; (800) 328–0200.

NACBA-Ledger, National Association of Church Business Administration, 7001 Grapevine Highway, Suite 324, Fort Worth, TX 76180; (817) 284–1732.

Profile: The Church Office Professional's Information Source, Success System, Inc., 13004 South Pratt Road, Lee's Summit, MO 64086; (816) 524–8161.

Books and Articles

Bloss, Julie L. *Church Guide to Employment Law.* Matthews, N.C.: Christian Ministry Resources, 1993.

Bloss, Julie L. "Wage and Hour Laws: Part One" *Clergy Journal,* Aug. 1995a, pp. 38–41.

Bloss, Julie L. "Wage and Hour Laws: Part Two" *Clergy Journal,* Sept. 1995b, pp. 37–41.

Bloss, Julie L. "Being Sued by Employees." *Clergy Journal,* Mar. 1996a, pp. 36–38.

Bloss, Julie L. "Interview Update: What You Can and Can't Ask." *Clergy Journal,* July 1996b, pp. 34–36.

Bloss, Julie L. "Religious Discrimination." *Clergy Journal,* May/June 1996c, pp. 27–29.

Bullis, Ronald K., and Mazur, Cynthia S. "Church Liability for Staff Conduct." *Christian Ministry,* Mar./Apr. 1996, pp. 15–18.

Busby, Daniel D. "Paying by the Rules." *Your Church,* Mar./Apr. 1994, pp. 16–17.

Busby, Daniel D. *The Zondervan Church and Nonprofit Organization Tax and Financial Guide.* Grand Rapids, Mich.: Zondervan, published annually.

Calendar and Workbook for Church Secretaries. Nashville, Tenn.: Abingdon Press, published annually.

Cobble, James, Jr., and Hammar, Richard. *The National Church Safety Program.* Matthews, N.C.: 1996a. (A kit of resources.)

Cobble, James, Jr., and Hammar, Richard. *Selecting and Screening Church Workers.* Mattthews, N.C.: Christian Ministry Resources, 1996b.

Cobble, James, Jr., and Hammar, Richard. *The Compensation Handbook for Church Staff.* Matthews, N.C.: Christian Ministry Resources, published annually.

DeKruyter, Arthur. "Hiring and Firing." In Leith Anderson, Don Cousins, and Arthur DeKruyter, *Mastering Church Management*. Portland, Ore./Carol Stream, Ill.: Multnomah Press/Christianity Today, 1992.

Hammar, Richard. *Pastor, Church and Law*. (2nd ed.) Matthews, N.C.: Christian Ministry Resources, 1991.

Hammar, Richard. "The Personal Liability of Church Officers for Uncollected or Unpaid Payroll Taxes." *Church Law and Tax Report*, Jan./Feb. 1992a, pp. 12–14.

Hammar, Richard. "Sexual Abuse in the Church Nursery." *Church Law and Tax Report*, May/June 1992b, pp. 11–14.

Hammar, Richard. "Tips on Completing 1991 W-2 and 1099 Forms." *Church Law and Tax Report*, Jan./Feb. 1992c, pp. 7–12.

Hammar, Richard. "Tax Court Rules That a Methodist Minister Is an Employee for Income Tax Reporting Purposes." *Church Law and Tax Report*, Nov./Dec. 1994, pp. 1–11.

Hammar, Richard. "How to Give a Negative Reference—Safely." *Your Church*, Mar./Apr. 1995a, pp. 21–25.

Hammar, Richard. "Tax Court Rules That a Pentecostal Holiness Minister Is Self-Employed for Income Tax Reporting Purposes." *Church Law and Tax Report*, Jan./Feb. 1995b, pp. 14–20.

Hammar, Richard. *Church and Clergy Tax Guide*. Christian Ministry Resources, Matthews, N.C.: updated annually.

Hilligoss, Gayle. "What Church Secretaries Are Paid." *Your Church*, Jan./Feb. 1995, p. 64.

LaRue, John C., Jr. "Technology in Today's Churches." *Your Church*, July/Aug. 1994, p. 40.

Rueter, Alvin C. *Personnel Management in the Church*. Minneapolis: Augsburg Fortress, 1984.

Watkins, Charles. "Employee or Independent Contractor?" *Clergy Journal*, Jan. 1996, pp. 12–16.

7

CONTRACTING WITH SERVICE PROVIDERS FROM INSIDE AND OUTSIDE THE CONGREGATION

PROPERTY MANAGEMENT, including risk management, may be the absolutely last consideration in the mind of any seminarian; but in most congregations, it comes with the territory. It may come as second nature to some: overseeing one or more buildings, knowing how all the details are handled, knowing whom to call and when, and building relationships with professionals who specialize in the physical, legal, and financial aspects of corporate life. For the rest of us, it is pea soup.

Yet this is an important arena for leaders, and not just because these people are service providers who make our lives easier or tougher, depending on the relationship. Equally important, they offer a web of connections to the community that hosts your congregation. Each instance, each meeting offers a personal contact, offers to serve the congregation's best interests in one or more ways.

Frequently, worshiping communities are blessed with lay people or custodians who are handy. They offer the tender care that keeps a building and its property clean, safe, and continually maintained. For larger maintenance tasks or major repairs, volunteers better oversee than actually do the work involved. Anyone who volunteers for work normally done by those in professional building trades should be specifically included in the congregation's insurance or workers' compensation coverage.

Discourage volunteers from doing anything dangerous. An uninsured volunteer painter who falls from a stepladder, if seriously injured, may sue the congregation for medical costs, pain and suffering, lawyers' fees, or workers' compensation payments. Several remedies exist to protect the congregation and the volunteer. First, check to see if the congregation's insurance policy covers injury to volunteers. Many do. Both the individual and the institution are protected by the addition of significant liability coverage to the congregation's policy. That is also helpful for covering legal fees when a congregation is sued by a volunteer or anyone else. A leader's best legal and ethical behavior cannot protect against expensive litigation when someone takes the congregation to court. Many congregations, when they do purchase such coverage, have a $1 million limit per incident. In the worst of circumstances, $1 million of coverage is not enough—$3 million or $5 million is safer.

Workers' compensation coverage can be purchased for volunteers in a few states. In this case, workers' compensation rather than liability insurance may become the exclusive remedy for injury and loss.

Relating to Service Providers

Just as families develop relationships with baby-sitters, plumbers, and lawyers, so congregations, particularly those owning their own facilities, develop relationships with a variety of service providers and professionals. These people butter their daily bread with this work and have high standards concerning the quality of their effort. Blind trust in outside contractors is folly, but be sensitive to their concerns and willing to build friendly relationships. Your congregation's bills may usually get paid at the end of each month; but do not ask a professional painter to wait for a check once the work is complete and approved.

Selecting Contractors

Painting, carpeting, and all kinds of construction need to be governed by well-written contracts. Servicing energy systems, appliances, and electronic, mechanical equipment usually involves contractual relationships between a congregation and those offering the services. Many congregations contract with a custodial firm instead of hiring a janitor. Good relationships with professionals such as realtors and lawyers are governed by clear agreements.

It is not unusual for a worshiping community to maintain business relationships with dozens of firms in the building trades, professions, and service industries. Following some simple suggestions can make these relationships a pleasure most of the time. Ignoring them increases the risk of shoddy work, broken agreements, overpayment, or even litigation.

By itself, the word *contractor* is usually associated with the building trades, probably because the complexity of construction requires particularly detailed clear agreements. Any construction job that is big, complicated, or dangerous needs insured professionals guided by a good contract reviewed by an attorney before it is signed. Over the years, congregations often develop working relationships with contractors whose skills in masonry, carpentry, painting, roofing, plumbing, electrical systems, and stained glass distinguish them as experts. States classify and license building contractors. California, for instance, has forty-one different categories in the construction trades. Anyone licensed in at least three classifications can advertise as a "general contractor."

SUGGESTIONS FOR SELECTING A CONTRACTOR

○ Once a job requiring a contractor has been defined, interview three or more contractors who are interested in working with you. If the job is big enough to warrant asking for bids, get at least three.

○ Check references and examine prior work, if appropriate. Ask former clients about their overall satisfaction with the work. Were there any scheduling problems? Was the contractor sensitive to problems or special concerns and willing to make corrections?

○ Resist the pressure a salesperson may bring to your decision, and beware of those who offer a special price if you decide today. The offer of a referral fee to induce a decision may be illegal and is a red flag. Avoid all "pay in advance" schemes. In some states, they are illegal.

○ Always work with licensed contractors. Ask to see their license, get the number, and check them out with your state's contract license board, asking if any complaints have been received. If you make the decision to work with an unlicensed contractor, the state has little leverage and will probably offer little help if you have a complaint. You may also end up in trouble with your local municipality. Some jurisdictions require work done without a permit to be removed and redone.

○ Subcontractors are the licensed professionals hired by licensed contractors who need their services for a particular part of a larger project. Ask prospective contractors whether they use subcontractors, and which ones may be called upon for work on the project. For big jobs, an evaluation of the subcontractors is a good idea.

○ Beware of the lowest bid. Before accepting it, determine what the other bids might offer that this one does not. You have no legal obligation to select the lowest bidder, and prudence suggests that your invitation to bid should affirm your right to reject any and all bids received.

o After your comparative evaluation is complete and the bidding
   done, choose a contractor on the basis of reputation, experience,
   and financial stability.

o Be sure the contractor and any subcontractors have workers' compensation as well as liability insurance coverage with adequate limits of liability. The story of the painting contractor with $100,000
   of insurance protection accidentally burning down a $3 million
   sanctuary has been told over and over again. The congregation
   should be added to the contractor's liability coverage as "an additional insured in a primary position," with confirmation in writing.
   This means that in the case of an adverse financial judgment, the
   contractor's coverage would be primarily responsible, the congregation's secondarily. If a worker falls from a ladder, for instance, and
   sues everyone in sight, the contractor's protection would pick up
   most or all of the bill.

o The contract should require from the contractor a thirty-day notice
   of cancellation or material changes made in the contractor's insurance policy.

In addition to checking the prospective contractor's workers' compensation
and liability coverage, prudent leaders secure a bond when any big project
is planned. Without a meeting of minds, goodwill, and lots of luck, problems occur during construction. Sometimes, they can be financially devastating. Bonds provide a project with varying degrees of financial protection.

A *contractor's license bond* is required of contractors in some states; it
can provide financial relief for poor or incomplete work. But if a number
of claims are filed against a particular contractor, a very limited pie is
divided up, reducing everyone's compensation. A *performance bond* guarantees a project's completion according to plans and specifications. A *payment bond* guarantees that all labor and materials will be paid for. A
contract bond guarantees both job completion and the payment for all labor
and materials. It provides the best protection and is the most expensive.

Bonds should be secured from a reputable insurance company with at
least an A rating. Bonds do not usually pay more than their face value, and
most require the owner to hold back part of the project payment, usually
10 percent, until the project's completion. Bonds may not be available if the
congregation plans to work with a new or inexperienced contractor.

The Art of Agreement

In the business community, people work with each other on the basis of
legal agreements called contracts. A contract is an agreement between two

or more parties for services or materials and their payment. Contracts should never be signed for a worshiping community except by appropriate officers accurately representing the decisions of the congregation's governing body. Always consult a competent attorney when writing and signing major contracts.

Four elements usually can be found in a contract: (1) the parties making the agreement, (2) a preamble that indicates why the parties are making an agreement, (3) the details of what each party is promising, and (4) protections for each party, which may include an end date, the consequences of a failure to perform, and agreements about how to handle disputes.

The quality of any contract, then, depends on the amount of clear, precise detail it contains. Large or small, a contractual effort often needs to be conceived, defined, planned in detail, scheduled, bid, and "completed" on paper before a single hammer falls or service visit is scheduled. A computer service contract is relatively simple if the details are straightforward, clear, and complete. But before a contract for major construction is signed, architects, engineers, bankers, and city planners all have work to do with the congregation. Major repairs usually benefit from prior consultation with architects and engineers.

A contract is the fruit of the planning process, stating all agreements in detailed order, defining the precise responsibilities of the various parties. Once signed by the appropriate parties, a contract is a legally binding instrument.

Contracts are an everyday part of congregational life. Painting a building, servicing a furnace, installing new carpet, these are all tasks best governed under the terms of a contract. Without such documentation, the worshiping community has little recourse in the face of poor or incomplete work. A well-written contract can save untold misery and bad feelings.

How and When to Sign a Contract

Congregational leaders need to be particularly careful about signing contracts. They may be personally vulnerable when "breach of contract" is alleged. A few safeguards help protect leaders from personal liability when doing a congregation's business with a contractor:

SUGGESTIONS FOR SIGNING CONTRACTS

- Never sign a contract for the community without having been given the authority to do so by the congregation's governing body.
- Before signing a contract on behalf of a congregation, (1) understand it in all its detail, and (2) be convinced that all the necessary work preceding the signing has been completed.

○ Avoid signing simply as an individual, which could make you personally liable. Immediately above the signature on a contract, identify the name of the institution. Below, write "by" before the signature, and indicate the role of the signer (for example, "chairperson of a committee," "trustee," "or administrator") following the name. Thus:

FIRST CHURCH
BY JOAN DOE, TREASURER

○ If a contract is complicated, particularly if it involves construction, have it reviewed by an attorney before it is signed.

Entering into a contract and receiving services brings its own responsibilities. Whenever a congregation pays an individual $600 or more in one year for services rendered, its officers are legally required to notify the federal government for tax purposes on IRS Form 1099, with a copy sent to the contractor. As long as the money was paid for work done, it must be reported, whether or not there was a signed contract. Requests to forget about the 1099 represent invitations to cooperate in income tax evasion.

Building Professional Relationships

We tell lawyer jokes, gasp at the size of medical malpractice premiums, and nod in agreement when old-timers complain about young MBAs fresh out of business school. But for all the grief they take, professionals bring extraordinary skills and services to the nonprofit community in general, and churches and temples in particular.

Employed wisely, professionals have information and resources to empower those with whom they work. Using professionals unwisely, on the other hand, is expensive and can be destructive.

Knowing *when* to call on professional services is critical. Most of us know when to dial a doctor, but the same cannot be said about lawyers, insurance agents, and other professional providers. The following discussion makes some specific suggestions about working with different kinds of professionals. One easy guideline to follow whenever you work with them: *let professionals take responsibility for the work they are trained to do.* A minister playing lawyer is as effective as a choir director with a surgeon's scalpel in hand. Choose professionals you can trust, then do not make a habit of second-guessing them.

Professionals are expensive precisely because they know so much. Nickel-and-diming, complaining about their fees, and ignoring them when the treasury is low are all poor strategies for coping with the cost. Instead, prepare yourself before meeting them, know what you need, do not ask them to do your busywork, and stay focused when the service begins. This way, you benefit while keeping cost to a minimum.

Initiating Professional Relationships

Careful shopping best serves a congregation needing professional services. Start the selection process by spending time on the telephone asking people you trust for their recommendations. Other congregations, local businesspeople, bankers, attorneys, and nonprofit agency directors all may have suggestions.

SUGGESTIONS FOR SELECTING PROFESSIONAL SERVICES

○ When interviewing potential service providers, do not be shy about asking questions, and listen carefully (take notes!) to the answers.

○ Always compare the work of at least two or three before hiring one.

○ Ask for references and check them out.

○ Look for recent satisfied clients rather than depending on someone's reputation.

○ Clarify in writing exactly what services are being provided, along with all details of the billing process.

○ Satisfy yourself that the professional can explain his or her work in lay language. When lawyers use Latin phrases without explaining them, watch out.

○ Highly opinionated, inflexible professionals can be difficult to work with. Mutual respect and a friendly working relationship are important factors when soliciting expert resources.

○ Have the congregation's attorney review all complicated contracts before they are signed.

○ Consider waiving the right to a jury trial and appeal by agreeing to arbitrate any disputes that arise between the congregation and the professional.

Bumping into Conflicts

Professionals are people with special training and certification offering important services. Congregations are best served by professionals chosen for their particular competence and experience, not their membership or acquaintance with a member. In fact, entering a contractual relationship with one of your own members can be risky. Asking for professional accountability is more difficult from an old friend than from an outsider. Even free services can be problematic—how do you evaluate the services of a member who does the work "for expenses"? Paying prevailing fees makes it easier to insist on satisfaction from professionals.

A church near Chicago burned to the ground. Only then did members discover that their building was insured for less than 5 percent of its value. It was a case of negligence on the part of their insurance agent, a long-time member. The agent had failed to update the policy, in spite of several church council requests. Because the congregation decided not to sue the agent for more than the limits of his professional liability insurance, it was not able to rebuild the sanctuary.

Thousands of inadequate congregational insurance policies begin with an agent who is unfamiliar with the appropriate sector of the industry. Institutional property and casualty insurance is a highly specialized field, and the stakes are extremely high. A congregation may only have one serious fire in one hundred or two hundred years, but when it happens, the consequences for the poorly protected institution and its leaders are devastating. And it can happen on anyone's watch.

Breaking through the old-buddy, big-giver networks in a congregation may not be easy. But approached with tact it can be done, while protecting both the congregation and the member-professional or member–business owner. Whenever a member is considered for professional services or approached as a vendor, establishing the following understanding can mitigate the potential conflict of interest. Through no fault of their own, and regardless of the quality of work and its costs, professionals sometimes find themselves caught in a conflict of loyalties. When this happens in a worshiping community, it can be understood that

- The member will not be discriminated against, but will be expected to compete in the marketplace by (1) bidding against competitors and (2) not taking it personally if someone else gets the business.
- If the member is able to stand the scrutiny of comparative shopping for professional services and win the bid, the details of the relationship will be communicated to the membership and the completed work or purchase will be expected to meet "professional" standards.
- Talent, not cost, will be the primary consideration in retaining a professional.

Cutting corners when contracting professional services or making major purchases usually is harmful in the long run. Whether proposals and purchasing opportunities come from members or outsiders, decision makers need to be wary of unusually low prices. Penny-wise-and-pound-foolish behavior can break a congregation's treasury.

As a general rule, congregational officers should never benefit financially from the congregation by accepting professional fees, serving as vendors, or providing services.

Learning Professional Habits

Working with professionals tends to be expensive. A leader's good habits can keep waste out of the budget.

SUGGESTIONS FOR WORKING WITH PROFESSIONALS

- Assign one person as the official communications link to the professional. Then welcome occasional visits and in-person reports from the professional (lawyer, agent, vendor, contractor, and so on) to committee or council meetings.

- Leave a paper trail, documenting in writing all meetings, decisions, assignments, and time lines. Be clear and precise about details, agreements, and chronology.

- Stay in contact without becoming an annoyance.

- Be sure bills are paid in a timely manner.

Congregations need certain professional services only occasionally. Working with an architect or a contractor may be very complex. But once the work is done, the relationship is concluded. This is true with professionals in the building trades, real estate agents, and various consultants.

Choosing an architect requires particular care. The American Institute of Architects (AIA) will send you *Building Relationships: A Guide for Institutions on How to Work with an Architect. Faith and Form,* a beautiful quarterly publication of the AIA, publishes a list of church architects every other issue. Read the AIA literature, but when contracting with an architect, use your lawyer's form, not the standard AIA form. Forms published by an association of professionals for themselves sometimes protect the professionals better than they do you.

In the areas of financial management, legal counsel, and insurance coverage, long-term relationships do develop. To be effective, they need nurturing and periodic evaluation.

FINANCE. Most communities have a number of banking options. Congregational leaders profit from shopping to discover which institutions offer the best benefits. Many congregations also invest money through stock brokers and financial advisers. Choose reputable firms that steer their clients toward a diversified portfolio, provide ongoing educational information about investing, and are willing to discuss the ethical implications of specific investments.

Dozens of sources of financial advice sit poised to serve congregations. Some are useful, and a few, if you can identify them, can be incredibly valuable to the needs and possibilities in your congregation. (Chapter Five catalogues the kinds of professional financial advice available and surveys financial opportunities and their attendant dangers.)

LEGAL COUNSEL. Fortunately, most congregations require legal assistance only occasionally. Nonetheless, knowing a lawyer who is familiar with the congregation, reviews contracts, and offers occasional advice over the telephone can be an important resource for clergy and officers. Some congregations are happy to depend on the guidance of members who happen to be attorneys, though this can create possible conflict of interest problems. If a lawyer works for certain members of the congregation, it may be inappropriate for him or her to simultaneously represent the congregation.

Doing *favors* for anyone, including the congregation, is a mistake when establishing professional relationships. The only appropriate favor for your attorney is pointing out the congregation's copy of Richard Hammar's *Pastor, Church and Law* (1991) or Richard Couser's *Ministry and the American Legal System* (1993b). An attorney who does not want to have one or both of these books on hand is probably the wrong attorney for you. *The Legal Defense Handbook: For Christians in Ministry*, by Carl Lansing (1992), explores the nature of the law, congregation-attorney relationships, and litigation against churches. Written from an evangelical point of view, the book's information is helpful to the legally uninitiated regardless of their tradition, especially when first selecting an attorney.

A congregation's attorney needs to be willing and able to call in specialized legal talent when appropriate. Threatened litigation, real estate development, personnel problems, tax questions, copyright infringement, professional malpractice, workers' compensation—these are a few areas where congregations need a specialist's legal expertise.

Never retain a lawyer to respond to litigation against a church without first talking to your insurance agent. Insurance policies sometimes cover attorney's fees, but insurance companies insist on being the ones to hire anyone they pay in the matter. If there is any reservation of rights by the carrier, you may be able to hire your own attorney at the carrier's expense.

This attorney is called a *Cumis* lawyer, from the name of the case establishing this right.

Before retaining any kind of expert, be sure he or she has specific experience in your area of concern. Ask for an estimate of how long it will take to resolve the problem at hand and a preview of the major steps along the way.

Lawyers employ various billing methods:

○ Often they charge a flat fee for a specific task, such as reviewing a contract.

○ Sometimes they will work for a contingency fee to be received only if a particular suit concludes successfully.

○ If they do a large amount of work on a regular basis, they may receive a monthly retainer.

○ Most attorneys bill by the hour or fraction thereof. Typically, they charge anywhere from $50 to $300 per hour and up, depending on experience and expertise. Large firms, offering a range of capabilities, generally charge more than sole practitioners.

○ For the good of individuals and institutions they care about, attorneys sometimes do a certain amount of work for free, called *pro bono* work.

When hiring a lawyer, be sure to obtain in writing all details of the services offered and how they will be invoiced. The more precise the working agreement the better, with any court costs and "extra" charges understood at the outset.

INSURANCE AGENTS. Insurance coverage costs money each month, each year. The agent who receives a commission from each premium is as close to a congregation's finances as someone on the payroll. Being a member may hinder rather than enhance an insurance agent's ability to write insurance for a congregation. An inherent conflict of interest exists between the agent's loyalty to the congregation and desire to do business.

The agent whose business is primarily property and liability insurance serves a congregation better than one who works mostly with health and life coverages. Indeed, the "property and casualty" industry is its own discipline with its own literature, practices, and associations. Choose an agent who can help educate your leadership about the many different dimensions of protecting your members and property. The insurance agent who specializes in medical or life insurance is about as helpful as a plumber when you secure church or temple coverage. Congregations need agents who specialize in *property, liability,* and *nonprofit* coverages. A specialty in churches and temples is a bonus.

Resist the enormous temptation to favor the agent with the lowest cost of coverage. One church underwriter tells of refusing to bid on a Pennsylvania church because the trustees, seeking to save money, refused to value the church's property at more than $1.4 million. They were forced to acknowledge the actual value—over $3 million—when the building burned to the ground a year later. Thousands of fires each year destroy seriously underinsured congregations. Buying insurance on the basis of its cost rather than the quality of its coverage means playing Russian roulette with the future of the community. Accountable leadership requires something better.

Finding the right agent is worth the time and energy it takes, because, as the ad says, the person you choose holds the future of your congregation in her or his hands. In a 1996 survey of nine hundred congregations, a quarter of those responding said their current insurance agent is not helpful in assessing their property risks. The figure went up to 30 percent regarding liability risks (Hammar, 1996a). Congregational leaders who feel stranded this way need to call other qualified agents. Give them a photocopy of your current policy, ask what they can offer by comparison, and then ask lots of questions.

Loss prevention and *risk management* are two phrases from the insurance industry becoming familiar to institutional leaders throughout the nonprofit community. Both point to the realities beyond paying a premium and honoring a claim. Both call for systematic, careful attention to creating a safer world. One of the first publications available specifically addressing insurance for congregations was *Risk Management: A Guide to Insurance, Accident Prevention, Property Protection, and Maintenance for Churches.* It is a short, inexpensive introduction to the subject from the National Association of Church Business Administration, full of good advice and including a safety checklist.

Early in the 1990s, the two authors who wrote the classic texts on clergy, congregations, and American law each weighed in with a risk management workbook. Richard Couser's, titled *Managing Risks: First Steps in Identifying Congregational Liability* (1993a), came first, followed by *Risk Management for Churches: A Self-Directed Audit* (1994) by Richard Hammar, George Grange, and James Cobble Jr. Though the books overlap a bit, the wise steward will buy both. Including postage, the total outlay is less than $20.

Do the self-study the books call for. It will be the most cost-effective money ever spent by your congregation. The fire averted, the lawsuit avoided, make these short workbooks incredibly valuable resources. Though no substitute for insurance, they contribute quite a bit more to your congregation's day-to-day safety. Neither workbook publisher markets these resources through bookstores, so call the publishers to secure them.

Except for these few exceptions, most loss-prevention literature for churches and temples is published by the insurance underwriters that have provided congregations with coverage over the decades—including such major players as Brotherhood Mutual, Church Mutual, and Preferred Risk Mutual. These particular underwriters all have long commitments to religious institutions and see education as part of their responsibility. Their policies tend to be better tailored and more reliable than coverage from companies without a historical commitment to local worshiping communities. Ask your agent for loss-prevention literature and use it. It reduces accidents, saves money, and is a measure of your underwriter's long-term commitment to real safety.

The historical task of church and temple insurance has been protection from fires. With over seven sanctuary fires on an average day in the United States, property protection remains critical to all worshiping communities. Fire safety is straightforward, an important part of any congregation's operation.

Beginning in the late 1970s, liability protection became increasingly important for congregations, including coverage for professional malpractice, directors and officers liability, and sexual molestation. Starting in the late 1980s, the American Bar Association started scheduling workshops at its continuing education meetings tracking and studying trends in litigation against congregations! Liability has become a subject with dozens of implications, many of them important to leaders who want to maintain a safe congregation.

A personally disciplined sense of accountability in leaders is the best loss-prevention remedy available. Besides bringing an informed ethical point of view to what we do, accountable practices translate into a safer environment and save money. At the same time, trustworthy insurance coverage is an enormously valuable safeguard. Excellent leaders sometimes fail to be accountable, accidents happen in spite of safe habits, and insurance provides a safety net.

The most important factor in congregational insurance is not how much it costs, though thousands of trustee boards act as though this were so. The important considerations are the terms and limits of coverage, deductibles, blanket limits, *claims paid* coverage as opposed to *occurrence* coverage, and the level of your co-insurance, which is the percentage the congregation contributes toward making up a major loss. A good agent will be happy to educate trustees about all these issues. The more comprehensive the coverage, the safer the pledge to your children and grandchildren that they will enjoy the same benefits you do from this congregation.

"What Your Insurance May Not Cover" by Patrick Moreland (1994) is a particularly useful article for congregations. He points out that "replacement cost" is much more valuable than "actual cash value," that a pastor's personal property is generally not covered in a church policy, and that new building codes may mean it will take much more money than projected to repair a partially damaged building. Occurrences like earthquakes, floods, boiler damage, and sewer backups and congregation valuables like antiques (including stained glass windows) are all areas that need special attention, because they may not be covered by your basic policy.

On the liability side, ask your agent about sexual misconduct and molestation coverage (hard to get and expensive, but important), *errors and omissions* insurance, medical expenses coverage (after injury to members, friends, and visitors), and *directors and officers* coverage in case these leaders are named in a suit and need legal counsel. These coverages are worth knowing about and securing.

Leaders responsible for a number of congregations need to know about *ascending liability*. This is liability that accrues to a parent organization for injury or damage done by a member congregation. In litigation, parent organizations, with more funds at their disposal than individual congregations, become popular targets. Establishing ascending liability usually depends on the nature of the relationship between the parent body and the particular congregation in a given case.

Edward Gaffney Jr. and Philip Sorenson have written a book on this subject, titled *Ascending Liability in Religious and Other Nonprofit Organizations* (1984). Liability issues including ascending liability are also covered in the church and law texts by Couser and Hammar, Grange, and Cobble listed below. At this writing, the most up-to-date information is in Hammar's "Liability of Churches and Denominational Agencies for the Sexual Misconduct of Ministers" (1996b).

Going the Next Step

The most important next step with service providers and professionals is building friendly relationships with as many as possible, preferably before you have to hire one or sign a contract. Trustworthiness is the currency, and building mutual respect is the first step in earning it.

Published resources about relationships congregations have with contractors and professionals are even fewer than the resources about employment listed in the previous chapter. It is remarkable that congregations pay the insurance industry over $1 billion a year for coverage, and yet a major text has not yet appeared on the subject.

The one agency with a strong record of producing helpful resources in this arena is the Nonprofit Risk Management Center (NoRMaC), until recently known as the National Center for Community Risk Management and Insurance. It was founded by Charles Tremper, a pioneer in nonprofit financial protection, who has written many of its best publications.

Melanie Herman became NoRMaC executive director in 1996 and says the agency is studying the possibility of targeting the religious community. Almost all of the legal, financial information NoRMaC publishes for its secular nonprofit constituency is equally useful to those responsible for property in the religious community. NoRMaC's three-times-a-year newsletter *Community Risk Management and Insurance* is sent to you free for the asking and is the best way to keep up on the center's other publications.

Resources for Contracting with Service Providers

Agencies

American Institute of Architects, 1735 New York Avenue, NW, Washington, DC 20006; (202) 626–7461.
National Association of Church Business Administration (NACBA), 7001 Grapevine Highway, Suite 324, Fort Worth, TX 76180; (817) 284–1732.
Nonprofit Risk Management Center, 1001 Connecticut Avenue, NW, Suite 900, Washington, DC 20036; (202) 785–3891.

Periodicals

Community Risk Management and Insurance, Nonprofit Risk Management Center, 1001 Connecticut Avenue, NW, Suite 900, Washington, DC 20036; (212) 785–3891.
Faith and Form, American Institute of Architects, 1735 New York Avenue, NW, Washington, DC 20006; (202) 626–7461.
NACBA-Ledger, National Association of Church Business Administration, 7001 Grapevine Highway, Suite 324, Fort Worth, TX 76180; (817) 284–1732.

Books and Articles

"'Are Your Volunteers Covered?'—Board Members." *Community Risk Management and Insurance,* Jan. 1993, pp. 8–9.

Bloss, Julie. "What Ministers Should Know About Churches." *Clergy Journal,* July 1993, pp. 13–17.

Building Relationships: A Guide for Institutions on How to Work with an Architect. Washington, D.C.: American Institute of Architects, Public Affairs Department, n.d.

Couser, Richard B. *Managing Risks: First Steps in Identifying Congregational Liability.* Minneapolis: Augsburg Fortress, 1993a. (To order, call (800) 328–4648.)

Couser, Richard B. *Ministry and the American Legal System.* Minneapolis: Augsburg Fortress, 1993b.

Gaffney, Edward M., Jr., and Sorenson, Philip C. *Ascending Liability in Religious and Other Nonprofit Organizations.* Waco, Tex.: J. M. Dawson Institute for Church-State Studies, Baylor University, 1984.

Hammar, Richard. "Tort and Religion: The American Bar Association Conference on Church Litigation." *Church Law and Tax Report,* July/Aug. 1990, pp. 2–5.

Hammar, Richard. *Pastor, Church and Law.* (2nd ed.) Matthews, N.C.: Christian Ministry Resources, 1991.

Hammar, Richard. "Denomination Found Liable for Pastor's Misconduct." *Church Law and Tax Report,* May/June 1994, pp. 1–13.

Hammar, Richard. "A Legal Profile of American Churches." *Church Law and Tax Report,* July/Aug. 1996a, p. 30.

Hammar, Richard. "Liability of Churches and Denominational Agencies for the Sexual Misconduct of Ministers." *Church Law and Tax Report,* July/Aug. 1996b, pp. 16–19.

Hammar, Richard, Grange, George R., II, and Cobble, James F., Jr. *Risk Management for Churches: A Self-Directed Audit.* Matthews, N.C.: Christian Ministry Resources, 1994. (To order, call (704) 841–8066.)

Lansing, Carl F. *The Legal Defense Handbook: For Christians in Ministry.* Colorado Springs, Colo.: NavPress, 1992.

Moreland, Patrick M. "What Your Insurance May Not Cover." *Your Church,* May/June 1994, pp. 36–39.

Patterson, John, and Seidman, Anna. *Kidding Around? Be Serious: A Commitment to Safe Service Opportunities for Young Children.* Washington, D.C.: Nonprofit Risk Management Center, 1996.

Risk Management: A Guide to Insurance, Accident Prevention, Property Protection, and Maintenance for Churches. Fort Worth, Tex.: National Association of Church Business Administration, 1989.

Rypkema, Paula. *Healthy Nonprofits: Conserving Scarce Resources Through Effective Internal Controls.* Washington, D.C.: Nonprofit Risk Management Center, 1996.

PART THREE

TENDING TO INVISIBLE WOUNDS WITHIN THE CONGREGATION

SIN IS NOT HURTFUL because it is forbidden, but it is forbidden because it is hurtful.

—Benjamin Franklin

THE DEADLIEST SINS were the consciousness of no sin.

—Thomas Carlyle

8

ZERO TOLERANCE
FOR ABUSIVE BEHAVIOR

THE ROLE OF THE SANCTUARY as a safe place is ancient and holy. People meeting in the name of God expect to feel secure. The faithful community, we hope, is made up of caring sisters and brothers, trusting parents and children. We share forgiveness, experience *shalom*, a sense of peace and connectedness.

In the last quarter century, this high vision has encountered another ancient reality—private violence in our families and institutions. Private abuse is at least as old as the story of Lot's incest with his daughters in the book of Genesis.

Until the 1990s, religious institutions mostly turned their eyes away from such violence, ignoring the evidence and denying complicity. Leadership in religious institutions has been dominated by men, and 98 percent of abusers are men. Commentators point out that lifting the veil from private violence is part of the current revolution in how we value women and children in this culture. What may be most stunning is the *size* of the problem. Statistics from the Center for the Prevention of Sexual and Domestic Violence fall on our ears in a terrible barrage.

- One girl in three and one boy in seven is sexually abused by the age of eighteen. Half of this violence is done by family members.
- One million children in the United States are physically abused by parents or guardians every year. Fifteen hundred will die of the abuse.
- Over two million women are physically abused every year.
- One million elders are abused by their adult children each year.
- One marriage in four suffers from spousal abuse.

- ○ Eighty-eight percent of women in the workplace have experienced sexual harassment.
- ○ Forty-four percent of women in one study have been subjected to rape or attempted rape, nine out of ten times by someone they knew, not a stranger.
- ○ Most abusers were abused themselves as children.

This once-secret plague spans the population. Hidden violence does not discriminate by faith, race, class, economics, or neighborhood. Members of the clergy as well as church staff and volunteers have been abusers. Worshiping communities are as susceptible as secular to abusive situations, sometimes more so, because the open fellowship most congregations enjoy and promote can be a magnet to a potential abuser.

Consider, for instance, the 2.3 million children who go to day care or private schools in churches and temples during the week. Clearly hundreds of thousands of these youngsters suffer abusive behavior at home. Just as clearly, in some situations, both children and adults, usually women, are abused by employees and volunteers given positions of responsibility by the worshiping community.

The legal and financial ramifications of this tragedy can be nearly as profound as the personal, moral, and theological issues. The good news is that consciousness of the problem and strategies to make life safer for people have begun to emerge.

In 1964, the first child abuse reporting laws in this country were passed. From 1974 to 1984, five hundred shelters for battered women were established, and now there are over two thousand. As awareness increases, so do those willing to speak out, and the figures continue to escalate. The National Committee to Prevent Child Abuse reports that in the ten-year period from 1986 to 1995, reported cases of child abuse and neglect rose from 2.1 to 3.1 million ("Current Trends in Child Abuse Reporting and Fatalities," 1996). For the last five years in the study, the figure went up 4 percent each year, in part because education continues to bring survivors forward to make reports. On average, four children die each day from abuse, nearly half of them under the age of one.

The National Child Protection Act of 1993 could be a great leap forward in the religious community's ability to keep children out of the hands of abusers. The legislation allows states to set rules requiring qualified child-care providers to seek FBI checks for employees working with children. The check could be completed on the telephone, and the FBI response would be nothing except yes or no: no story, no accusation, just approval or no approval of the prospective employee.

The law was designed so that congregations could be listed as qualified providers. To date, few states have taken advantage of the act. A number require criminal background checks for child-care center employees, including those at congregation-sponsored centers. But most states make no such requirement of employees or volunteers working with children in a congregation. The absence of an easy legally mandated way to check someone's background makes the *National Church Safety Program* (1996), reviewed in Chapter Six, all the more valuable.

Before 1980, the idea that one might write a whole book about violence in the congregation would have been shocking, unthinkable. As this hidden tragedy has moved from the shadows, dozens of articles and a handful of books have gone a long distance in waking up the religious community and in identifying what is required to turn violence around and reclaim the sanctuary as a safe place. Several of these books were published in the 1980s. The earliest is *Sexual Violence—The Unmentionable Sin: An Ethical and Pastoral Perspective* (1983), the first of a number of superb resources from the pen of Marie Fortune, the founder of the Center for the Prevention of Sexual and Domestic Violence. The first half of this book studies the ethics of sexual violence. The second focuses on pastoral responses.

Four years later came *Sexual Assault and Abuse: A Handbook for Clergy and Religion Professionals,* edited by Mary Pellauer, Barbara Chester, and Jane Boyajian (1987), a 278-page anthology of resources rich in theological, devotional, and practical advice for dealing with abuse in the worshiping community. Both books are dated in the sense that so much work has been done since then. However, these were the trailblazers, and their work holds up well.

Moving Beyond Denial

Throughout the 1980s, Fortune and a handful of others began bringing visibility to the problem and its relationship to the worshiping community. They were part of a larger community of concerned parents and professionals across the nation who were first to respond when the scope of private violence in our culture surfaced. In 1987, *Christianity and Crisis* published an extraordinary essay by Mary Pellauer titled "Sex, Power, and the Family of God." It surveys abuse within congregations, raising most of the important issues that since have received increasing attention. In 1993, "The Worst Sexual Sin: Sexual Violence and the Church," by Christine Gudorf, returns to much of the same material. But Gudorf's particular focus is how a congregation can respond to this epidemic, an approach that, we will see, has received considerable attention in the mid-1990s.

Making a congregation safe for all, including the abused and abusers, is the continuing challenge. Religious institutions have been slow in recognizing personal violence. But the sheer magnitude of the suffering and the ethical imperative to offer relief, whatever one's religious tradition, are finally bringing attention to this invisible plague. Institutional awareness and response take time and are not easy.

Personal violence is only one form of misconduct suffered within worshiping communities. Vandalism, embezzlement, and arson, for instance, can do enormous damage to a worshiping family. Emotional, physical, and sexual abuse, however, are more insidious because they persist in our midst invisibly and because personal violence is endemic in our culture.

In the worshiping community, the number of people who violate others—physically, emotionally, or sexually—may be small, but no institution is immune. A single case can rock a congregation, the larger community, and related denominational bodies. Early in the 1990s, sexual abuse in the religious community started making "most important religious stories of the year" lists. In 1990, Marie Fortune asserted that three to five new allegations of sexual abuse by clergy are made every week somewhere in the nation (Higgens, 1990).

Denial is the first difficult hurdle facing worshiping communities. Until truth-telling, in all its complexity, can rule the day, congregations passively serve to abet abuse instead of helping the abused. At a clergy training workshop in California, one story sketched the potential tragedy when leaders are ill-informed and afraid of the truth.

A mother and her daughter visited their pastor with a nightmare tale of an abusing father. The father was brought into the counseling environment and confessed the abuse with tears of repentance and pleas for forgiveness. After several sessions of appropriate contrition, the pastor assumed the problem was solved. After five more years of continuing abuse, when the daughter failed in a suicide attempt, she was asked at the hospital, "Didn't you ever tell anyone what was happening to you?" She replied, "Only my pastor."

This failure is legal as well as ethical. California, like many other states, does not exempt clergy from child abuse reporting laws. These laws, explored further later in the chapter, typically require reporting within forty-eight hours.

A lawsuit is remarkably enlivening where denial prevails. A court awarded a $1.5 million judgment against a denominational mission board because it had not informed a woman that her husband was molesting their daughters. Board executives apparently knew the truth but denied it.

In the most reprehensible cases, leaders have been known to add false witness to denial. Cases are documented of clergy, sexually involved with members, receiving high recommendations for a new, faraway job; these recommendations have come from leaders who see no other way to rid themselves of a problem pastor. In 1992, a Minnesota court gave $187,000 in punitive damages and $850,000 in compensatory damages in a clergy misconduct case. Despite a priest's history as an abuser, church officials had repeatedly placed him in situations where he was able to abuse youngsters sexually.

If this kind of deception can be established, congregations *and* their officers become extremely vulnerable to large financial judgments. In no other area of life is the state so willing to enter the sanctuary, bringing the law to bear before criminal as well as civil courts, particularly if the offense includes abusing children sexually.

From the late 1980s on, the legal vulnerability of religious communities to sexual abuse allegations, both true and false, has taken thousands of congregations to court. The best introductions to congregational liability are "Church Legal Liability," Chapter Twelve of *Pastor, Church and Law*, by Richard Hammar (1991a), and "Risk Management Issues," Part Three of Richard Couser's *Ministry and the American Legal System* (1993).

More specifically, Hammar is averaging three feature articles a year in *Church Law and Tax Report* on church liability regarding abuse and molestation. Each article examines some new nuance to emerge from the courts. For instance, in 1995 a Wisconsin court found for a church that had been the site of child molestation by a teacher ("The Liability of Churches for Acts of Child Molestation," 1996d). The church was found innocent because the victim could not prove any abuse after the church was notified. The clear warning: treat accusations seriously and with dispatch.

Liability insurance is an important factor in this climate. It can be a safety net against bankruptcy and can help guarantee that the mistakes of an individual will not bring an institution to its knees financially. Unfortunately, not all insurance companies offering liability protection to churches provide sexual abuse coverage.

However important, insurance is only one responsibility, a back-up system when abuse prevention efforts fail. Leadership's responsibility is to create as safe an environment as possible. This begins with learning. For the integrity of the worshiping community and for the sake of those who suffer, leaders need to be educated about what constitutes abuse, what warning indicators to look for, and how to confront abusive situations.

Many allegations of abuse are true. However, false accusation can be equally destructive to the life of a community. Vigilance is important, but it needs to be defined in the context of nonviolence, building reliable trust, guaranteeing due process, and truth-telling.

Congregations will differ in the degree to which they can be a witness and influence for personal safety in the world. But if the worshiping community fails to address the protection of children, wives, battered women and men, or elders in pain, who will stand up for them?

A curious *warning* is important at this point. The incidence of secret abuse is so high that whenever a religious leader draws serious attention to the subject, a number of people come forward with tragic stories. This has been documented regarding both spousal and child abuse. An uneducated sensitivity to the subject can cause a crisis that no one knows how to handle. When clergy raise issues of abuse and a call goes out for the end of private violence, clergy also need to be educated about vulnerability and know how to respond appropriately.

The suggestions that follow are only a beginning. Special training is required to secure the leadership skills to adequately cope with allegations of abuse. Leaders need to talk to people who know more than they do. Even experts rely on a network of other caregivers in dealing with specific abuse situations. The emotional, legal, and financial realities related to abusive situations require multiple resources for an effective healing ministry.

Leaders encountering abuse in the worshiping community for the first time need to stay particularly attentive to two issues—the well-being of the victim and the congregation's vulnerability, including legal liability. From the personal to the institutional, everyone loses when abuse occurs.

Discerning Abuse

"Surely as I attended church school classes, someone must have noticed the pain and terror in my eyes, the hopelessness with which I moved, my withdrawal into isolation, or, at least, the swelling in my hands and feet" (Quinn, 1984). Noticing an abused person is the first step toward bringing hidden suffering to an end. Most of us look, but fail to see. This addiction to denial wreaks havoc with our perceptions and judgments. Until it is overcome, we are insulated, blind to each other's pain. Hurt, embarrassed, and afraid, the victim usually hides the pain. In caring for people, pushing past denial allows us to recognize what we have been looking at all along.

In a religious setting, clergy often contribute to the conspiracy of silence. Clergy can honestly claim the subject "has never been raised" in their presence. Concluding, therefore, that it does not exist is the error. Given the statistics, *any* large group of people has a number of members who have been sexually assaulted, and a large proportion of them will be caught in a long-term cycle of violence. The phenomenon is not at issue, just our silence and when it will be broken.

The victim of assault, meanwhile, is caught in the tortured grip of pain, fear, anxiety, guilt, and shame. Denial is absolutely natural, seeming to be the only safe harbor from forces of violence. Thus, the caring person is discerning, willing to notice and ask about the signs of violence even when it is denied. Discernment is not enough, of course; to be accountable, discernment needs an education.

The emergency room doctor receiving the victim of a freeway collision does not sling the body over a shoulder and head to the operating room, does not ask the patient to explain the details of what happened. With survivors of abuse, *assuming a pastoral role without an educated sensitivity* is the psychological equivalent of slinging the freeway victim over your shoulder. It is extremely easy to underestimate or be blind to the scope and severity of the wound the invisibly violated person carries around all the time, awake or asleep. These are people who look exactly like everybody else, but *they have been betrayed and seriously violated for months and years on end.* Their survival is a testimony to enormous courage.

The next few pages are tough reading and are not for everyone. For leaders in a position of responsibility, however, the indicators of abuse described here offer important information for discerning the suffering of the most vulnerable among us. One or two indicators prove nothing by themselves, but each provides information worth noticing. When a number of indicators apply, it may be time to seek expert advice. If you are legally obligated as a professional to report abuse, this may be the time to do so. The indicators are adapted from those in the *Child Abuse Handbook for Professionals* (1986), published by Los Angeles County, and from *Victims: A Manual for Clergy and Congregations*, by David Delaplane (1996). Delaplane's book, in its fifth edition, is an extraordinary file of information for educating local religious leaders about ministry to abused people. It developed out of clergy workshops offered by the Spiritual Dimension in Victim Services, a nonprofit agency in Denver that provides consulting and training for congregations and clergy regarding victim services.

We focus first on the issue of neglect, an arena people mistakenly take less seriously than abuse. Neglect is a form of abuse and can be as damaging as overt violation. Following neglect, various indicators are listed for child abuse, domestic abuse, elder abuse, and ritual abuse.

Neglect

Nearly three million children are neglected and abused each year in this country, nearly half of them five years old and younger. *Child neglect* occurs when a child suffers through the inattentiveness and negligence of a parent or caregiver or when the child is not offered an adequate context for growth and development.

A number of factors may point toward neglect. Any single particular indicator may not be significant. If a number of indicators seem to fit, though, the child may well be neglected. A child is possibly neglected when he or she

- Is consistently dirty, unwashed, hungry, or inappropriately dressed
- Goes without supervision for extended periods of time or is engaged in dangerous activities
- Is constantly tired or listless
- Suffers unattended physical problems or receives no routine medical care
- Is exploited, overworked, or kept from attending school
- Begs or steals food

A parent or caregiver is possibly neglectful when he or she

- Misuses alcohol or other drugs
- Maintains a chaotic home life
- Evidences apathy or futility
- Is mentally ill or of diminished intelligence
- Has a history of neglect as a child
- Lacks involvement with others
- Is unable to plan or to control impulses

Child Abuse

Abuse is injury to people who lack the ability or the will to protect themselves. Congregational leaders who have a handle on dealing with abusive situations can be an enormous influence for alleviating the pain so many children experience.

The first step is to recognize the problem. Coming to a quick judgment can be a mistake unless there is clear, strong evidence convincing you that abuse is happening. Discernment needs to be ongoing and conscientious. Most states legally require professionals working with children, including teachers, counselors, and often clergy, to report any child abuse they discover.

Children can be abused in different ways. Physical abuse is often the first for which indicators are noticed. A child is possibly abused when he or she

- Has bruises or welts, especially if they are in various stages of healing or in unusual patterns or clusters
- Has bites or burns on the body
- Has cuts and abrasions, especially on the face
- Is wary toward adults
- Is apprehensive when children cry
- Shows extreme aggressiveness or withdrawal
- Seems fearful of parents
- Has concealed injuries

A parent or caregiver is possibly abusive when he or she

- Has a history of abuse as a child
- Administers inappropriately harsh discipline
- Has unrealistic performance expectations
- Lacks concern for the child
- Misperceives the child as "bad" or a "monster"
- Is psychotic or otherwise psychologically ill
- Misuses alcohol or other drugs
- Gives illogical, unconvincing, contradictory, or inadequate explanations of an injury

Neglect and physical violence are two ways children can suffer from adults. Even worse is sexual abuse. Between 80 and 90 percent of sexual abuse against children is by family members or close acquaintances.

Incest and pedophilia, that is, sexual attraction to children, are the most common forms the injury takes. A pedophile is often drawn to children the same age he was when he was first abused.

Single mothers, looking for male role models for their kids, and congregations, with their welcome mats out to strangers, are particularly vulnerable to abusers. Clergy, religious educators, day-care staff, and youth counselors all need to be able to identify sexual abuse if they are to do anything about alleviating it. A child is possibly being sexually abused when he or she

○ Has torn, stained, or bloody underclothing

○ Has pain, itching, bruises, or bleeding in genital or anal regions

○ Exhibits withdrawn appearance or preoccupation with fantasy or infantile behavior

○ Shows poor peer relationships

○ Is unwilling to participate in physical activities

○ Engages in delinquent behavior or running away

○ Makes accusations of sexual assault

A person is possibly a sexual abuser when he or she

○ Is extremely jealous or protective of a child

○ Encourages sexual activity from a child

○ Has been sexually abused as a child

○ Misuses alcohol or other drugs

○ Is frequently absent from home

○ Experiences marital difficulties

Emotional abuse may be the most difficult to discern. The parent who repeatedly tells a child he or she is rotten can do enormous damage with little risk of ever being called to account or prosecuted. Sarcastic words of condemnation rivet themselves so deeply within us as children that the healing process, when it happens, may take decades.

When emotional abuse is identified, if the emotionally abusive parent is able to grasp the damage being done and prays to rectify it, appropriate counseling can help clean out the emotional bad will and may free love to begin growing again. Professionals working with abused children, however, report that parents have difficulty overcoming verbal abuse. A child is possibly emotionally abused when he or she

○ Acts overly compliant, passive, and undemanding

○ Shows extreme aggression, emotional demands, and rage

○ Shows overly adaptive behaviors, inappropriately adult ("parenting" other children) or infantile (sucks thumb, rocks constantly)

○ Lags in physical, emotional, and intellectual development

○ Shows suicidal behavior

A person is possibly an emotional abuser when he or she

○ Blames or belittles the child

○ Is cold and rejecting, withholding love

○ Treats siblings unequally

○ Terrorizes a child

○ Is unconcerned about the child's problems

○ Displays extremely inconsistent behavior and discipline

Domestic Violence

Nowhere is an effective worshiping community needed so much as when a battered woman goes to her clergy and asks for help. One-quarter of all homes in this country are involved. People who seem altogether normal may in fact be victims or victimizers in the quagmire of hidden violence.

The traditional advice from church and synagogue too often has been stern, accusatorial, and judgmental. Women who leave their husbands after repeated severe beatings have been shunned and expelled from congregations. Women were accused of evoking the violence and told to learn to be "subject to their husbands" as the scripture requires. In fact, studies show that *husbands* provoke the violence in domestic conflicts 85 percent of the time. A woman's steadfast faith, by itself, lacking the support of a discerning, loving community, clearly does not save thousands of abused women from enduring extended histories of violence.

This is not to underestimate the tragedy or need for similar care when husbands are violated. Virtue and fault come mixed in us all, in any case, and whoever suffers violation deserves attention. Nonetheless, men usually are the perpetrators, and a conspiracy of silence about what wives suffer has blinded us for centuries.

One rural county government for years depended on a single pastor, a woman, to do all the counseling for severely battered women in the county. She could not interest any of the other dozen local clergy in addressing the problem. Finally, another congregation opened itself to the issue, but only after its associate pastor was thrown in jail for battering his wife.

Beaten women often cooperate with their violators to conceal the abuse, so it can be difficult to discern the problem. Nonetheless, most abuse does leave clues or indicators behind. A woman is possibly abused when she

○ Feels shame, guilt, self-hatred, and pain

○ Holds rigid values about home, family, and gender roles

○ Accepts responsibility for the batterer's behavior

○ Feels low self-esteem

o Expresses martyr-like endurance and passive acceptance

o Holds unrealistic hopes about change

o Acts compliant, helpless, and powerless

o Defines herself in terms of others' needs

o Is prone to addiction

o Exhibits stress disorders, depression, and psychosomatic complaints

Children who are at risk also provide important clues that domestic violence has struck. A child has possibly witnessed domestic violence when he or she

o Is sad, fearful, depressed, or anxious

o Is aggressively defiant or passively compliant

o Shows limited tolerance for frustration and stress

o Tends toward withdrawal and isolation

o Has poor impulse control

o Has feelings of powerlessness

o Has low self-esteem

o Takes on parental roles

o Is at risk for substance abuse, sexual acting out, running away

Frequently, the worshiping community is the only place a wounded wife can come for help. Taking responsibility for discerning abuse is initially a tough assignment. It brings bodings of confrontation and the fear of broken confidentialities, potential involvement of the law, and emotional firestorms.

Far easier to tell violated people, "Be more patient and prayerful, find out what you're doing wrong, and try to be a better wife." People who render such advice are likely to quote chapter and verse to justify this approach. The fact remains, such counsel leads to a deeper sense of despair, continued abuse, and untold suffering.

Elder Abuse

The tragedy of abuse strikes in every sector of society, and few situations are so sad as families whose elders are abused. The psalmist cries out, "Do not cast me off in the time of old age; forsake me not when my strength is spent" (Psalm 71:9). With continuing growth in the senior population, the problem will increase. An elderly person is possibly abused or neglected when he or she

- Is malnourished or dehydrated
- Displays poor personal hygiene
- Has unclean clothes or bedding
- Has untreated physical or mental health problems
- Has inadequate heating or cooling
- Is not given prescribed drugs by caregiver
- Is overmedicated by caregiver
- Has a caregiver with exaggerated defensiveness or hostility
- Has head injuries
- Has multiple injuries, burns, or bruises
- Has "imprint injuries," bruises that retain the shape of whatever caused the bruise, particularly on the inner arm or thigh
- Gives vague explanations or denials in view of obvious injury
- Gives conflicting or illogical explanations of injury
- Is unwilling to discuss problem or injuries with caregiver or in caregiver's presence
- Acts fearful toward caretaker but anxious to please
- Fails to meet basic subsistence needs despite adequate income
- Has a caregiver who relies on elder's income for caregiver's personal needs
- Has signed legal document he or she is incapable of understanding

Churches and synagogues have a particularly good vantage point from which to minister to this sector of society. Seniors receive precious little care from anyone else. Clergy and other visitors from the worshiping community are often in a unique position to notice when a number of the indicators of abuse appear. Visitors can be advocates when they observe a number of indicators.

Elder advocacy is one of the easiest ways to express faithful service, and the need is enormous. Friendship is an important ministry to our elders. But if and when abuse is identified, it needs to be challenged. Your local Department of Social Services, sometimes called Adult Protective Services, or your state or area agency on aging can be called into intolerable situations that resist change.

Ritual Abuse and Incest

A newly identified expression of private violence is ritual abuse, which indulges in Satan worship, killing animals, sexual molestation, and torture. The frequent repetition of abuse typical in these cases does enormous psychological damage, particularly to children. Expert counselors to the traumatically abused warn pastors to be emotionally and spiritually prepared before listening to these stories with a pastoral ear. Counselors hear ghastly, unbelievable narratives from ritually abused clients and, unprepared, can become angry, overwhelmed, and otherwise out of control emotionally. Although quite natural, such knee-jerk emotional responses can reinforce rather than diminish the survivor's suffering.

For protection, many ritually abused children, like many incest victims, *dissociate* the terrifying experiences from their consciousness, creating a multiple personality disorder. Highly specialized psychological counseling becomes critical for emotionally healing the ritually abused.

It is particularly important not to ask leading questions when talking to people who dissociate their terrifying experience from their normal personality. Survivors have difficulty identifying their feelings. Do not through suggestion help the survivor name the feeling. The survivor, not the therapist, needs to name the feelings involved. Leading questions about the abuse can be particularly destructive with the traumatically abused. Dissociative personalities are extremely prone to suggestion. The abused person may remember your query (for example, "Did he touch you where he should not have?") as something that actually happened simply because you asked.

In short, be pastoral, be kind, and respect the special training required before offering formal counsel. Lean on your friendly professionals in this setting, working together to find dependable specialists. The size of the personal damage means working with experienced experts. When children are involved, of course, report to human service professionals and law enforcement authorities, and ask them as well for reliable references.

A Pastoral Response to Abuse

What is the appropriate response when indicators suggest a person is being abused or when a member brings tales of violation to the clergy as counselor?

First and foremost, seriously abused individuals, particularly those with a history of abuse, should be referred to professionally trained counselors. This does not at all preclude a pastoral relationship, but it shares the responsibility at a professional level. Lone rangers make terrible mistakes in this arena. The role of the clergy is to open the door to the possibility of safety and healing.

Second, become educated about how clergy can help the abused and their abusers. The library of print and videotape resources is rapidly growing. A useful essay, "Helping the Sexually Abused," by Michael E. Phillips (1989), is the firsthand story of a pastor who ran into the problem before he knew how to handle it. "Domestic Violence: A Spiritual Epidemic," by James Leehan (1992), offers a helpful perspective on a local congregation's response to abuse. At the end of this chapter is a bookshelf of excellent resources. Though most of them have a Christian orientation, this literature can be helpful to any worshiping community. A rare interfaith exception is a monograph edited by Maryviolet Burns, *The Speaking Profits Us: Violence in the Lives of Women of Color.*

It goes beyond the scope of this survey, but a considerable and growing library is available concerning pastoral counseling. Those seriously drawn to the subject can pursue various degree programs and join professional groups. The value of dialogue with professionals cannot be overemphasized when you first swim into the deep waters of pastoral counseling, particularly when abuse is a factor. The American Association of Pastoral Counselors is a good place for information about the state of the art, and most seminaries include the subject in their curriculum.

Third, learn to be extremely sensitive to people when talking about abuse from the pulpit, casually, or in a counseling environment. People who are being or have been hurt on a regular basis live with a nightmare of fears that are staggering to anyone unacquainted with such suffering. Along with the myriad fears come guilt and shame. Victims tend to blame themselves, and victimizers reinforce the perverse judgment.

Ongoing prayer for openness, discernment, and guidance is the appropriate soil in which to grow the suggestions below. They apply most specifically to spousal violence, the most likely kind of violence to be discerned in a worshiping community. But the same sensitivities and many of the same suggestions apply for rape victims, families who suffer child abuse, elders suffering from institutions or family members, or people who have suffered the sudden loss of a loved one from death on the highway or criminal behavior.

Honoring appropriate boundaries is an idea we visited in the second "standard of care" (see Chapter One) and is a constant refrain in the following pages. In an article about biological cell walls, Thomas Harries (1992) compares the importance of the protective membrane surrounding biological cells to appropriate personal boundaries. Boundaries are not always good, but they can be critical. Take away the cell's membrane, and the cell is destroyed. The same can happen to people. Mary Pellauer

(1987), one of the first to expose hidden violence in congregations, writes, "Boundaries are sacred." Listing different kinds of broken boundaries makes the point. For instance, murder, adultery, and false witness are classic examples of broken boundaries. (Chapter Nine looks more closely at the role of boundaries in the pastor-parishioner relationship.)

Approaching the Subject of Abuse

Make it easy for a person to speak to you. When someone comes to be counseled with a story of assault or loss, listen nonjudgmentally and with caring concern. People who hurt, until they discover their anger, tend to be shy. Telling the story can be embarrassing and painful. *Active* listening, attentive listening, accepting the tears, honoring the silences in the story, are important if you are to be of use.

Many violated people, victims of repeated assault, live in denial. Ask simple questions when you discern a wounded person: Are you safe? Are you hurt? Are the children in danger from your husband? Gentle but persevering curiosity in the privacy of counseling is appropriate. At the same time, avoid a battery of questions, and avoid leading questions. Respect the boundaries of the person's privacy. In conversation, focus your attention on the person's safety, not the details of the story.

Abused people are usually telling the truth when they confess to being violated. Believe what they tell you. It is much more likely to be understated than exaggerated, due to shame, fear that the story will not be believed, and fear that the abuser may hear that the secret is out. Keep an eye out for panic or severe depression, and turn to medical and psychiatric professionals for advice and special resources.

Beware of your own outrage and anger when you hear about abuse. Your shock and upset can be perceived by the victim as an accusation, though that is not your intention. Stay away from quick agreement. Make no rush to judgment about the aggressor. Rely on empathetic listening.

Establish an appropriately confidential context and agreement about the counseling relationship and honor it unequivocally. (Later in this chapter, I review such an agreement.)

Learn to listen more deeply. Discover what the person fears most, and take the fear seriously. The danger may well be greater than the victim suggests. People who feel safe easily inflate their fears; people who suffer abuse, though, tend to underestimate the dangers, because they have already survived such tribulation. Work together on solutions to reduce the cause of the fear. Focus on safe places and how to create them.

Acknowledge and affirm the person's courage in reaching out for help. The dream of the abused and the goal of a confessed abuser committed to transformation is *violence-free living*. Clergy need to assert this vision, resolutely insisting that violence is never OK in a relationship. This rule is the foundation for liberating the abused and converting the abuser.

Developing a Pastoral Relationship

Be conscious and beware of any messianic impulse, and reject it. Playing the "rescuer" is inappropriate and destructive when pastoring to people who have been violated. Abuse tends to run cyclically through decades of a family's history, so even expert therapists do not work by themselves. Create a team response instead of working solo.

Reject any kind of temptation to take advantage of the person on the basis of the trusting relationship developed. Doing so is unethical, unprofessional, and destructive. Do not be surprised when the victim seeks considerable attention and care. People under professional counsel often idealize the helper, transferring all their affections to the person. *Accepting and interacting personally with these affections shuts down the healing process*, magnifies the suffering, and may be deemed malpractice. Instead, gently insist on appropriate boundaries.

Identify community resources that might help the abused and the abuser. Visit law enforcement agencies and ask how they can help when violence threatens or actually happens. Identify city and county programs addressed to domestic and sexual violence, and become acquainted with the professional therapeutic community, including women clergy, psychiatrists, and counselors. Visit homes for battered women and children, and ask about support groups.

Learn to refer, to introduce, to seek out resources. Most clergy have not developed this outreach and can vastly improve their therapeutic effectiveness with a couple of dozen telephone calls.

Typical marriage and family counseling is *inappropriate* in an abusive domestic situation. If anything, marriage counseling will prove destructive rather than healing. Any honest expression of pain and suffering from the victim can feed the victimizer's internal rationale for violence. So until violent behavior has been banished from a relationship, the battered wife's vulnerability is extended, not decreased, in marriage counseling. It lends the abusing husband a legitimacy and power he does not deserve and can misuse.

Counseling the Abuser

Clergy are often in a good position to confront a person who allegedly committed abuse. The usual response is denial, whether or not the abuse occurred. If the person is innocent, due process does everyone a favor as people struggle for the truth. Clergy with strong fears about such a confrontation should turn to professionals for advice and assistance.

Unhappily, abuse allegations frequently are true. Elaborate excuses and long explanations typically preface a gradual confession. The abuser rationalizes his behavior. Sometimes the violence is simply not acknowledged within the abuser's consciousness, happily compartmentalized and self-justified. In some cases memory is actually repressed, dissociated.

It is tempting at this point to remain the abuser's primary counseling resource; if repentance and conversion occur, can't the matter be put to rest? Probably not. Unless you have extensive professional training, the responsibility for the abuser's healing is not an appropriate pastoral task.

Instead, the clergy's role can be, first, to insist on violence-free living as a mandatory condition for personal relationships. The clergy can champion safety and campaign for it, whatever the cost. Personal violence against the weak by the strong is intolerable, and clergy are the logical ones to insist on this basic boundary. The clergy can elicit such a promise and regularly monitor it with the abuser.

Second, clergy can urge abusers to take responsibility for their own emotional healing, to enroll in services for domestic violence and find professional counsel. Refer the abuser with the same vigor with which you refer the abused.

The Sex Offender: Corrections, Treatment and Legal Practices, edited by Barbara Schwartz and Henry Cellini (1995), is a pricey but hefty study of offenders. Its thirty chapters by thirteen contributors are organized in five major sections: the psychodynamics of the offender, implementing and administering programs, treatment, aftercare, and legal issues. In an arena with few resources, this is a major contribution for those who counsel offenders.

Supporting the Healing Process

Do not ask victims to take responsibility for changing the behavior of victimizers. In relationships, we do not change others. Asking an injured person to provide the key to transforming a violator into a peaceful person is unfair and ineffective.

Understanding a person's story through and through is important. But focusing on *blame,* though tempting, can inhibit rather than support the healing process. The victim, trapped in the culture's sexual mythology, may well blame herself or himself. Questioning this blame is appropriate, but expressing anger at the abuser is not. A victim, feeling a mixture of love and hate for the abuser, may spring to the abuser's defense if the abuser is criticized by the counselor.

Violation usually crushes self-esteem, and many kinds of healing have to happen to restore this precious element to a person's self-consciousness. Clergy can assist, but do not make quick and easy promises about getting through the problem.

Together, survey any resources an abused person can claim, including skills she or he has, the support of family and friends, access to support groups, help within the community, counselors, and state-funded help. In the campaign for nonviolence, remind the abused that leaving the abuser is always one avenue to safety. With a child, the state takes over to guarantee this safety. For battered wives, leaving is preferable to continued assault and is profitably considered if the abuser is in denial or refuses therapy.

Identify the person's strengths and consider how they might be useful. Seek opportunities within the life of the congregation that might nurture a sense of self-confidence in the person. Consider introducing the person to another member who has gone through the pain of violation, is recovering, and is willing to help. Be sensitive to confidentiality issues however.

Explore what the victim wants besides respite. If you can understand the person's point of view, you will begin to see how that person might define the life she or he would like to live. Often violated people wear blinders to what they want in order to save them from the disappointment of not having it. Explore personal goals with the person, considering as many options as possible, and talk about how to achieve those which are most desirable.

Give up quick solutions and discern and appreciate the different phases of healing and growth. Encourage the survivor to forge her or his own decisions on her or his own time line, in dialogue with any other professional resources and family supporters the person chooses. Then practice patience, welcoming uncertainty as a way of trusting the process. Keep learning to listen and discern. Be safe to talk to.

Trying to solve someone else's problems and making decisions for that person detracts from the restoration of self-esteem. For instance, it may be appropriate to suggest that returning home is a dangerous option. Respect the considered decision to do so, however, and discuss ways to make the return as safe as possible.

An important role clergy can play is to keep in touch with all parties. Even if the primary counseling relationship is transferred to others, keep in touch with the therapist, the abused, and the abuser.

Warnings About Pastoral Counseling

First, *protect yourself through relationships with those doing the same ministry.* Clergy need their own support groups, a safe place to share the insights as well as the stress of pastoral counseling. Everyone needs feedback, and your peers understand the size of the task. If your *whole* attention is captured by a difficult case of abuse, you become an ineffective leader. Colleagues can help.

Second, *establish a confidentiality agreement with counselors.* It is fair and appropriate to ask for an agreement clarifying what confidentiality means (see the example in Exhibit 8.1). However structured, these agreements honor the confidence, except when it is necessary for the counselor to act to protect a person from abuse or its serious threat. Some pastoral counselors publish a policy to this effect and give it to all who come for counsel. Others simply establish the agreement verbally. Counselors of adults should know about their reporting requirements regarding child abuse in case child abuse becomes an issue. A confidentiality agreement is equally important when working with children. Otherwise, children may feel badly betrayed (and additionally wounded) if and when you report the abuse they suffer.

Third, *stay away from situations that could be compromising.* In particular, find ways to protect one-on-one encounters such as pastoral counseling from temptation as well as false allegation.

Fourth, *watch for red flags in your own feelings and behavior.* While counseling, if you find yourself using threats, getting angry, waxing judgmental, arguing a lot, or becoming personally attached to a survivor of abuse looking for help, you are probably in over your head and need to find other help and other counseling opportunities for the person.

Finally, *be careful with your theology.* Talking with colleagues, not counselors, is the best way to explore abuse from a theological point of view. Theologizing off the top of your head or relying on religious cliches in the counseling environment can be particularly harmful. Consider the following examples:

"God will never give you anything you cannot handle" admits to at least two meanings. It may helpfully suggest, "God will provide the courage and options needed for your safety." But the perceived meaning to the victim may be, "God is protecting you, so put up with the abuse."

Forgiveness is at the heart of the healing process when one person harms another. But expecting forgiveness immediately is like asking a flower to bloom before the seed sinks roots into the soil, before the leaves

---

Whatever is said in our sessions together is confidential, with the following exceptions. If it seems to me that someone is hurting you, or that you are about to hurt yourself or someone else, I will have to have help, which means bringing others into our discussion.

Exhibit 8.1. Sample Confidentiality Agreement for Counseling.

and stem have a chance to grow. Urging forgiveness too early in the healing process misuses this most important gift in human relationship.

Theological understanding of misconduct, injury, and loss is more appropriate for a study group than a pastoral relationship. In a relationship, it can be a diversion from the primary tasks at hand: to minister to victims seeking safety and well-being and to challenge abusers to honor personal boundaries and seek professional help.

Religious therapists with the most experience serving the invisibly wounded suggest abandoning all pulpit tones and waiting for the theological implications to grow through the healing process. Gradually, faith issues and insights emerge in the survivor's consciousness if, like flower seeds, they are quietly nurtured and not preempted by a pastor's "message."

The Legal Obligation to Report Child Abuse

Failure to report child abuse can create severe consequences for worshiping communities and their leaders. In Washington state, two lay counselors "called to serve and shepherd members of their congregation" were criminally prosecuted and convicted for failing to report violence against children that had been disclosed during counseling sessions. A third counselor from the congregation was convicted but had the judgment reversed because he is ordained. The appellate court noted that Washington lawmakers specifically excluded "clergy" from those required to report. The court bowed to the choice of the lawmakers but went out of its way to reject any argument that clergy-penitent relationships automatically excuse the clergy from reporting (Hammar, 1990a).

All states have child abuse reporting laws. A number of states exempt clergy. Whatever the law, however, clergy have a moral responsibility to help protect children and prevent their abuse. Hard though it may seem, the best way to begin the process is through reporting. To be sure, not everyone agrees. One retired minister reviewing this manuscript expressed grave reservations about reporting. "My own personal experience," he said, "has been that our court system cannot handle the problem properly. I have seen a child taken from a non-abusive parent and given to the abusive parent. I have seen a person who rescued three very abused children tried for kidnapping. I have a lawyer friend that defends persons accused by Child Protective Services, and though many are guilty, he tells of the many that are unjustly accused by the system." This witness notwithstanding, professionals charged with the safety of children consistently argue that reporting is the best of the few opportunities available for preventing continuing abuse.

Continuing abuse and criminal prosecution represent only a part of the risk for failing to report. Clergy and their calling bodies are also vulnerable to civil suits, particularly from children whose suffering continued because responsible individuals failed to report. The statute of limitations for such violations can extend a victim's right to sue for decades after the actual abuse occurred.

SUGGESTIONS FOR REPORTING CHILD ABUSE

- Obey the law. In most states, providing professional care and services to children legally obliges a person to report within forty-eight hours his or her knowledge or "reasonable suspicion" that a person under eighteen years of age has been abused. Abuse means severe neglect, as well as physical, emotional, or sexual abuse. Most states have a telephone number for reporting abuse. Usually, it is listed under the child protection division of a county's department of social or human services.

- In the report, include the names of the abuser and the abused, the extent of injury discerned, and any other relevant information. Be as specific as possible. (People who report abuse are exempted from any liability for doing so, unless the report is made maliciously or untruthfully.)

- Provide the written report that is typically requested following the call.

- Clergy in some states can report anonymously by asking that their names not be divulged without permission. However, refusing to name yourself can cause problems months or years later in a court of law. People who refuse to name themselves when reporting could also find it difficult to prove their report was actually filed. To remain anonymous and still be able to demonstrate your compliance with your own concern and the law's demand, make the report in a lawyer's office with the lawyer listening. If you are asked to provide proof later, the lawyer can be called to attest that the call was made.

- Discuss with a lawyer your obligations and options when reporting child abuse in your state, preferably before the need ever arises.

The difficulties of confidentiality in a religious context are dramatized by child abuse reporting law. Suppose a trustee approaches you, his pastor, and says: "I've been abusing my daughter sexually; my wife caught me, and she's going to turn me in if I don't get help. So I'm coming to you for help. I need it, and our family needs this to remain confidential, or it will ruin us all. I'm sorry. Please help us!" What is the appropriate response?

You could argue the following:

> The molester is repentant and confessing, looking for a way to stop this evil.
>
> Having the father sent to jail or removing the daughter to a foster family might destroy the family.
>
> Making the issue public will be an emotional bombshell for the family and the worshiping community and may get written up in the local paper.
>
> The abuse has not gone on for long, and the father is ready to make some agreements about stopping the abuse and counseling with me regularly.
>
> Therefore, I'm in a position to respect the family's confidentiality and provide the counseling that will save them from being destroyed. I will not report.

Just such arguments tragically prevail in thousands of situations. The result is continuing abuse, lifetime emotional scars for the victims, and sometimes suicide. Usually the clergyperson is *not* in a position to be the family's savior; the father is more frightened than repentant; the abuse has a much longer history than admitted; the family as fantasized by the clergy was destroyed long ago, if it ever existed; and the molester's primary tool, secrecy, has been guaranteed. Further, the available resources for really helping the abused and the abuser are neglected. In sum, beware of the role of clergy as rescuer. And be ready for the extraordinary manipulative skills many abusers bring to relationships.

This is not to devalue confidentiality as an important component in most pastoral counseling or confessional situations. This value, though, needs to be put next to another value—the safety of the victim from violence. To ease this conflict of values, some clergy educate their membership about reporting laws, letting them know in advance that ordained clergy will follow the law when they learn about child abuse, even if it was confessed in the privacy of the pastoral study. Some clergy ease the bind by letting the abuser know that reporting is going forward. A penetrating discussion by Marie Fortune about confidentiality and reporting is included in *Sexual Assault and Abuse: A Handbook for Clergy and Religious Professionals* (Pellauer, Chester, and Boyajian, 1987).

Fortune points out that the abused child has the most to fear in the reporting process. If the child tells the clergy about the abuse, he or she may well be terrified that the abuser will find out and become enraged and violent. The clergy's point must be that getting help from other people is the *only* way to stop the violence. Clinically this is true. Tell the child of your own concerns and explain how the reporting is designed to increase safety, not take it away.

The best description of legally mandated child abuse reporting is "Clergy Reporting of Child Abuse" (Hammar, 1990a). As the resources at the end of this chapter indicate, Hammar has returned to the subject a couple of times, the most important being "Personal Liability of Clergy for Failure to Report Child Abuse" (1994). He points out that even in states that do not require clergy to report, personal liability may follow the pastor who fails to report. An Indiana appeals court said that where there is a "special relationship," that is, a close, meaningful relationship between a clergyperson and a child, a special responsibility to report exists. The law may not accuse you for failing to report, but years later the victim may sue for damages. This article is important for clergy, staff, and volunteers who spend considerable time with minors.

Turning the Tide

The best news about this tragic subject is that a handful of people have begun effectively teaching us in the religious community what we can do about it. Two small agencies have been the moving force in convincing the religious community in this country to examine the tough issues described in this chapter and the next two. The most important is the Center for the Prevention of Sexual and Domestic Violence. The center offers consulting and training and publishes several dozen resources for the local congregation, including workbooks, curricula, and videotapes created by founder Marie Fortune and an increasingly large group of excellent coauthors. Their work comes in many formats. For instance, the center publishes a modest brochure titled "What You in the Congregation Need to Know About Clergy Misconduct: Sexual Abuse in the Ministerial Relationship." Using a question-and-answer format, it is a superb discussion resource on a single piece of paper.

The center mostly leaves aside the legal and financial realities attending abuse. Christian Ministry Resources takes up the slack with a variety of resources designed to protect everyone involved. CMR goes far beyond the legal self-help approach, however utilitarian its publications. Anyone seriously interested in justice, law, and faith, for instance, will be saddened but deeply informed and stimulated by the detailed journey Richard Hammar charts in the twenty articles listed in the resources about violence and responsibility in the worshiping community. More than one doctoral dissertation will unpack the difficult truths hidden in the details of this legal development. Until then, the best summary of much of this material can be found in Hammar's own "Clergy Sexual Misconduct: Risks and Responses" (1996b). (Chapter Nine examines this article in some detail.)

In the mid-1990s a third agency has emerged that holds promise of becoming an equally important contributor. A 1993 interfaith conference called by Abbot Timothy at Saint John's Abbey and University in Collegeville, Minnesota, inspired formation of the Interfaith Sexual Trauma Institute (ISTI) now housed there. In its mission statement, ISTI "affirms the goodness of human sexuality and advocates respectful relationships through the appropriate use of power within communities of all religious traditions." Though still new, it promises to become a third major center devoted to mitigating invisible violence in the religious community.

The *ISTI Sun*, a quarterly newsletter, has excellent short articles about particular issues—for instance, sexuality training in seminaries, models of reconciliation after abuse, and power, gender, and religion. It also features book reviews of important new contributions not much noticed elsewhere due to their narrow focus. A particularly helpful *ISTI Sun* feature is publishing on occasion the names, addresses, and telephone numbers of particular service provider groups, a networker's dream. In recent issues, it has listed forty-nine survivor organizations and agencies in this country (Sept. 1995), thirteen newsletters addressing sexual abuse in the congregations (Sept. 1995), and thirty-seven treatment programs for survivors and offenders (Jan. 1996). ISTI also has an inexpensive bibliography, available on paper or CD, with about two thousand entries. One of the first books to emerge from the group behind ISTI is *Restoring the Soul of a Church* (Hopkins and Laaser, 1995).

The Center for the Prevention of Sexual and Domestic Violence, CMR, and ISTI are by no means the only contributors to the critical study of abuse. Many denominations have excellent resources designed for their own congregations, often with the help of people like Marie Fortune and Richard Hammar. The Alban Institute's most recent catalogue lists seven books on the "dilemmas of sexuality and ministry" (several are examined in Chapter Ten). And most religious publishing houses now have one or more books about abuse in the family and congregation.

Going the Next Step

The proliferation of excellent resources is a sign that the issues in abuse and violence are finally receiving needed attention. This is ground-breaking work from authors who have chosen faithfulness over rage, confident that faith families can be healed if they are willing to take responsibility for creating safe congregations and ministering to the abused. Care for the victims, appropriately enough, is an early focus of attention. Particularly recommended are *Pastoral Care of Battered Women,* by Rita-Lou Clarke (1986), and *Battered Women: From a Theology of Suffering to an Ethic of Empowerment,* by Joy Bussert (1986).

Sexual Abuse in Christian Homes and Churches, by Carolyn Heggen (1993), is wholly devoted to developing a congregation's ability to minister to the abused. For the parish pastor who needs a reliable handbook when taking on these issues, Heggen's remains an excellent starting place. Theological, pastoral, liturgical, therapeutic, and organizational issues all receive attention, with the focus always on the local congregation. In Chapter Ten, we will look more closely at Heggen's contribution and at the more recent *Restoring the Soul of a Church* (Hopkins and Laaser, 1995), an anthology of resources for the wounded congregation.

Two contributions published in 1995 considerably deepen our understanding of religion and violence against women and children. *Violence Against Women and Children: A Christian Theological Handbook* is a five hundred–page anthology, edited by Carol Adams and Marie Fortune, that should become a standard textbook. The thirty-one contributors address the theological foundations of violence against women, relevant biblical concepts, and an ethical appraisal, reexamining history and the present in terms of what we now know, and the church's ability to deal with the tragedy of violence. The book is full of pastoral and theological resources and is aimed at preparing people entering ministry.

The Cry of Tamar: Violence Against Women and the Church's Response, by Pamela Cooper-White (1995), is one person's in-depth analysis of violence, the forms it takes, and how the church can work to mitigate the evil. Cooper-White, an Episcopal priest, has extensive experience with women who have suffered abuse from clergy, and her work benefits from an awesome grasp of the relevant literature. In this extremely emotional arena, Cooper-White's impulse is pastoral, offering the means for healing anyone wounded by hidden violence. After drawing a conceptual framework, she spends the second half of the book studying how congregations can respond to the violence both inside and outside their membership.

Family Fallout: A Handbook for Families of Adult Sexual Abuse Survivors, by Dorothy Beaulieu Landry (1992), and *Adults Molested as Children: A Survivor's Manual for Women and Men,* by Euan Bear (1988), are both useful. Published by the New York State Council of Churches under the sponsorship of the Safer Society Foundation, they are designed to support members of stricken families.

The Safer Society Foundation will send you a resource list regarding ritual abuse. One resource listed is Believe the Children, a group organized by survivors and parents of survivors of abuse in child-care settings. It offers specific resources and references in situations where ritual abuse is alleged. (*The Cry of Tamar* also devotes a chapter to ritual abuse.)

A particularly helpful publication, *The National Victims Resource Directory*, is available from the National Victims Resource Center. The directory profiles dozens of organizations serving survivors of all kinds of violence. It offers an instant network of concerned experts, telephone hot lines, and resource and service providers throughout the nation.

Even reviewing this material briefly is a painful experience. One can easily be overwhelmed emotionally. The best protection from the information's assault is glimpsing the light at the end of this tunnel. Happy, healthy children are the joy of every community. A world safe from violence, public or private, is a driving vision for peacemakers. Accountable leaders are not being simply utopian when they try to help their congregations be an influence for reducing abuse and for responding to the invisibly wounded. When one child's suffering is alleviated, God is happier for it, and that joy is ours to share and celebrate.

Resources for Dealing with Abuse and Violence

Agencies

American Association of Pastoral Counselors, 9504-A Lee Highway, Fairfax, VA 22031; (703) 385–6967.

Believe the Children, P.O. Box 797, Cary, IL 60013; (630) 515–5432.

Center for the Prevention of Sexual and Domestic Violence, 1914 North 34th Street, Suite 105, Seattle, WA 98103; (206) 634–1903.

Christian Ministry Resources, P.O. Box 1098, Matthews, NC 28106; (704) 841–8066.

Interfaith Sexual Trauma Institute, Saint John's Abbey and University, Collegeville, MN 56321–2000; (320) 363–3931.

National Coalition Against Sexual Assault, 912 North Second Street, Harrisburg, PA 17102–8119; (717) 232–7460. (Provides referrals to rape crisis centers.)

National Committee to Prevent Child Abuse, 332 South Michigan Avenue, Suite 1600, Chicago, IL 60604–4357; (312) 663–3520.

National Resource Center on Child Abuse, 2204 Whitesburg Drive, No. 200, Huntsville, AL 35801; (800) 543–7006.

National Victims Resource Center, P.O. Box 6000, Rockville, MD 20850; (301) 251–5000; (800) 627–6872.

Safer Society Foundation, P.O. Box 340, Brandon, VT 05733; (802) 247–3132. (At this number, the foundation also offers a free telephone service

providing assessment and treatment referrals to victim-survivors
and offenders.)

Spiritual Dimension in Victim Services, P.O. Box 6736, Denver, CO 80206;
(303) 333–8810.

Periodicals and Resource Packages

In addition to the publications here, the periodicals listed at the end of
Chapter One occasionally publish articles about abuse and violence in the
congregation.

The *ISTI Sun,* quarterly newsletter of the Interfaith Sexual Trauma Institute,
Saint John's Abbey and University, Collegeville, MN 56321–2000;
(320) 363–3931.

National Church Safety Program, Christian Ministry Resource, P.O. Box 1098,
Matthews, NC 28106; (704) 841–8066.

Working Together, quarterly newsletter of the Center for the Prevention of Sexual and Domestic Violence, 1914 North 34th Street, Suite 105, Seattle,
WA 98103; (206) 634–1903.

Books and Articles

Adams, Carol, and Fortune, Marie (eds.). *Violence Against Women and
Children: A Christian Theological Handbook.* New York: Continuum,
1995.

"A Trail of Abuse." *Christian Century,* Dec. 22, 1993, p. 1294.

Bear, Euan. *Adults Molested as Children: A Survivor's Manual for Women and
Men.* New York State Council of Churches, 1988. Available from the
Safer Society Foundation.

Branding, Ronice E. "Churches Need to Become Involved in Invisible Issue."
United Church News, Dec. 1987, p. 10.

Burns, Maryviolet C. (ed.). *The Speaking Profits Us: Violence in the Lives of
Women of Color.* Seattle: Center for the Prevention of Sexual and Domestic Violence, n.d. (Available in Spanish or English.)

Bussert, Joy. *Battered Women: From a Theology of Suffering to an Ethic of
Empowerment.* New York: Lutheran Church in America, Division for
Mission in North America, 1986.

Child Abuse Handbook for Professionals. Los Angeles: County of Los Angeles
Interagency Council on Child Abuse and Neglect (ICAN), 1986.

Clarke, Rita-Lou. *Pastoral Care of Battered Women.* Louisville, Ky.:
Westminster/John Knox, 1986.

Cooper-White, Pamela. *The Cry of Tamar: Violence Against Women and the Church's Response.* Minneapolis: Augsburg Fortress, 1995.

Couser, Richard B. *Ministry and the American Legal System.* Minneapolis: Augsburg Fortress, 1993.

"Current Trends in Child Abuse Reporting and Fatalities: The Results of the 1995 Annual Fifty State Survey." Chicago: National Committee to Prevent Child Abuse, 1996.

Delaplane, David. *Victims: A Manual for Clergy and Congregations.* (5th ed.) Denver, Colo.: Spiritual Dimension in Victim Services, 1996.

Fortune, Marie. *Sexual Violence—The Unmentionable Sin: An Ethical and Pastoral Perspective.* Cleveland, Ohio: Pilgrim Press, 1983.

Fortune, Marie. *Is Nothing Sacred? When Sex Invades the Pastoral Relationship.* San Francisco: Harper San Francisco, 1989.

Gil, Eliana. *The California Child Abuse Reporting Law.* Sacramento: State of California Department of Social Services, 1986.

Glaz, Maxine. "Reconstructing the Pastoral Care of Women." *Second Opinion,* Oct. 1991, pp. 94–107.

Greeley, Andrew M. "Religion Has Role in Grim New Statistics on Violence Against Women." *National Christian Reporter,* June 6, 1994, p. 2.

Gudorf, Christine E. "The Worst Sexual Sin: Sexual Violence and the Church." *Christian Century,* Jan. 6, 1993, pp. 19–21.

Hammar, Richard. "Clergy Malpractice: The Nally Case." *Church Law and Tax Report,* Jan./Feb. 1988, pp. 2–6. (For reprints of Richard Hammar's articles in *Church Law and Tax Report,* write to the publisher, Christian Ministry Resources, P.O. Box 1098, Matthews, NC 28106.)

Hammar, Richard. "Sexual Molestation of Children by Church Workers." *Church Law and Tax Report,* July/Aug. 1989a, pp. 1–7.

Hammar, Richard. "Sexual Molestation of Children by Church Workers, Part II." *Church Law and Tax Report,* Sept./Oct. 1989b, pp. 7–8.

Hammar, Richard. "Clergy Reporting of Child Abuse." *Church Law and Tax Report,* Sept./Oct. 1990a, pp. 1–5.

Hammar, Richard. "Tort and Religion: The American Bar Association Conference on Church Litigation." *Church Law and Tax Report,* July/Aug. 1990b, pp. 2–5.

Hammar, Richard. "Church Legal Liability." In Richard Hammar, *Pastor, Church and Law.* (2nd ed.) Matthews, N.C.: Christian Ministry Resources, 1991a.

Hammar, Richard. "Sexual Seduction by Youth Workers." *Church Law and Tax Report,* May/June 1991b, pp. 1–4.

Hammar, Richard. "Punitive Damage Awards for Acts of Child Molestation." *Church Law and Tax Report,* July/Aug. 1992a, pp. 11–15.

Hammar, Richard. "Sexual Abuse in the Church Nursery." *Church Law and Tax Report,* May/June 1992b, pp. 11–14.

Hammar, Richard. "Sexual Harassment." *Church Law and Tax Report,* Mar./Apr. 1992c, pp. 1–6.

Hammar, Richard. "Personal Liability of Clergy for Failure to Report Child Abuse." *Church Law and Tax Report,* Sept./Oct. 1994, pp. 1–8.

Hammar, Richard. "Child Abuse Reporting and Confidentiality." *Church Law and Tax Report,* May/June 1995a, pp. 7–13.

Hammar, Richard. "Church Liability for Sexual Assaults Committed by Children." *Church Law and Tax Report,* July/Aug. 1995b, pp. 8–14.

Hammar, Richard. "Liability for Acts of Child Molestation on Church Premises." *Church Law and Tax Report,* Nov./Dec. 1995c, pp. 8–13.

Hammar, Richard. "Liability for Child Molestation Occurring on Church Premises." *Church Law and Tax Report,* Mar./Apr. 1995d, pp. 1–7.

Hammar, Richard. "Two States Respond to Child Protection Act." *Church Law and Tax Report,* July/Aug. 1995e, pp. 23–25.

Hammar, Richard. "Church Liability for Acts of Child Molestation." *Church Law and Tax Report,* Jan./Feb. 1996a, pp. 9–13.

Hammar, Richard. "Clergy Sexual Misconduct: Risks and Responses." *Clergy Journal,* Feb. 1996b, pp. 45–47.

Hammar, Richard. "A Legal Profile of American Churches." *Church Law and Tax Report,* July/Aug. 1996c, pp. 30.

Hammar, Richard. "The Liability of Churches for Acts of Child Molestation." *Church Law and Tax Report,* May/June 1996d, pp. 7–13.

Hammar, Richard. "The National Child Protection Act: An Update." *Church Law and Tax Report,* July/Aug. 1996e, pp. 1–15.

Harries, Thomas. "The Cell Wall: a Metaphor for Good Boundaries." *Congregations,* Nov./Dec. 1992, pp. 14–15.

Heggen, Carolyn H. *Sexual Abuse in Christian Homes and Churches.* Scottdale, Pa.: Herald Press, 1993. (Order from Herald Press, 1616 Walnut Avenue, Scottdale, PA 15683; (800) 759–4447.)

Higgens, Richard. "Abuse by Clergy: Dirty Secret Surfaces." *Boston Globe,* May 11, 1990.

Hopkins, Nancy Myer, and Laaser, Mark (eds.). *Restoring the Soul of a Church: Healing Congregations Wounded by Clergy Sexual Misconduct.* Collegeville, Minn.: Liturgical Press, 1995.

Kennedy, John W. "$1.75 Million Paid to Abuse Victims." *Christianity Today,* June 20, 1994, p. 56.

Landry, Dorothy Beaulieu. *Family Fallout: A Handbook for Families of Adult Sexual Abuse Survivors.* New York: New York State Council of Churches, 1992. (Order from the Safer Society Foundation.)

Leehan, James. "Domestic Violence: A Spiritual Epidemic." *Christian Ministry,* May-June 1992, pp. 15–18.

Livezey, Lois Gehr. "Sexual and Family Violence: A Growing Issue for the Churches." *Christian Century,* Oct. 28, 1987, pp. 938–942.

The National Victims Resource Directory. Rockville, Md.: National Victims Resource Center.

Pellauer, Mary. "Sex, Power, and the Family of God." *Christianity and Crisis,* Feb. 10, 1987, pp. 47–50.

Pellauer, Mary, Chester, Barbara, and Boyajian, Jane (eds.). *Sexual Assault and Abuse: A Handbook for Clergy and Religious Professionals.* San Francisco: Harper San Francisco, 1987.

Phillips, Michael E. "Helping the Sexually Abused." *Leadership,* Summer 1989, pp. 65–72.

Quinn, Phil. *Cry Out.* Nashville, Tenn.: Abingdon Press, 1984.

Schwartz, Barbara K., and Cellini, Henry R. (eds.). *The Sex Offender: Corrections, Treatment and Legal Practices.* Kingston, N.J.: Civic Research Institute, 1995.

9

PREVENTING
CLERGY MISCONDUCT

WHEN CLERGY ARE INVOLVED in sexual abuse, the size of the tragedy increases. Clergy abuse can range from harassment in the office to sexual relationships with parishioners to pedophilia, all hidden from sight and categorically denied. In 1983, a United Church of Christ clergyperson named Marie Fortune published a book titled *Sexual Violence—The Unmentionable Sin: An Ethical and Pastoral Perspective*. On the opening page she writes, "Ironically, we have not heard about sexual violence in the Church because we have not spoken about it." The book surveys various kinds of violation that can happen in a worshiping community. Fortune's most important insight is that sexual violence is much more about power, anger, and control than sexuality. Until this is grasped, responding to sexual violence in any creative, effective, compassionate way is impossible.

Fortune published an equally courageous book in 1989, this time focusing specifically on clergy misconduct. *Is Nothing Sacred? When Sex Invades the Pastoral Relationship* is the classic case study of clergy abuse. In great detail, changing only the names, the book tells the story of "Peter Donovan," pastor at a large mainline congregation who sexually abused dozens of women in his care. Along with the story, Fortune provides an extended analysis of the church's inaction in addressing the problem. She also provides a concise, sturdy definition of appropriate sexual boundaries: "Consent to sexual activity, in order to be authentic, must take place in a context of mutuality, choice, full knowledge, and equal power, and in the absence of coercion or fear."

Until Fortune published her books, the perception of clergy abuse was negligible—once in a blue moon, one might guess, but nothing more than an aberration. And Fortune's books were not the only call to account. Forty thousand new law school graduates each year, with perspectives and interests quite different from hers, also contribute to the housecleaning religious institutions have been going through for over a decade.

The idea of suing a congregation or member of the clergy was planted in the furor over medical malpractice in the 1970s. Medical malpractice cases became a cash cow for the legal community, but most of these litigation opportunities faded at the end of the decade when the insurance and medical industries began cooperating in support of each other's protection.

In early 1979, insurance companies wrote the first clergy malpractice coverage. The first clergy malpractice lawsuit was filed in 1980 (Schaefer, 1987). In 1982, the Christian Legal Society published a monograph titled *Clergy Malpractice: An Illegal Legal Theory* by Samuel Ericsson. He argues against the idea of clergy malpractice on the basis of the separation of church and state, a proposition that has not swayed the courts. Nevertheless, there has never been a successful prosecution of clergy *malpractice*. Establishing malpractice, where the clergyperson is breaking professional standards (but not necessarily breaking the law), is a difficult task that requires addressing issues the court feels are outside its jurisdiction, and the attempt has never succeeded.

Shifting the focus from malpractice to sexual misconduct (ranging from sexual harassment to rape) brings the court to full attention. One 1990 estimate suggested that three thousand cases alleging clergy sexual misconduct were in the courts at the time (Culver, 1991). Christian Ministry Resource's research (Hammar, 1996b) indicates that 4 percent of polled congregations have had at least one allegation of child molestation (though not necessarily by clergy) in the past five years. Conservatively, that suggests that 2,400 congregations have allegations each year, of which 18 percent, or about 430, end up in court.

As tragic as these figures are, many perpetrators, no doubt, have managed to keep their secret. A 1990 study by the Park Ridge Center for the Study of Health, Faith and Ethics, in Chicago, found "that one in every ten clergy" has had sexual intercourse with a member of the congregation, "while one in four has had some kind of sexual contact with a parishioner" (Spohn, 1991, p. 1). Another expert in preventing clergy misconduct observes that the 10 percent (his estimate) who have been sexually inappropriate must be seen along with another 15 percent of "clergy hanging over the cliff just waiting for a triggering incident to push them into malfeasance" (Rediger, 1990, p. 42).

Sexual harassment is another prevalent form of the disease, with the religious community mirroring the violations in the business community.

A 1992 survey by the National Association of Female Executives found 60 percent of women executives have experienced sexual harassment ("Getting Serious About Sexual Harassment," 1992). A United Methodist Church poll found that 42 percent of clergywomen "had been sexually harassed by other pastors or colleagues and that 17 percent of laywomen had been sexually harassed by their own pastors" (Spohn, 1991, p. 1).

These tragic statistics should not lead us to condemn the vocation. The large majority of clergy have evaded the temptations the profession offers. In one large church insurance program, 60 percent of the sexual abuse claims had nothing to do with clergy. However, because 40 percent of them do include allegations against clergy, it is important for congregations to know about the problem and support prevention measures that make life safer for all.

Knowing why clergy are vulnerable is an important step in this process. In the worshiping community, people relate to one another intimately, especially to the clergy. Over time, feelings of warmth and attraction can grow. The friendship can seem a consolation from the frustrations of religious vocation or a troubled marriage. Without the grounding of a clear ethical perspective, the pastoral *and* personal kind of relationship is about as safe as speeding down Main Street at noon.

Understanding the dynamic when professional and personal relationships overlap is important. From the power of the pulpit or from giving some sage advice or any other ordinary act of ministry, the ordained person is idealized in the eyes of many, "fallen in love with." Some members invest a total kind of trust in the clergy. This is the point of vulnerability for the troubled clergy who lack a strong ethical framework. A sexual relationship can be a real temptation.

Such illicit relationships are not only immoral, they are set to self-destruct and badly hurt any number of people close by. The love that grows out of idealizing a religious leader is utterly different from the love that knows the other person through and through, warts and all. When the idealization fades, the parishioner is in for a hard landing. Often the relationship is exposed with devastating effects on the congregation. Equally tragic, some clergy manage to get away with such a scenario a number of times, and sexual addiction may mean a gradually accelerating sickness, with new victims created all the while.

For the sake of every well-intentioned pastor, and for the sake of every congregation, the potential personal problems that lead clergy down the destructive path should be known before the tragedy occurs. Knowing the warning signs can encourage appropriate behavior.

Factors that may contribute to clergy misconduct are

○ Being "on duty" twenty-four hours a day, responsible whenever a call for help comes

○ Putting in fifty- or sixty-hour workweeks and falling into worka-holic patterns

○ Lacking ability to delegate, to empower a team approach to ministry

○ Being responsible for administrative tasks, usually the least appreciated chore in an overworked schedule

○ Feeling stress from being called for crisis intervention with the dangerous, the suicidal, and the depressed without support structures in place

○ Feeling stress from budgetary difficulties and decreasing attendance or membership

○ Feeling stress because of a lack of conflict resolution skills

○ Having a loner approach to ministry, cut off from most personal support systems

○ Having a sense of isolation in spite of support systems

Job stress is one thing, the clergy committing adultery quite another, some might say. To be sure, sexual activity outside of marriage is condemned by most traditions, but this judgment is *not* a universal ethical standard for ordained leaders, married or single, conservative or liberal. We should not be surprised by this in a culture preoccupied with sexuality.

Research suggests that many religious leaders intuitively sense that sexual intimacy with parishioners is inappropriate without being able to explain why. A primary commitment to a spouse or covenanted partner keeps many from acting out sexual attraction to a parishioner. Others have a sense of professional obligation, claiming it just wouldn't "feel right." But a reliance on feeling right is not adequate when drawing boundaries for professional behavior. In a therapeutic context, the critical boundary is professional. The counselor, therapist, psychologist, or healer works for the best interests of the counselee, offering guidance and wisdom not as a peer but as someone with special expertise. Getting romantically involved, or even developing a close friendship, violates the therapeutic relationship and is inappropriate, a violation of the counselor's accountability.

This specific issue was hotly debated after Carter Heyward, a respected feminist theologian and Episcopal priest, wrote *When Boundaries Betray Us: Beyond Illusions of What Is Ethical in Therapy and Life* (1993). Heyward argues that it is wrong to ban friendship from the therapeutic relationship. She is thoroughly rebutted in Marie Fortune's review (1994) of the book in *Christian Century,* and the two authors continued their debate in a piece called "Boundaries or Barriers?" (Fortune and Heyward, 1994).

Obviously not all boundaries are bad—few of us would be happy with a short tether on our imaginations. Nevertheless, with wounded people, recognizing and respecting particular boundaries is crucial. Indeed, professional counselors working with abused people observe that the ethical importance of boundaries parallels their therapeutic importance. For a good, nuanced discussion of boundaries, read "Setting Healthy Boundaries" by David Selzer (1995). It is a pastoral-clinical-theological reflection, written with care and full of wise suggestions and warnings about a pastor's point of view.

Another factor influencing clergy misconduct is the failure of vocational expectations and a shift in the public perception of clergy. In 1992, the Princeton Religion Research Center reported that only 54 percent of the public gives clergy high marks for ethics and honesty, an all-time low, 12 percent less than pharmacists ("Clergy's Image," 1992). The awe and automatic respect that put the clergy on a pedestal is receding in our increasingly secular culture. Pastoral clergy once wielded great influence as pillars of the community. Today, their function has narrowed in the public eye, and esteem must be earned.

Religious leadership, fortunately, is not cut from a single mold. Different ministries require different gifts. In our splintered religious community, in a culture reeling from future shock and struggling with ethical norms in every sector, knowledge of what is required after ordination can be fuzzy and vague. Expectations shift from one tradition, setting, or generation to the next. Those who attended seminary twenty or thirty years ago may find themselves particularly disconcerted by what members expect of them today.

Only 53 percent of mainline Protestant clergy strongly affirm a sense of satisfaction for their work, according to a Minnesota study. Sixty-six percent of evangelical-fundamentalist pastors were equally happy with their work, as well as 75 percent of all Catholic priests (Thorkelson, 1991). For many clergy, then, the task is disappointingly different from what they once imagined.

The question of a continuing ministry for clergy guilty of sexual misconduct is difficult. Child abusers should never again be allowed to work with children, experts agree, because children are so vulnerable. With other kinds of professional misconduct, unless there is a long history of abuse, the possibility of successful rehabilitation is taken seriously by some. A symposium of eight respected clergy talked about "Traits of a Sexually Healthy Pastor" (1995) for the periodical *Leadership*. Five of them responded to the specific question of abusers' returning to ministry. The four men each suggest a nuanced "maybe"; the woman says an abuser should look for a new vocation.

Whoever you agree with, the pattern of the response makes one remember it was an old-boys network that kept this tragedy secret so long. Perhaps character *can* be authentically reformed. That possibility by itself does little to mitigate the potential financial liability of hiring a known offender, a factor that will discourage most congregational search committees from considering such clergy.

Appropriate Behavior for Single Clergy

Single clergy in noncelibate traditions face special problems. What happens when a single pastor and a parishioner fall in love and explore the possibility of marriage? Many pastors have become engaged and married in just such a manner. Genuine perils attend this path, even when people feel their relationship is "made in heaven."

When clergy and parishioners become romantically inclined, the couple's romance is preceded by a professional, pastoral relationship. Two kinds of relationship coexist when this happens: one personal, one professional. Often, this results in confusion. Is an amorous kiss between two people who hope to wed appropriate behavior? Of course. Is an amorous kiss between clergy and parishioner appropriate behavior? Ethicists make a strong case that it *never* is (Cooper-White, 1991). First, they point out, appropriately certified clergy are conferred authority in the community of faith, vested with power by the pastored. Using the role and its power for personal advantage is the danger. Abuse can occur in spite of the integrity and best intentions of those involved.

Second, a healthy romantic relationship is between *equals*. The clergyperson's intrinsic authority means that she or he will never be "equal" to those being pastored. The conclusion: maintaining a healthy pastoral relationship and a healthy romantic relationship are mutually exclusive. If the pastoral relationship included counseling, the role confusion is significantly more serious.

What are single clergy and parishioners to do when they fall in love? One suggestion is that the couple redefine their relationship to escape the double bind. This suggestion comes from a continuing experiment in defining appropriate standards for single clergy. In early 1990s, the Northern California Nevada Conference of the United Church of Christ began developing guidelines for single clergy. It based its work on the analysis of power, role, and relationship in *Sex in the Parish*, by Ronald

Barton and Karen Lebacqz (1991). When a pastor and parishioner fall in love, the parishioner is assisted in finding new pastoral leadership. The new pastor relieves the couple of their double bind. Freed to be "equals," they can pursue a personal relationship.

This step opens up the possibility of "valid consent," an ethical concept based on the belief that good romantic relationships are between equals, free from unfair manipulation and mixed agendas. One hopes the new pastor can provide good counsel to the two people exploring their commitment and care for each other. They need guidance when their idealization rubs off and they examine the sterner stuff of courtship and marriage.

In addition, the couple lets the congregation or its leaders know they share more than an ordinary friendship, instead of hiding their relationship.

Life is too complicated for anyone to suggest that this approach will instantly clear the way for an ordinary relationship. After all, relationships are rarely ordinary between people who spend their lives together. But this approach may allow people to sort out their roles and keep those roles from bumping into each other.

Nevertheless, expect strong arguments from some against *any* kind of romantic relationship between clergy and members of the parishes where they work. Opponents will point to the field of psychotherapy. A study of secular therapists who admitted to romantic relationships with their patients indicated that 25 percent of the patients so involved were later hospitalized for depression or behaved suicidally. Kenneth Pope, former chairman of the ethics committee of the American Psychological Association, did the study. He says, "When a therapist engages in sex with a patient, he or she is engaging in a potentially homicidal activity, far more than getting into a car drunk and driving" (Beck, 1992). Such tragedies led California to make it a felony for a therapist to have a sexual relationship with a patient.

The Ethical Requirements of Ministry

Denominational bodies are paying new attention to the sad scenario of clergy misconduct (Spohn, 1991). The Presbyterian Church USA, the Episcopal Church, the Evangelical Lutheran Church of America, the Seventh Day Adventists, and the United Church of Christ have been among the first to respond. Standards of accountability are being scrutinized. New denominational policies prohibiting misconduct have been affirmed. Complaint procedures are being established. Educational packages and resources are being produced and promoted. And Richard Hammar's articles on denominational liability in *Church Law and Tax Report*, beginning in 1990, have provided a legal commentary as new cases make their way through the courts.

Simultaneously, seminaries have been rethinking the preparation of the clergy. One denominational executive who teaches practical ministry in Boston told me, "We've been dealing with sexual misconduct cases for the past three or four years in which clergy have violated the office they hold. These situations have raised issues of power and its inherent responsibilities. And it comes down to being able to define boundaries."

Clergy professional ethics became an issue in the 1980s. *Professional Ethics, Power, and Paradox* helped bring attention to the subject in 1984. Written by Christian ethicist Karen Lebacqz, of the Pacific School of Religion, it focuses on the problem of confidentiality, eventually proposing a framework for making decisions around issues relating to professional ethics. Lebacqz once expressed the dilemma to me this way: "How should a pastor respond if a teenager comes forward saying I'm pregnant, I want an abortion, and I don't want my parents to know? How should the clergy respond?"

Confidentiality is but one item on the professional ethics agenda:

SUGGESTIONS FOR AN ETHICAL AGENDA

○ What is truth-telling and how does it work in a worshiping community? Do we cover up problems, as addicted people do, or address them?

○ What is the difference between using and abusing authority?

○ What is the difference between leadership through control and leadership through empowerment?

○ What is harassment and how should a congregation respond to it?

○ How are interim clergy responsible to the clergy yet to be called?

○ What does financial integrity mean to the clergy?

One could write a book about why we have so ignored these questions. In the 1960s, hypocrisy became associated with traditional values, giving values a black eye and lowering most of the boundaries that sexual mores had raised for earlier generations. The ethos of the 1970s and 1980s, driven so much by greed, was little help in holding up ethical behavior and leadership. The cultural consequences of a weak moral compass surround us with thousands of congregational tragedies, so finally, these questions are being asked and answered.

At the heart of the matter, clerical ethics examines the dynamics of interpersonal power and vulnerability. The pastoral role automatically confers power, accompanied by specific ethical responsibilities, particularly regarding boundaries. However obvious this may seem to some, it has not been clear to others. "Many people have been unsure about sexual morality," Karen Lebacqz once observed to me. "People say, 'Everything's OK with two consenting adults.' That's the way to *avoid* the power issues."

Power is the critical issue. It is the same proposition we confronted in romances between single ministers or rabbis and parishioners in their care. By dint of call, commitment, and ordination, clergy are given a certain kind of authority (and therefore accountability) in all their relationships with parishioners. *Power Analysis of a Congregation*, by Roy Oswald (1981), provides a way to understand and be more comfortable with power in your congregation.

Clergy wield the professional power of the role as well as a *numinous* power, a God-given mantle of authority. Added to this is the clout men often wield over women in a sexist society. No wonder then, a power gap inevitably prevails between clergy and parishioner. This gap undermines the validity of mutual consent, particularly between male clergy and female parishioners. Because mutual consent is at the root of ethical sexual contact, power disparities ethically preclude such relationships.

Peter Rutter, a psychiatrist, has written a well-received best-seller, now in paperback, titled *Sex in the Forbidden Zone: When Men in Power—Therapists, Doctors, Clergy, Teachers, and Others—Betray Women's Trust* (1991). It studies this same disparity of power and sexual abuse throughout our culture. Rutter's thesis is that sexual relations are inappropriate and destructive whenever two people enjoy a special professionally defined relationship of power and trust. Pastor, therapist, lawyer, teacher, and doctor all serve with an ethical imperative to respect the boundaries established by the special trust they enjoy from their congregants, clients, students, and patients. Rutter has studied thousands of instances where power became sexually abusive in specially trusting relationships. His wry conclusion: "Some people survive these relationships, but it's like a plane crash. We're happy for the survivors, but that doesn't save us from the loss of the others."

The temptation to abuse power is greater in larger congregations than small ones for several reasons. It is more difficult to keep secrets in small congregations, to begin with. "Big church pastors are particularly vulnerable," James Nelson, who teaches ethics at Union Theological Seminary of the Twin Cities in Minnesota, observed to me. "When one has a strong sense of one's own power and charisma, it can be very self-deceptive and deluding. That's one reason why it's important for clergy to have support groups and counseling for themselves. Ethically, we need moral communities. The toughest issues are genuinely ambiguous, and clergy need the support and counsel of colleagues in a confidential, supportive community."

Realizing that power rather than sex is the underlying issue, Nancy Hopkins calls clergy misconduct a "dominance sin" rather than a "sexual sin" (1996). Taking unfair advantage of power can happen in all sorts of arenas. It can come from a perverse grasp of authority. It can be about bullying, about manipulation and disrespect, about stealing money, about sexual harassment and rape, and worse.

Before power problems arise, as you train for this difficult, blessed vocation, a good place to start is by crafting your own working code of ethics, a code you might ask a congregation to endorse. A code of ethics can signal to all that safety from misconduct is a high congregational priority and goal. The following suggestions are adapted from a variety of codes found in researching this study. Ask clergy in your community for other codes from their own traditions and compare them with what you believe. Use your own in your congregation's education curriculum.

SUGGESTIONS FOR ETHICAL PRINCIPLES FOR LEADERS

- I will regard all persons with equal respect and care and undertake to lead/minister impartially.

- I will honor all confidences shared with me, except when keeping such confidence means putting someone at risk of injury.

- I will not use my position, power, or authority to exploit any person, nor betray the appropriate boundaries that hold my relationships accountable and keep them vital and healthy.

- I will not use my position for personal financial gain, nor will I misuse the finances of the institution that I serve.

- I will not perform leadership or pastoral services within a parish or for a member of a parish without the consent of the leadership or clergy of that parish.

- I will deal honorably with the record of my predecessor and the opportunities of my successor in leadership.

- I will not, upon my termination and departure from my current role, interfere with nor intrude upon the leadership and ministry of my successor.

If you keep your code short enough to memorize and hold it close, its focus can provide a strong safety net for your ministry. But it is not a panacea, nor will it save you from experience's hardest tests, so commit yourself to lifelong learning.

In 1995 and 1996, several new voices emerged in the clergy misconduct discussion, people like Nancy Hopkins (quoted earlier in these pages), Mark Laaser (coeditor with Hopkins of *Restoring the Soul of a Church*, discussed in Chapter Eight), Jonathan Sams, and David Selzer. They have studied the subtle nuances of pastoral boundaries, a subject we keep turning back to.

Selzer's "Setting Healthy Boundaries" (1995) offers a full-blown defense of the idea of helpful boundaries for clergy as a natural extension of promoting justice and peace for all. Going further, Selzer says boundaries are "key in understanding what we are about not only as clergy, but as baptized members of the Body of Christ." The whole aim, as far as Selzer is concerned, is to appreciate boundaries as a gift that can keep us trustworthy in all sorts of ways on both sides of the clergy-parishioner relationship.

Equally valuable are "Clergy Sexual Ethics: A New Puritanism?" by Jonathan Sams (1996), and "Re-Thinking Sexual Misconduct: A Response to Jonathan Sams," by Nancy Hopkins (1996). What sounds like a debate is not, though Sams and Hopkins have some small disagreements. In different ways, both see the issue of pastoral boundaries as a milestone in understanding the evolution of religious leadership today.

Sams applauds the new codes of ethics being written, the legal calling to account, the cry for standards. But his main point is that the word *boundaries* has been used indiscriminately. Some kinds of fences make good neighbors, but others cut us off from each other entirely; the history of religion is replete with religious leaders' use of boundaries to keep people from each other, including spiritual leaders from their followers. In fact, the literature about sexual violence in congregations does tend to talk about boundaries without clarifying well enough what the word means. The articles by Sams and Hopkins begin to detail various meanings. An interesting suggestion from Sams is that leaders periodically ask others if their behavior is "overly familiar" or "overly reserved." Sams does this himself, and finds it helps build strong relationships.

Hopkins has a book's worth of ideas in her article, including the suggestion that we move from an ethics inspired by a "set of rules governing behavior" to a new emphasis on the "quality of a relationship." She offers a convincing discussion of why hugging deserves discussion, whether or not your congregation practices it, and she includes an excellent summary of why and how the psychological realities of *transference, projection,* and *differentiation* make boundaries so important in the pastor-parishioner relationship. She also captures the extraordinary pain and difficulty generated when laypeople and clergy misuse their power against each other simultaneously. This is religious life at its worst, a travesty that harms everyone involved. There is a silver lining—the quality of the work by people like Selzer, Sams, and Hopkins takes us all a step forward. In the long term, it will reduce the number of congregations suffering from bad leadership.

Addressing the Inherent Risks of Ordained Leadership

Like doctors and nurses, clergy face certain inherent risks in their work. A code of ethics, along with the best advice, still may not save a priest, rabbi, or minister from accusation and litigation. Failure to report child abuse, even with "good" intentions, can result in a civil judgment for thousands of dollars many years after the abuse has occurred. This is not to bemoan the profession. Whose calling comes without risks? Understanding the risks can inspire ways to protect our integrity and stay accountable to ourselves and everyone else.

A dose of humility (to be distinguished from low self-esteem!) is good for all of us. Back in 1971, Adolf Guggenbuhl-Craig wrote a short, penetrating book called *Power in the Helping Professions*. It suggests that most of us entering the helping professions do so for mixed, ambiguous reasons. He advises facing up to the ambiguity and provides imaginative ways to do so. A Swiss Jungian psychiatrist, Guggenbuhl-Craig puts his finger on the critical issue separating healthy and abusive leadership—how we use power. In pastor-parishioner type relationships, he contends, "Quite frequently, the issue at stake appears to be not the welfare of the protected but the power of the protector" (p. 9). Getting perspective on this mix-up, being able to discern where one misuses or abuses power, opens the door to cleaning up one's act before more harm is done.

The Risk of Misconduct

Discounting the risk of your own potential misconduct is folly, whatever your character development. All are tempted, no one is perfect, and each of us is responsible for himself or herself and those he or she has vowed to care for. Realizing the scope of the risk for clergy misconduct, most denominations and their judicatories have developed policies, procedures, and educational programs to reduce the problem and mitigate injury when it happens.

One of the best ways to be trustworthy and so recognized is to build that other treasure, a happy marriage. Thriving matrimony is rated by happy clergy as a primary asset in doing accountable, effective ministry; a failing marriage, by contrast, raises the risk of misconduct.

But marriage is no requirement nor any guarantee that you will not sometimes abuse the power conferred with leadership. Along with a sophisticated sense of pastoral boundaries, both single and married clergy have plenty of resources for evading misconduct as well as its accusation. Spiritual practice, trustworthy colleagues, continuing education, expert advice, healthy self-esteem, and self-care all help enormously. Burnout is all too often a risk in religious vocations, so taking advantages of tool kits like Anthony Pappas's *Pastoral Stress: Sources of Tension, Resources for Transformation* (1995) is smart.

The Risk of Counseling

Issues associated with clergy as *counselors* are additionally complex. Professional pastoral counselors often face the same legal and financial liability vulnerability as psychologists and other therapists who are required to meet standards of care. For instance, the parents of a youth in serious counseling may sue the pastoral counselor if their child commits suicide.

In fact, the suicide of Kenneth Nally, twenty-four, on April 2, 1979, led to a protracted suit (*Nally v. Grace Community Church of the Valley*). Church leadership was exonerated eventually, but only after years in court and a half-million-dollar defense. Unless there is clear evidence of abuse, judges are never happy pursuing accusations involving religious counseling. Secular counselors have normative therapeutic models; but in the religious context, healing usually comes with a theological explanation. Thomas Jefferson said that the purpose of the First Amendment to the U.S. Constitution was to build a wall between religion and the state. Few judges are willing to breach that wall by entering into a theological discussion. Nonetheless, the Nally case calls forth some commonsense suggestions for clergy and any others offering counsel on behalf of a worshiping community:

SUGGESTIONS WHEN A PERSON THREATENS SUICIDE

o Suggest and try to arrange for medical and/or psychiatric assistance whenever a counselee is actually threatening suicide, particularly if the threat takes place in a counseling environment.

o If the person resists the suggestion, contact a licensed counselor who will be aware of the necessary steps to discern whether the threat is serious.

Congregations are well advised to have a *written* policy regarding these two issues, which should be given to anyone counseling on behalf of the congregation.

Risk management specialists in recent years have issued a number of other warnings. Screen, select, and train lay counselors with great care, and ask your insurance agent about liability coverage for them. Volunteers need training to discern which clients are a threat to themselves or others, and to be prepared to make references to licensed psychologists and psychiatrists.

Along with getting the right professional degrees, anyone in professional pastoral counseling should own copies of *Legal Issues and Religious Counseling*, by Ronald Bullis and Cynthia Mazur (1993), and *Law for the Christian Counselor*, by George Ohlschlager and Peter Mosgofian (1993). (Both are reviewed in Chapter Two.)

The Risk of False Accusation

The risk that someone will falsely accuse you of abuse is a possibility that comes with ordained religious leadership. As Nancy Hopkins puts it, "Laity can—and do—abuse their secular power." One of a handful of writers who have begun looking at congregations from a "systems" point of view, Hopkins observes that "from a systems perspective, the clergyperson can be in a very vulnerable position" (1996, p. 8). Just as the authority and power conferred with ordination can be betrayed, the power of lay leadership is corruptible.

The lack of good data on how many misconduct accusations are false is no surprise; figuring out an adequate viable research methodology boggles the mind. Most guesses in the literature reflect the writer's interests. Those involved with therapeutic solutions for transforming sexual abuse victims into survivors think that very few accusations are false. Anecdotal evidence, however, can establish that false witness is a real phenomenon.

People of integrity who suffer the fire of false indictment, as did Cardinal Joseph Bernardin of Chicago in 1993, pay painfully for their faith and vocation. Bernardin was accused of sexually abusing a teenage boy seventeen years earlier. Steven Cook, the accuser, claimed a "repressed memory" of the abuse had surfaced. Bernardin claimed his innocence from the beginning, received enormous support from those who trusted his integrity, and waited until Cook's story fell apart and he confessed to making it all up. As James Wall, editor of *Christian Century* put it, Cardinal Bernardin was fortunate for his tradition's belief "that unwarranted suffering has its purpose" (Wall, 1993, p. 1196).

Whoever in a congregation works with minors or provides one-on-one counseling needs to know the intrinsic risks in the work and proactively work to build trust. In allegations of misconduct behind closed doors, it is one person's word against another's. In response, youth leaders work in pairs, and some counselors leave the door open. Clergy sometimes invite their spouses to be a third party to counseling sessions. Some openly tape-record counseling sessions after the initial one. Some limit counseling sessions to forty minutes and only do three or four before referring a person or couple to a professional counselor. Having windows between offices protects privacy better than open doors, rendering counseling public in a manner that protects both the counselor and the parishioner in his or her trust.

We feel bad that we cannot trust each other more easily, and should. After that, it becomes a "been there, done that" situation. Being smart means moving forward to identify and explore your own integrity and live up to it. Here are some suggestions along the way:

SUGGESTIONS FOR AVOIDING MISCONDUCT AND FALSE ACCUSATION

- If single, never date parishioners.
- If married, pay more attention to your spouse.
- Be sure that at least one other adult joins you in youth leadership responsibilities, particularly when trips are involved.
- Refrain from counseling in isolated settings.
- Put limits on your counseling availability, emphasizing referrals for any serious counseling unless you do the study and clinical work to keep yourself accountable in dealing with serious psychological problems.
- Draft and use confidentiality agreements when counseling (see Exhibit 8.1).
- In public and private, refrain from any speech or physical act that could in any way be construed sexually or romantically.
- When accusations or threats *are* made, during counseling or publicly, inform your insurance agent and attorney.

The Risk of Criminal and Financial Liability

By now it should be clear that law and the courts have had a great deal to say about clergy misconduct. And anyone concerned with justice might hesitate before castigating the legal community. Donald Clark, an attorney who represents a number of religious organizations, writes, "The law is filling a void, a vacuum of leadership caused by the religious community's failure to act promptly and adequately. . . . I think the law is doing what it historically does best: empowering the powerless" (Clark, 1993, p. 396).

Child abuse brings the court's harshest judgment. It is criminal, and victims can sue the perpetrators. Sexual relationships between clergy and adult parishioners form a considerably more complex arena. Richard Hammar (1996a) surveys this legal liability in "Clergy Sexual Misconduct: Risks and Responses," from the vantage point of early 1996. At that time, he reports, most clergy sexual misconduct issues concerned sexual relations between male clergy and unaccompanied adult female counselees.

In most states, the law does not forbid clergy from having sexual relations with a "consenting" adult who happens to be a parishioner. Nevertheless, it has become generally acknowledged, as discussed earlier, that a pastor and parishioner have an inherently unequal relationship, precluding genuine "consent." At this writing, a number of states are contemplating adding clergy to the list of those professionals for whom it is a crime to have sexual relationships with a client. In Texas, for instance, a new law distinguishes between religious and secular counseling. Clergy doing "secular" counseling in that state (that is, those using "professional" rather than "religious" standards) now are criminally liable for inviting or accepting a sexual relationship with a counselee.

The theory of *professional malpractice* often used against clergy has regularly been rejected by the courts on the grounds that the separation of church and state precludes the state from defining professional clergy standards. That does not let the abusing pastor off the legal hook from other established forms of liability—such as for assault and battery, sexual harassment, and negligent or intentional infliction of emotional distress. When injury is involved or alleged, an accused clergyperson, usually male, assumes considerable personal risk. In a number of cases, courts have set aside the statute of limitations if a counseled person realizes and can establish that an injury was done long ago through sexual manipulation in a pastoral counseling context. Church insurance, typically, will not defend one so accused.

The Risk of Bad Apples

Practicing clergy have to put up with the risks of the profession, including what commentator G. Lloyd Rediger (1996) calls "killers of congregations," the few bad apples who put us all at risk. Bad apples come in different flavors. Some are sluggards, some are obsessed with power and control, some have no moral keel, some are sexual predators, and some are otherwise violent. We have few reliable statistics here. Andrew Greeley, a priest and well-known scholar and novelist, whose sociological research is well respected, suggests that 2,000 to 4,000 of 53,000 Catholic priests in this country have abused minors ("Clergy Sex Abuse," 1993). A

Fuller Institute of Church Growth clergy survey found that 37 percent of those responding had been involved in inappropriate sexual behavior at least once with a parishioner (London and Wiseman, 1993, p. 22).

Whatever the numbers, bad apples represent a small minority of ordained leaders, whose influence is disproportionate to their numbers. The problem in confronting the bad apple is that he or she can be powerful, dangerous, and difficult to dislodge. Extreme examples, such as Jim Jones and David Koresh, have led their congregations into the valley of death, and no one, least of all the government of the United States, was able to stave off these terrible consequences.

So it is appropriate to stay educated about the differences between healthy and pathological behavior. Starting in the 1980s and continuing late into the 1990s, religious institutions have been scrambling to put together the workshops, resources, policies, and procedures that allow the worshiping community to call harmful clergy to account. Coping with difficult, harmful lay leaders has received much less attention so far, but expect new resources as we approach the end of the century.

Even with all the procedures in place, the role of local bishop or conference minister these days is one of the toughest tasks in the religious community, whatever your tradition. Margaret Morris's "Judging Clergy Misconduct: A Woman's Viewpoint" (1995) tells the roller-coaster story of being responsible for maintaining church accountability at the regional level, responsible, too, for taking action whenever a breach of trust is alleged.

Most religions give high priority to the value of compassion, and just such compassion toward abused people as well as the perpetrators must direct us in all we do to reduce the harm. The agencies described in Chapter One that support and advise fired clergy also offer services to those who have seriously misbehaved or simply need counseling or career guidance. Failure is often our best teacher, and lives can be transformed. Good people who are violent can become good people who are not violent.

At the same time, we must affirm there is no room in the sanctuary for abusive leaders, and compassion's first call must be for those who suffer abuse. The integrity of the entire religious community is caught up in how well we address those who, one way or another, have been violated. The painful story has finally been told by survivors cutting through their fears and laying bare their suffering. "I did not know" is no longer an adequate position for accountable leaders in the worshiping community.

Going the Next Step

This discussion of clergy misconduct has been a continuation of Chapter Eight's subject of hidden violence and the congregation, and many of the resources listed in that chapter can be used to provide a context for the more specialized bibliography for this chapter.

By the beginning of the 1990s, national and regional religious leadership realized that the sexual scandals unfolding all over the country were symbolic of a vocation in crisis. There has been a swift response from many quarters.

Denominational publishing houses have worked overtime on these issues, creating excellent workshops, curricula, books, and multimedia products. The sad part is that no distribution system currently exists allowing us to take advantage of the variety of good sectarian materials. Even though these materials tend to be designed for "family," and outsiders would not be comfortable with most of them, some of them could be of wider use.

Agencies like the Center for the Prevention of Sexual and Domestic Violence have done an extraordinary job at filling the gap. Get the center's catalog of over two dozen books, workbooks, curricula, and tapes. A good example of its best work is the resource package *Prevention of Clergy Misconduct: Sexual Abuse in the Ministerial Relationship,* produced by Marie Fortune. A leading expert in the subject called it a "tour de force" educational project (Schoener, 1992). It includes two videotapes, awareness brochures, and a trainer's manual and detailed curriculum.

A much more modest and older but still useful publication is an eleven-page monograph titled *Sexual Contact by Pastors and Pastoral Counselors in Professional Relationships* (1984) prepared and published by the Washington Association of Churches. The result of an ecumenical study, again involving Marie Fortune, it takes on the issue straightforwardly, including how to proceed when allegations of abuse have been made. If you are just beginning to formulate policy and procedure, this is a good place to start.

It may sound like an old refrain by now, but the Alban Institute catalogue is a treasury of inexpensive resources and expert hands-on authors and consultants who systematically address most of the issues that put clergy at risk. Though it is largely a creation of the liberal community, like most Alban resources, the materials are user-friendly for everyone in the religious community. For instance, the personal temperament of those in religious vocation is a major influence on their success and effectiveness, an issue explored in *Personality Type and Religious Leadership,* by Alban consultant Roy Oswald (1988).

Two particularly important Alban contributions are *Clergy and the Sexual Revolution,* by Ruth Barnhouse (1994), and *Clergy Sexual Misconduct: A Systems Perspective,* edited by Nancy Hopkins (1993). Barnhouse is an Episcopal priest and psychiatrist and covers a diversity of sexual issues, including divorce, adultery, homosexuality, and premarital relationships, all from the perspective of a clergyperson. Hopkins' anthology contains ten articles by various authors. It narrows the focus to clergy misconduct, taking the subject apart issue by issue to convey the full complexity of the tragedy. Both reports are recommended for anyone dealing with a particular situation of misconduct or professionally connected to the subject.

Pastors at Risk, edited by H. B. London Jr. and Neil Wiseman (1993), is specifically written for male clergy in an increasingly risky vocation. Seven colleagues join the team to untangle the crisis; they focus on marriage, spirituality (personal holiness), money, stress and burnout, and the clergy-spouse role.

One of the rare legal reports in this field not from the pen of Richard Hammar is Anne Underwood's book *An Attorney Looks at the Secular Foundation for Clergy Sexual Misconduct Policies* (1994). It focuses on the legal issues surrounding a congregation's policies regarding clergy misconduct and sexual harassment, a subject to be surveyed in the next chapter.

An important factor in clergy vulnerability is spiritual health. Every tradition has rich resources in this regard for those who seek them out. A valuable tool is *Spiritual Wholeness for Clergy: A New Psychology of Intimacy with God, Self, and Others* (1993), by Donald Hands and Wayne Fehr. Based on the counseling of four hundred clergy over five years, the book identifies the problems, traps, and temptations of ordained leadership. It goes on to suggest integrating theology, psychology, and an understanding of human frailty in such a way that everyone is better protected. Anthony Pappas's *Pastoral Stress,* mentioned earlier, is another well-received self-health resource.

Theological ethicists have weighed in with important contributions, some of them shifting their focus from the theoretical to the practical. *Ethics in Ministry: A Guide for the Professional,* by Walter Weist and Elan Smith (1990), is a thoughtful discussion of ministerial ethics, focusing on the complexities of truth-telling, the problem of authority, and the quality of pastoral relationships. More recently *Ethics in Pastoral Ministry,* by Richard Gula (1996), takes into account the scandal of abuse and the resources that have emerged. Character, professional duties, sexuality, confidentiality, and a proposed code of ethics are all major themes in a text that has been reviewed as a good seminary textbook.

A good resource in the search for appropriate ethical standards is *Power and Change in Parish Ministry: Reflections on the Cure of Souls,* by Michael Jinkins and Deborah Bradshaw Jinkins (1991). It seeks to improve how leaders relate to authority, power, and change. *As One with Authority,* by Jackson Carroll (1992), studies the meaning of "sacramental presence and trust" and builds a case for "reflective leadership," a healthy rather than abusive use of authority. Celia Hahn's more recent *Growing in Authority, Relinquishing Control* (1994), surveyed in Chapter One, specifically seeks an authority that is shared and supportive, not harmful.

Recidivism in Sex Offender Treatment is a packet of professional articles on the subject and is available from the Safer Society Foundation. Safer Society also provides a nationwide, telephone-only referral service (not a hot line) for the treatment of juvenile and adult sex offenders. Names are not asked when help is solicited from Safer Society at (802) 247–3132. Safer Society is connected with 1,600 counselors around the nation trained to work with sexual offenders.

Resources for Preventing Clergy Misconduct

Agencies

Alban Institute, Suite 433 North, 4550 Montgomery Avenue, Bethesda, MD 20814; (800) 486–1318.

American Association of Pastoral Counselors, 9504-A Lee Highway, Fairfax, VA 22031; (703) 385–6967.

Center for the Prevention of Sexual and Domestic Violence, 1914 North 34th Street, Suite 105, Seattle, WA 98103; (206) 634–1903.

National Coalition Against Sexual Assault, 912 North Second Street, Harrisburg, PA 17102–8119; (717) 232–7460. (Provides referrals to rape crisis centers.)

Safer Society Foundation, P.O. Box 340, Brandon, VT 05733; (800) 247–3132. (At this number, the foundation also offers a free telephone service providing assessment and treatment referrals to victims-survivors and offenders.)

Resource Packages

Crossing the Boundary: Professional Sexual Abuse, U.S. Women's Concerns of the Mennonite Central Committee at 21 South 12th Street, P.O. Box 500, Akron, PA 17501. (Multimedia package.)

Prevention of Clergy Misconduct: Sexual Abuse in the Ministerial Relationship, Center for the Prevention of Sexual and Domestic Violence, 1914 North 34th Street, Suite 105, Seattle, WA 98103; (206) 634–1903. (Multimedia package.)

Recidivism in Sex Offender Treatment, Safer Society Foundation, P.O. Box 340, Brandon, VT 05733; (802) 247–3132. (Packet of professional articles.)

Books and Articles

Barnhouse, Ruth Tiffany. *Clergy and the Sexual Revolution.* Washington, DC: Alban Institute, 1994.

Barton, Ronald, and Karen Lebacqz. *Sex in the Parish.* Louisville, Ky.: Westminster/John Knox, 1991.

Beck, Melinda. "Sex and Psychotherapy: A Current Affair." *Newsweek,* Apr. 13, 1992, pp. 52–57.

Berry, Jason. *Lead Us Not into Temptation: Catholic Priests and the Sexual Abuse of Children.* New York: Doubleday, 1992.

Bullis, Ronald K., and Mazur, Cynthia S. *Legal Issues and Religious Counseling.* Louisville, Ky.: Westminster/John Knox, 1993.

Carroll, Jackson W. *As One with Authority.* Louisville, Ky.: Westminster/John Knox, 1992.

Clark, Donald C., Jr. "Sexual Abuse in the Church: The Law Steps In." *Christian Century,* Apr. 14, 1993, p. 396.

Clarke, Rita-Lou. *Pastoral Care of Battered Women.* Louisville, Ky.: Westminster/John Knox, 1986.

"Clergy Sex Abuse Widespread, Says Priest." *Christian Century,* Apr. 14, 1993, pp. 392–393.

"Clergy's Image Sinks to All-Time Survey Low." *National Christian Reporter,* Nov. 11, 1992, p. 1.

Cooper-White, Pamela. "Soul Stealing: Power Relations in Pastoral Sexual Abuse." *Christian Century,* Feb. 20, 1991, pp. 196–199.

Culver, Virginia. "More and More Churches Face Sexual Misconduct Suits." *Denver Post,* Sept. 7, 1991, p. 1B.

Eckert, Jerry. "Beware of Witch Hunts on Clergy Sex-Abuse Charges." *National Christian Reporter,* Dec. 3, 1993, p. 2.

Ericsson, Samuel, E. *Clergy Malpractice: An Illegal Legal Theory.* Christian Legal Society, 1982. (Order from the Center for Law and Religious Freedom, P.O. Box 1492, Merrifield, VA 22116; (703) 642–1070.)

Fortune, Marie. *Sexual Violence—The Unmentionable Sin: An Ethical and Pastoral Perspective.* Cleveland, Ohio: Pilgrim Press, 1983.

Fortune, Marie. *Is Nothing Sacred? When Sex Invades the Pastoral Relationship.* San Francisco: Harper San Francisco, 1989.

Fortune, Marie. "Therapy and Intimacy: Confused About Boundaries." Review of *When Boundaries Betray Us,* by Carter Heyward. *Christian Century,* May 18, 1994, pp. 524–525.

Fortune, Marie, and Heyward, Carter. "Boundaries or Barriers? An Exchange." *Christian Century,* June 1, 1994, pp. 579–582.

"Getting Serious About Sexual Harassment." *Business Week,* Nov. 9, 1992, p. 78.

Guggenbuhl-Craig, Adolf. *Power in the Helping Professions*. Dallas, Tex.: Spring, 1971.

Gula, Richard M. *Ethics in Pastoral Ministry*. Mahwah, N.J.: Paulist Press, 1996.

Hahn, Celia Allison. *Growing in Authority, Relinquishing Control: A New Approach to Faithful Leadership*. Bethesda, Md.: Alban Institute, 1994.

Hammar, Richard H. "Clergy Malpractice: The Nally Case." *Church Law and Tax Report*, Jan./Feb. 1988, pp. 2–6. (For reprints of Richard Hammar's articles in *Church Law and Tax Report*, write to the publisher, Christian Ministry Resources, P.O. Box 1098, Matthews, NC 28106.)

Hammar, Richard H. "Clergy Malpractice." *Church Law and Tax Report*, Mar./Apr. 1989a, pp. 1–4.

Hammar, Richard H. "Sexual Seduction of Church Members by Clergy." *Church Law and Tax Report*, May/June 1989b, pp. 5–7.

Hammar, Richard H. "Denominational Liability for Acts of Local Clergy." *Church Law and Tax Report*, July/Aug. 1990, pp. 6–9.

Hammar, Richard H. "Church and Denominational Liability for the Sexual Misconduct of Clergy." *Church Law and Tax Report*, Sept./Oct. 1991a, pp. 4–7.

Hammar, Richard H. "Sexual Seduction by Youth Workers." *Church Law and Tax Report*, May/June 1991b, pp. 1–4.

Hammar, Richard H. "Liability of a Church and Parent Denomination for Acts of Sexual Harassment by Clergy." *Church Law and Tax Report*, July/Aug. 1992, pp. 15–17.

Hammar, Richard H. "Church Liability for Clergy Sexual Misconduct: Case #1 and Case #2." *Church Law and Tax Report*, July/Aug. 1994, pp. 1–9.

Hammar, Richard H. "Church Liability for the Sexual Misconduct of Clergy." *Church Law and Tax Report*, Sept./Oct. 1995, pp. 14–20.

Hammar, Richard H. "Clergy Sexual Misconduct: Risks and Responses." *Clergy Journal*, Feb. 1996a, pp. 45–47.

Hammar, Richard H. "A Legal Profile of American Churches." *Church Law and Tax Report*, July/Aug. 1996b, p. 30.

Hammar, Richard H. "Texas Statute Imposes Liability on Some Ministers and Churches." *Church Law and Tax Report*, Mar./Apr. 1996c, pp. 10–13.

Hands, Donald R., and Fehr, Wayne L. *Spiritual Wholeness for Clergy: A New Psychology of Intimacy with God, Self, and Others*. Bethesda, Md.: Alban Institute, 1993.

Heyward, Carter. *When Boundaries Betray Us: Beyond Illusions of What Is Ethical in Therapy and Life*. San Francisco: Harper San Francisco, 1993.

Hopkins, Nancy Myer. *Clergy Sexual Misconduct: A Systems Perspective*. Bethesda, Md.: Alban Institute, 1993.

Hopkins, Nancy Myer. "Re-Thinking Sexual Misconduct: A Response to Jonathan Sams." *Congregations,* July/Aug. 1996, pp. 8–12.

Jinkins, Michael, and Jinkins, Deborah Bradshaw. *Power and Change in Parish Ministry: Reflections on the Cure of Souls.* Bethesda, Md.: Alban Institute, 1991.

Karf, Samuel E. "Religious Leadership." *Christian Century,* Mar. 23, 1994, pp. 300–302.

Lebacqz, Karen. *Professional Ethics, Power, and Paradox.* Nashville, Tenn.: Abingdon Press, 1984.

London, H. B., Jr., and Wiseman, Neil B. (eds.). *Pastors at Risk: Help for Pastors, Hope for the Church.* Wheaton, Ill.: Victor Books, 1993.

Morris, Margaret Z. "Judging Clergy Misconduct: A Woman's Viewpoint." *Clergy Journal,* Apr. 1995, pp. 8–9, 35.

Ohlschlager, George, and Mosgofian, Peter. *Law for the Christian Counselor.* Irving, Tex.: Word, 1993.

Oswald, Roy. *Power Analysis of a Congregation.* Bethesda, Md.: Alban Institute, 1981.

Oswald, Roy. *Personality Type and Religious Leadership.* Bethesda, Md.: Alban Institute, 1988.

Pappas, Anthony. *Pastoral Stress: Sources of Tension, Resources for Transformation.* Bethesda, Md.: Alban Institute, 1995.

"Pastors' Sex Lives." *Christian Ministry,* Jan. 1995, pp. 5–6.

Pellauer, Mary, Chester, Barbara, and Boyajian, Jane (eds.). *Sexual Assault and Abuse: A Handbook for Clergy and Religion Professionals.* San Francisco: Harper San Francisco, 1987.

Phillips, Michael E. "Helping the Sexually Abused." *Leadership,* Summer 1989, pp. 65–72.

Rediger, G. Lloyd. "It's More Than Scandal." *Clergy Journal,* Jan. 1990, p. 42.

Rediger, G. Lloyd. "Killers of Congregations." *Clergy Journal,* Apr. 1996, pp. 23–27.

Rutter, Peter. *Sex in the Forbidden Zone: When Men in Power—Therapists, Doctors, Clergy, Teachers, and Others—Betray Women's Trust.* New York: Fawcett, 1991.

Sams, Jonathan C. "Clergy Sexual Ethics: A New Puritanism?" *Congregations,* July/Aug. 1996, pp. 5–7.

Schaefer, Arthur Gross. "Divine Immunity: Should Clergy Be Subject to a Standard of Care?" *CPCU Journal,* Dec. 1987, pp. 217–218.

Schoener, Gary. "Prevention and Intervention in Cases of Professional Misconduct." *Minnesota Psychologist,* May 1992, pp. 9–10.

Selzer, David. "Setting Healthy Boundaries." *Clergy Journal,* Apr. 1995, pp. 10–12.

Sparks, James A., Ray, Robert O., and Houts, Donald C. "Sexual Misconduct in Ministry: What Clergy at Risk Are Doing About It." *Congregations,* Nov./Dec. 1992, pp. 3–8.

Spohn, Gustav. "Churches Take Bold Steps to Combat Clergy Sex Misconduct." *National Christian Reporter,* July 26, 1991, p. 1.

Thorkelson, Willmar. "Poll Says Catholic Priests More Satisfied at Work Than Mainline Protestant Clergy." *National Christian Reporter,* May 10, 1991, p. 1.

"Traits of a Sexually Healthy Pastor." (Symposium of eight clergy.) *Leadership,* Summer 1995, pp. 19–29.

Underwood, Anne. *An Attorney Looks at the Secular Foundation for Clergy Sexual Misconduct Policies.* Bethesda, Md.: Alban Institute, 1994.

United Church of Christ. "Code of Ethics." In *United Church of Christ Manual on Ministry: Perspectives and Procedures for Ecclesiastical Authorization of Ministry.* Cleveland, Ohio: United Church of Christ Office for Church Life and Leadership, 1986.

Wall, James M. "The Bernardin Factor." *Christian Century,* Dec. 1, 1993, pp. 1195–1196.

Washington Association of Churches. *Sexual Contact by Pastors and Pastoral Counselors in Professional Relationships.* Seattle: Washington Association of Churches, 1984. (Order from Washington Association of Churches, 149 Occidental South, Seattle, WA 98104; (206) 625–9790.)

Weist, Walter E., and Smith, Elan A. *Ethics in Ministry: A Guide for the Professional.* Minneapolis: Augsburg Fortress, 1990.

White, Gayle. "Episcopalians Rewrite Rules on Misconduct by Clergy." *National Christian Reporter,* Sept. 23, 1994, p. 1.

10

HEALING THE
WOUNDED CONGREGATION

MY GRANDFATHER, God rest his soul, happily served Presbyterian congregations throughout the state of Washington for over forty years. No doubt he saw instances of almost everything discussed in this book. Still, I wince at the thought of his reading the last two chapters, at the pain it would etch on his face, listening to the story so long denied in the worshiping community. The shock and pain evoked in so many by this plague of invisible violence is real, must be recognized and addressed, and sometimes can be healed.

In the quest to reestablish sanctuary in the houses of worship that dot the land, the stakes for the religious community are enormous, as they are for every individual congregation and its leaders. For millions of victims, the stakes include the continuing physical and emotional pain and harm beggaring anything the nonabused have experienced. Probably all of us, once upon a time or more, have felt the sting of abuse deeply enough to catch the flavor of terror abused people taste day and night. This reality constitutes the strongest mandate, the ethical admonition for moving past denial and toward therapeutic goals.

Yet something larger is also at stake. The tragedy in the worshiping community is the same we find throughout the culture, where violence turns out to be even better than sex for making money and influencing people. The soul of the nation is wrestling with power and the impulse to harm one another. The religious community—if it can adequately confront the tragedy in its own midst—is one of the last institutions left to model justice, peace, and health for all people and the planet. Two steps can help qualify the religious community for that role. First, we must clean house: we must reestablish trustworthiness and safety within the local congregation. Then we can institute the safeguards that sustain community health and vitality as well as personal faith.

Dressing the Wound

Hearing about harm and injury always disturbs a congregation, particularly when that harm is malicious rather than accidental. When accusations are made about anyone related to a congregation, the situation immediately becomes complicated in a number of ways. An accused leader, for instance, will be ineffective in his or her role until the matter is resolved, so a replacement needs to be secured. The pastoral response to the congregation as a whole becomes more complex, and the institution's legal and financial vulnerability increases. Cleaning and dressing a severe body wound is painful. If done well, it may also be life giving. So it is when people are wounded in a congregation.

The first step is for congregational clergy to get educated. Typically, this learning process begins in a crisis situation. The cliche about a little learning being dangerous applies here precisely, so—before allegation and violation surface—talk to colleagues and local experts, go to workshops, and start a library of resources. Reading *Sexual Abuse in Christian Homes and Churches,* by Carolyn Heggen (1993) (reviewed in Chapter Eight), is a good starting place.

From Heggen's fine contribution you can turn to a variety of tools in an increasingly sophisticated resource bank, most of it created within the past ten years. It includes forms, curricula, videotapes, brand-new research found in pamphlets and special reports, workshops, books, and periodicals, along with a cadre of hands-on expert consultants who have been through it all. Such consultants are available through the Alban Institute, the Center for the Prevention of Sexual and Domestic Violence, Christian Ministry Resources, and a number of other agencies, including judicatory and denominational offices. These institutions have also published their own research-based, user-friendly materials for congregations.

One finds very little overlap in the work of the big three agencies: Alban, the Center for the Prevention of Sexual and Domestic Violence, and CMR. Happily, and befitting their good faith, they price their products modestly. Consultants of any kind are expensive, of course. Going to workshops, though, now held all over the country, and spending a hundred dollars for a shelf of basic texts are within every congregation's treasury. Money spent like this does so much more than save time, money, and agony in a future crisis; it can cut short the suffering of children and other innocent people.

Study makes quickly apparent the need to recognize the gradations of injury people have received from each other. Bullying someone at a camp retreat has some of the same abusive features as rape; but because they are vastly different in other ways, an appropriate response to the two situations calls for different policies and procedures.

Freedom from harassment is the most basic standard of care we can expect from each other; without it, safety and trust are impossible.

Promoting Policies Prohibiting Harassment and Abuse

Harassment of anyone at any time in a worshiping community is inappropriate, whether it happens to come from a bully, a trustee who likes dirty jokes, or any other activity that demeans people. Harassment is different from abuse in degree, not in kind. It can be recognized whenever someone is made to feel embarrassed, afraid, ashamed, intimidated, helpless, vulnerable, inferior, or inadequate through words or actions. Harassment is about manipulating power, and because leaders have certain powers, perceived or not, harassment by them is as intolerable as the mugger, empowered with a gun, violating someone on the street.

Harassment comes in many guises. Sometimes it is an off-hand remark; when an occasional nasty comment becomes habitual, it is much more serious. Confronting the issue concisely and precisely, as in, "Please quit making comments about my clothes. It makes me feel bad, not good," often puts an end to abusive treatment. When that fails, the problem is more complicated.

Prudent, caring congregations, in support of justice and safety, will publish written policies (see Exhibit 10.1 for a sample policy) prohibiting harassment and offering people a means of safely complaining if and when they feel harassed. Bullied people are sorely tempted to remain silent, hoping the problem will simply abate. Usually, it does not, and in the silence, emotional wounds have no access to healing. Defining, endorsing, posting, and talking about policy periodically is an excellent beginning point. It offers the abused person an open door.

In addition to having a written policy, communities can offer these suggestions to people who suffer harassment.

To make ―――――――――――――― a safe place for all of us, harassment and abuse are prohibited here. Harassment is behavior that inappropriately invades, embarrasses, frightens, shames, intimidates, or threatens the safety or self-esteem of another person. It has no place in our congregation.

Anyone who feels harassed is encouraged to communicate this to the clergy, the moderator, or any other officer without fear of reprisal.

Exhibit 10.1. Sample Congregational Policy on Harassment and Abuse.

SUGGESTIONS FOR PEOPLE HARASSED IN THE
WORSHIPING COMMUNITY

o Clearly ask the harasser to cease the offending behavior. Many times this will bring a welcome change.

o If the request does no good, tell your trusted friends about the problem.

o Keep a file noting the harassing behavior in detail, along with the times and dates it occurs.

o Make an official complaint to the person or authority who can confront the harasser. (Congregations with a published policy can identify the appropriate names. Always have more than one authorized person, because the overseer may also be the accused.)

o If your congregation belongs to a denomination, contact and inform a regional clergy or an officer such as a bishop, district superintendent, or conference minister.

o Seek both legal and spiritual counsel.

Responding to Allegations

Responding to an allegation of harassment is a sensitive matter. Response should come quickly from someone who is educated about the range of abusive issues and how to respond to them. Such a person needs the support of policy and procedures. Confidentiality is important because if the abuse cannot be confirmed, inappropriate discussion of the allegation can inspire a lawsuit for libel. In talking to a victim, listen carefully; offer the benefit of the doubt without joining in the accusations; focus on specifics; and run down the who, what, when, where, and how questions, leaving aside why for the time being. Did anyone else witness the harassment? Has anyone else been told about the incident, and has it happened more than once? Do a thorough investigation and document the details from the start. The prospect of writing a statement can be intimidating for a complainant and should be handled with great sensitivity. But the sooner that it happens the less likely the *rumor* of allegation will do its unfair, usually untrue business. Many denominations require a statement as an early part of any investigation.

Do not encourage or discourage the accused from making the issue public; that is an extremely personal issue and comes with potential legal liability, particularly when there is no way to corroborate the accusation except through one person's word against another's. Explore the available options with the victim, including counseling to deal with the upset, confronting the individual accused, asking for the support of others, and seeking the advice of an attorney. If the issue involves anyone employed by the congregation, a complaint should be made directly to the pastor or the presiding lay leader, such as a council president. In any case, if clergy are not involved in the accusation, they should be kept informed about the investigation. If clergy are accused, the board chair or president should be kept informed.

When employees are involved—anyone from clergyperson to custodian—the law holds the institution responsible for their work, for a safe working place, an established, effective sexual harassment policy, and quick response to allegations of abuse.

Julie Bloss's two-part series titled "Sexual Harassment" (1996a, 1996b) explains the legal intricacies of employee-related sexual harassment. Her discussion suggests that harassment that creates a hostile workplace—a pattern of constant nitpicking, demeaning sarcasm, sexual innuendo—is much more prevalent than more specific sexual abuse. The law is particularly severe with those rarer cases where employment or a higher salary are promised for sexual favors. But if a choir director refuses to cease from oppressively flirting with the secretary, and if the leaders of the congregation pass her complaints off as a snit betwen prudery and an artistic sensibility, both congregation and the choir director could be in for an ugly lawsuit, to say nothing of the justice issues involved.

For the congregation, harassment and abuse by clergy is by far the most wounding kind of misconduct. Fortunately, we have new resources to turn to now for congregations that have been so victimized. First, it is worth noticing that unwelcome conduct by regular members is nearly as prevalent as clergy misconduct and harder to deal with in some ways. To date, we lack adequate tools, guidelines, policy, and procedures to harness the bad habits of an abuser who is a member of the congregation. The material about troublesome people surveyed in Chapter Three begins to address the issue. At a certain point, some troublesome people become intolerable.

One local church with a longtime member who started and refused to cease making demeaning sexual remarks to women in the congregation finally persuaded the member to leave after two years of painful meetings, private and public. Having a policy against harassment is one thing, but implementing it with an incorrigible offender can be tough. Kibbie Ruth writes of one church that acted on the strength of a New Testament passage (Matthew 18:15–17) to file a restraining order against a parishioner.

In that passage, Jesus suggests that abused individuals confront their abusers. If that fails to turn the person around, he continues, find others who witnessed the abuse, and if that does not help, tell the whole congregation. If you cannot convince the abuser to cease, Jesus concludes, insist on saying good-bye and close your door to the abuser. The advice is still good when faced with a person whose misbehavior resists reform after repeated interventions.

When clergy misconduct is involved, or any kind of child abuse connected to a congregation's facilities or activities, the complexity and liability are magnified. Dozens of civil and criminal issues raise their heads, many more people end up being wounded, and wounded deeply, so that the worshiping community as a whole suffers a body blow. Therefore, the guidelines for responding to these kinds of allegations are all the more important.

SUGGESTIONS FOR RESPONDING TO ALLEGATIONS OF MISCONDUCT AND CHILD ABUSE

- Take every allegation seriously, and be faithful to the policies and procedures that the congregation's leadership has endorsed.
- Bring denominational or trusted outside resources into the discussion whenever serious misconduct or criminal abuse is alleged, particularly when any employees or the congregation's property and program are involved.
- Bring the congregation's insurance agent and a lawyer expert in malpractice law into the discussion. Clergy and lay leaders should *not* try to act as lawyers. Cooperate with the professionals while focusing on pastoral needs. Typically, you can depend on the confidentiality of the professionals.
- Review with an attorney any confidentiality problems related to the case.
- Bring trusted experts into the situation, and share the responsibility of the situation. No one should have to play multiple roles in the situation. For instance, the clergy should not try to be counselor, spokesperson to the press, convener, judge, and decision maker—in addition to shepherding the congregation.
- Before allegations ever occur in your congregation, review the possibility with the congregation's leadership, attorney, and insurance agent.
- The victim and the victim's family, whether the allegation is true or not, need to receive pastoral care and professional counseling. Ethically and legally, the care and safety of the victim is paramount.
- Allow congregational and denominational councils and courts of law to do the judging. Clergy thrown into the role of judge cannot simultaneously provide pastoral care to those who need it. Alert leaders to shy away from blaming people in any crisis. Instead, support the process of discovery. Call for fairness for all involved, and

attend to whoever is hurting in and from the process. Typically, this includes the entire congregation.

o Give the accused due process, goodwill, and pastoral care and attention throughout, before judgments are made. Family members of the accused are particularly vulnerable and need support, not ostracism.

o The full details of any allegation and discovery process should not be communicated to the congregation at large. Instead, educate people about the process being followed, and depend on the process to guide the level of detail that is shared.

When judgments and decisions are made, they eventually need to be shared with the entire congregation as well as members of the press who inquire. Openness is the best antidote to rumor. During the crisis, and perhaps afterwards, there may be confidential information to maintain, such as the identity of the complainant, details of circumstances that could identify the complainant, and any official medical diagnosis. But the eventual resolution and the decision-making process along the way can be crystal clear and known by all. Without such openness, rumor and mistrust will fester.

The conclusion of most abuse investigations goes in one of three directions: the allegations are confessed, the allegations are denied, or often, one or two of five or six accusations are confessed, the others denied. The toughest situations are those where everything hangs on "he says" versus "she says." In these instances, we have to live with our opinions about credibility instead of any degree of certainty that we know what actually happened.

Once upon a time, this kind of puzzle encouraged sweeping the whole thing under the rug instead of "burdening" the community; that approach has been a boon to repeat offenders and rumormongers and is not one we can live with any longer. Those well experienced in these investigations suggest that the process of a congregational sexual abuse investigation and the results need to be shared with congregations, beginning with the board of directors, which then can respond as appropriate. The difficulties this process entails pale in comparison to keeping things secret.

The guidelines just given only begin to reflect the challenge to leaders who work at putting a worshiping community together after abuse on the inside. Indeed, a new word has been coined for the clergyperson who goes into a situation where another pastor has been removed for sexual misconduct. Such a person is now called the *afterpastor*, and the role is considered one of the toughest in parish ministry.

Anne Underwood, an attorney now writing for the Alban Institute, is responsible for a report titled *Considerations for Conducting an Investigation of Alleged Clergy Sexual Misconduct* (1996). It is a detailed map of the actual process of dealing with an allegation in your congregation. Alban will send it to you, even via overnight mail, if you ask. The process of the investigation, clearly defined roles, established policy and procedures, sensitivity to the rights of every person involved, a clear sense of what and when to communicate with people, including the congregation—these are the some of the elements that govern how well an investigation goes and influence the healing process afterward.

It is important to remember the warning associated with policy formation in Chapter Three. When specialists arrive at a congregation to begin a sexual abuse investigation and find policy that has been passed but not implemented, it is a red flag that the situation is not only tragic but a mess. Policy is like a rudder that aims an institution in the right direction. If the rudder is built, but flaps around because no one is holding it, that rudder is worse than useless. So remember to use the policy at your disposal to protect the wounded people, yourself, and everyone else involved.

Everyone writing about these dilemmas suggests that congregations embrace an educational regimen that raises consciousness and sensitizes people to how people harm each other and how to stay safe. The mid-1990s have been rich with excellent new resources. Perhaps the best is *Restoring the Soul of a Church: Congregations Wounded by Clergy Sexual Misconduct.* Edited by Nancy Hopkins and Mark Laaser (1995), the book was inspired by an interfaith group of people involved in various aspects of clergy abuse. Meeting in Minnesota at a 1989 conference titled Healing the Wounds, they made a commitment to work with each other in what became a pioneering study. Meeting regularly, they spent a year visiting Catholic, Jewish, and Protestant congregations that have endured clergy sexual misconduct. In-depth conversations were shared with members from these congregations.

Marie Fortune's early work threw open the door to invisible abuse in the sanctuary and told it like it is. *Restoring the Soul of a Church* walks us inside and shows us how to understand in some depth what has happened. The book is divided into three parts and analyzes the subject from a systems perspective, an approach mentioned several times now that is appearing in various areas of new congregational scholarship. Essentially, the congregational community is understood as a series of systems influencing each other. The first section of the book focuses on "primary victim survivors and offenders," that is, those involved in the situation itself. This includes those receiving the least attention of all, the families of offenders. The second section addresses "secondary victims," those in the congregation. This section includes an essay by Harold Hopkins on the effects of clergy abuse cases at regional and denominational levels, and one by Kevin McDonough on the harsh impact of the clergy abuse scandal on trustworthy clergy. Finally, long-term congregational healing is addressed. The wounds from clergy child abuse can fester silently for decades. Fourteen experts contributed to this anthology. For anyone involved in wounded congregations, it should always be within reach.

Excellent though it is, *Restoring the Soul of a Church* is a beginning, not the final word in this new arena of congregational studies. Good new materials appear each month. *Healing the Congregation: A Resource* (1995) is a curriculum written by Denise Tracy for leaders and consultants who regularly minister to congregations following clergy sexual misconduct. "Symbolic Church Fights: The Hidden Agenda When Clerical Trust Has Been Betrayed" (Hopkins, 1993) reports that in researcher Stephen Rosetti's analysis of 1,013 interviews with active Catholics about clergy abuse, 71 percent report being "very angry, very sad, or very disappointed" (p. 15). The closer a person has been to an abusive situation, the greater the anger he or she acknowledged.

So we know congregations suffering such a tragedy contain a deep reservoir of pain and aggravation. Unless the anger is defused, it gets aimed in all the wrong places, often beginning with the victim's being accused of inviting the abuse. The local bishop or whoever holds clerical authority often takes considerable heat, and the afterpastor is particularly vulnerable.

Sustaining a Healthy, Vital Congregation

Discussing congregational pain does not have to go on for long before the advantages of a proactive, precrisis strategy becomes dramatically clear. James Cobble Jr., Richard Hammar, and Steven Klipowicz have created a well-received multimedia package called *Reducing the Risk of Child Sexual Abuse in Your Church* (1993). The resource is most important for its defense of children and the guidance it provides for making a program safe for the kids it serves. The package is worth the modest price just for its detailed approach to screening procedures. The authors contend that the critical issue with screening is setting the process within a holistic pastoral-theological-legal context.

The goal is safety for all, for children and their parents, teachers, and pastors. If the right context is set, people will be inspired rather than fearful about screening. It will generate trust rather than anxiety. The accompanying videotape is moving, an empowering educational tool. Driven by no particular theology, the video compellingly invites care and trust from and for volunteers, employees, and all who are served by your congregation.

Marie Fortune's *Love Does No Harm: Sexual Ethics for the Rest of Us* (1995) is a perfect book for an adult study class. It focuses on establishing respect, honesty, love, loyalty, safety, acceptance, and support in our closest relationships. It explores the values of intimate family life with a depth that makes clear how shallow most of the public blustering about family values is these days.

Fortune and colleague Kathryn Reid are responsible for four curricula described in the resources for this chapter, each aimed at a different constituency, for studying issues associated with abuse and safety. Teaching children—and their parents—how to protect themselves before abuse happens is the primary goal. For those already hurt, the door can be opened to nonviolence and healing.

With adequate training and healing, worshiping communities can become safer places, sanctuaries from the pathological private violence this culture endures. The educated, well-managed congregation can deal with invisible abuse, restore the meaning of sanctuary, and move on to other issues. The plague is too much with us for us to give up vigilance and ongoing education, but it should not claim the center of our attention most of the time. If the issue has never been faced by a congregation, it cannot hurt to give a season or a year to the discussion.

To repeat an earlier admonition, before all else clergy need to be educated about the realities of abuse. Once lay leadership is brought into the discussion, classes and seminars can be planned, using the curricula and resources mentioned here and otherwise focusing on ways to make the worshiping community a safer place and our lives safer from violation.

Along with study groups, you can invite local community resource people to speak, set up support groups within the congregation, formalize support between the congregation and a crisis facility, set up safe homes for battered women and their children, learn about programs for offenders, and become an advocate for violence-free living. Defining, endorsing, and promoting a code of ethics, as discussed in the preceding chapter, is an important step. A well-educated congregation, with good policy and procedures in place, becomes a well-connected, accountable congregation, a safety net for victims of personal violence. We have hundreds of thousands of congregations in the nation's neighborhoods. Whenever one of them goes through an educational process, the suffering and injury to countless people, mostly children and women, is tangibly reduced. Good policy and an education lead to preventive strategies that help reinvest *sanctuary* with its original meaning.

Adopting an Attitude of Safety

Some aspects of living faithfully are inherently dangerous. Standing up for justice and love, for instance, is sometimes life threatening, as the biblical tradition attests time and again. But even the dangerous elements of faith can be safe in at least two ways. First, most religious traditions claim that our real source of safety comes from God. This sense of safety emerges from an internal realization, not necessarily our ability to overcome an external reality, however threatening. The peace that passes understanding led Daniel safely into the lion's den and can do the same for believers today. Ordinary people are daily called to act with enormous courage, and they need to be affirmed for it from the pulpit, in the counseling room, and in public when appropriate.

Knowing that *others in the worshiping community care about us* is another source of safety in a threatening environment. Leadership that articulates and authentically expresses this concern for *each* person gathered, including the most vulnerable, thereby discourages the possibility of abuse. Too often, though, this goal is held up in a community where people never meet each other except at coffee hour. Active care becomes real as it is expressed, and creative leaders can work to this end in many different ways.

Screening

Screening employees and volunteers is an excellent way to discourage abuse in the worshiping community. *Reducing the Risk of Child Sexual Abuse in Your Church,* reviewed earlier, has an excellent screening component (additional resources are surveyed in Chapter Six).

Supervising Children

Maintaining adequate supervision of children cannot be overemphasized as a factor in discouraging abuse and misconduct. The more-than-one rule regarding finances should also apply to youth: more than one adult should be responsible at any given time for the children's safety. This is especially true at any activity away from the facility or involving young children. Individuals should not be asked or allowed to drive children other than their own to or from programs without a second adult; policy should guide such a rule so that volunteers and staff do not have to bring up the issue on their own.

Taking Advantage of Civil Service Resources

Behind the faceless mask of city and county bureaucracies can be found caring individuals, professionally trained, who are able to provide critical resources for discouraging abuse and responding appropriately when it occurs. County health and education agencies, the local criminal justice system, and nonprofit human service agencies, such as a suicide hot-line program, all are staffed with individuals whose skills, experience, and charge include relating to worshiping communities and supporting them in the effort to keep citizens safe.

Traditionally, there has been a distrustful, arm's-length relationship between human service providers and clergy. In more recent years, most of the resistance seems to be coming from the clergy. The increasing violence in society, along with years of bare-bones budgeting, have made civil servants in the helping professions more anxious to find allies in their work. As the unhappy reality of abuse in the worshiping community receives more exposure, one hopes that more congregations will also shrug off their resistance to cooperation.

Essentially, every community has a "bank" of expertise that can be called on to deal with local tragedies of misconduct. Congregational leaders can serve the worshiping community well by being connected to these resources and taking advantage of them when appropriate. One proven strategy to further this rapport is to supply county health and education agencies with a site for their educational and counseling services.

Using Pastoral Relations Committees

Having a good pastoral relations committee is healthy for the clergy and the congregation and, incidentally, can help create a safer environment for all. A pastoral relations committee can make recommendations to the council and publish reports about its work. But the actual discussion in such groups is usually cloaked in the safety of confidentiality.

Thus, when the committee is effective, members have a protected way to make complaints. Clergy likewise can share their frustrations in a safe place. Problems identified by the committee have a context where they can be addressed without public accusation and acrimony. Additionally, clergy can be evaluated in a private context where accountability and confidentiality work together to provide a better leadership.

Choosing members to serve on a pastoral relations committee should not be a popularity contest, nor is the committee a platform for people who oppose the clergy. The best committee members are good listeners, in touch with a segment of the congregation, who are able to talk about difficult issues in an open, reasonable fashion. The most successful committees are usually chosen by a council from a list of names suggested by the clergy. Working from the clergy's suggestions is important because clergy *have* to feel comfortable with the group or it will fail. Conversely, the committee will fail if it simply becomes the clergy's lobby instead of a diverse group from the different segments of the congregation.

Using Evaluations

Earlier we considered the usefulness of evaluations in creating an effective congregation, but they are equally helpful in reducing bad feelings and conflict. Everyone has a silent opinion, but speaking the truth is often intimidating and impolitic. Sharing our wisdom and learning about ourselves is difficult unless procedures are in place to encourage the sharing of opinions in a safe environment. When procedures are not in place, unspoken criticism smoulders, and evaluation becomes personal and judgmental instead of analytical and useful.

Making valuations everyday and ordinary is one way to encourage corporate understanding and growth. At the end of a meeting, a line can be drawn down the middle of a blackboard, with "pro" written on one side, "con" on the other. A quick review of what people liked and disliked about the meeting can alleviate frustrations and make the next session more effective. Some leaders are so frightened about criticism that any such process is painful and discouraged. Nevertheless, the more habitual and ordinary valuation becomes, the more egos dissolve, the more we can laugh at ourselves, and the more healthy change can be furthered.

Purchasing Liability Insurance

The strategies described here cost much less than insurance in making the worshiping community a safer place. But just as fire sometimes strikes well-maintained buildings, so litigation can strike healthy congregations. From a financial point of view, and considering the litigation aimed at religious institutions today, having $5 million of umbrella liability coverage is a prudent measure for any congregation. Most carry less, and some live dangerously by having none.

Establishing loss prevention systems sometimes can be used in the marketplace to attract insurance underwriters willing to provide affordable umbrella coverage. Although with some companies this "good citizen" attitude will make no difference, with others it will. For those congregations who are willing to institute and promote a self-conscious effort to reduce liability risk exposure, the cost of insurance may be reduced.

When the Media Call

Whenever scandal, the loss of life, or violence occurs in a congregation, you can trust the reporter from your neighborhood paper or television station to give a call. Be prepared! It is much easier to reflect on your frame of reference professionally and institutionally *before* such an eventuality, than to receive the call unprepared. Sometimes, in fact, you first learn about a problem from an inquiring reporter. One minister who received several such calls over his career confided to me, "Each time, you gulp about three times and wonder if you should head for the hills. Then you begin wondering what to say."

SUGGESTIONS FOR HANDLING PRESS CALLS ABOUT A CRISIS

- When the call about a scandal or lawsuit comes, thank the reporter for calling and ask for his or her name and telephone number. If you do not know about the situation, let the reporter know and promise to call back. Turn the questions around and ask reporters for as many details as they know about the situation and how they heard about it.

- Find out what is going on. Be sure your facts are consistent and as complete as possible. Work in cooperation with and solicit advice from the congregation's staff and officers, legal counsel, your insurance agent, and anyone involved with the crisis personally or through the congregation before calling back.

- Designate a single spokesperson to handle communication with the press. This spokesperson should be able to develop a relationship of trust with reporters.

- The spokesperson can provide general information about the congregation, such as the size of its membership, the number of staff, and when it was founded.

- It is appropriate to briefly describe the congregation's governing body and other bodies of oversight with a say in the matter, such as a denominational committee on ministry. The procedures followed by these groups and an estimated time line of their activity may be communicated so that people understand the congregation is acting responsibly rather than hiding from the public eye.

- If a staff person is involved in allegations, the fact of the allegation can be shared, along with the person's name and his or her role in the congregation. Your lawyer will probably advise you not to comment further.

Your attorney will also remind you that detailing accusations in public or in an interview tends to be unwise. Communicating the eventual results once an investigation is complete and any necessary decisions made is appropriate unless the parties involved agree otherwise.

The best strategy includes building a friendly relationship with the media before you open the door and find television cameras aimed at you. Reporters are always looking for stories, so get to know them and suggest leads. If you can look back at positive articles written about the congregation, responding to an unhappy story becomes much easier.

Going the Next Step

This whole chapter has been about going the next step in banishing invisible violence and healing the wounded. Though difficult, facing these realities and going the next step each day lends your congregation authenticity, integrity, good health, and effectiveness. Remember the thousands of concerned professionals and institutions aimed at guiding you through these deep waters. Every mistake they have made becomes a learning in how to do things well, combining care and competence.

Resources for Healing the Wounded Congregation

Agencies

The agencies listed at the end of Chapters Eight and Nine can also be helpful with information and resources for creating healthy, nonviolent communities.

Periodicals and Resource Packages

The periodicals listed at the end of Chapters One, Four, Eight, and Nine are also resources for articles about recovery and healing for the worshiping community.

"Broken Vows": Religious Perspectives on Domestic Violence, Center for the Prevention of Sexual and Domestic Violence, 1914 North 34th Street, Suite 105, Seattle, WA 98103; (206) 634–1903. (This multimedia package contains a fifty-minute video, a study guide, and brochures for participants.)

A Clergy Abuse Survivor's Resource Packet, Center for Women and Religion, Graduate Theological Union, 2400 Ridge Road, Berkeley, CA 94709. (The package contains articles, definitions, guidelines for reporting, and a bibliography.)

Pastors Packet on Family Violence, Center for the Prevention of Sexual and Domestic Violence, 1914 North 34th Street, Suite 105, Seattle, WA 98103; (206) 634–1903. (The packet contains a collection of important publications.)

Reducing the Risk of Child Sexual Abuse in Your Church, Christian Ministry Resources, P.O. Box 1098, Matthews, NC 28106; (704) 841–8066. (This multimedia package contains a book and videotape, created in 1993 by James Cobble Jr., Richard Hammar, and Steven Klipowicz.)

The following curricula are available through the Center for the Prevention of Sexual and Domestic Violence, 1914 North 34th Street, Suite 105, Seattle, WA 98103; (206) 634–1903.

Fortune, Marie. *Sexual Abuse Prevention: A Study for Teenagers*. Cleveland, Ohio: Pilgrim Press, 1984. (For youth groups.)

Fortune, Marie. *Violence in the Family: A Workshop Curriculum for Clergy and Other Helpers*. Cleveland, Ohio: Pilgrim Press, 1991. (For clergy and lay leaders.)

Fortune, Marie, and Reid, Kathryn Goering. *Preventing Child Sexual Abuse*. Cleveland, Ohio: Pilgrim Press, 1989. (For children nine to twelve years of age.)

Reid, Kathryn Goering. *Preventing Child Sexual Abuse*. Cleveland, Ohio: United Church Press, 1994. (For children five to eight years of age.)

Books and Articles

Bloss, Julie. "Sexual Harassment." *Clergy Journal*, Jan. 1996a, pp. 33–36.

Bloss, Julie. "Sexual Harassment." *Clergy Journal*, Feb. 1996b, pp. 35–38.

Byerly, Carolyn M. *The Mother's Book: How to Survive the Molestation of Your Child*. Dubuque, Iowa: Kendall-Hunt, 1985.

Fortune, Marie. *Keeping the Faith: Questions and Answers for the Abused Woman*. San Francisco: Harper San Francisco, 1987.

Fortune, Marie. *Love Does No Harm: Sexual Ethics for the Rest of Us*. New York: Continuum, 1995.

Franklin, James L. "Congregations Need Help After Clergy Abuse." *National Christian Reporter*, May 21, 1993, p. 3.

Heggen, Carolyn H. *Sexual Abuse in Christian Homes and Churches*. Scottdale, Pa.: Herald Press, 1993. (Order from Herald Press, 1616 Walnut Avenue, Scottdale, PA 15683; (800) 759–4447.)

Hopkins, Nancy Myer. *The Congregation Is Also a Victim: Sexual Abuse and Violation of Pastoral Trust*. Bethesda, Md.: Alban Institute, 1992.

Hopkins, Nancy Myer. "Symbolic Church Fights: The Hidden Agenda When Clerical Trust Has Been Betrayed." *Congregations*, May/June 1993, pp. 15–18.

Hopkins, Nancy Myer, and Laaser, Mark (eds). *Restoring the Soul of a Church: Healing Congregations Wounded by Clergy Sexual Misconduct*. Collegeville, Minn.: Liturgical Press, 1995.

Miles, Al. "Preventing Child Abuse in Church." *Christian Ministry*, Mar./Apr. 1994, pp. 25–27.

Rediger, G. Lloyd. "Healthy Congregations." *Clergy Journal*, Mar. 1996, pp. 28–31.

Ruth, Kibbie. "Creating a Harassment-Free Church." *Leadership*, Summer 1995, pp. 67–68.

Shomon, Dan, Jr. "When *60 Minutes* Calls." *Your Church*, May/June 1996, p. 52.

Tracy, Denise D. *Healing the Congregation: A Resource*. Bethesda, Md.: Alban Institute, 1995.

Underwood, Anne. *Considerations for Conducting an Investigation of Alleged Clergy Sexual Misconduct*. Bethesda, Md.: Alban Institute, 1996.

AFTERWORD

WHAT DO WE NEED TO BEGIN?

Religion is a way of walking, not a way of talking.

—W. R. Inge, Dean of St. Paul's Cathedral, London, 1911–1934

THESE PAGES HAVE taken us a distant journey. Beginning with the individual leader, we looked to the need for courage, the need to know, the importance of standards, various legal responsibilities, and the role of decision makers. In Part Two, we turned to issues of community—administrative and financial systems, employer responsibilities, and relationships with the larger community.

Finally, in Part Three, our accountability to the invisibly wounded within sanctuary walls was raised. Congregations typically provide superb care for those who are publicly wounded—losing a parent, going through surgery, falling victim to a fire. For such difficulties, we visit the sick, take special offerings, deliver home-cooked meals, and go out of our way to provide care. It is the reverse for the invisibly wounded, whose pain we found easy to ignore in the past. Until this is remedied, accountable leaders give the tragedy of invisible wounding high priority.

The idea in all of this is not to absorb hundreds of suggestions and resources before assuming a leadership role. Rather, the hope is to provide resources to draw from that support your competence and accountability, whatever the particular call.

Before concluding, each of us needs to ask again, What do I need to begin? Knowing the scope and nature of the role you are accepting is important, these pages attest, but so is the attitude, *the point of view* you bring to leadership. Reflecting on your internal frame of reference and its influence on your behavior, in other words, may considerably improve your effectiveness.

For instance, a naturally shy person can consciously choose to be outgoing as a leader, to use the role as internal justification for asking engaging questions and initiating conversations, drawing people out, and finding new friends. The following suggestions offer similar ways in which our internal attitudes influence our action in the world.

Look at Everything As If for the First Time

Look at everything as if for the first time, beginning with the congregation's facilities. Most of us take the local environment for granted. Yet that same environment influences everything we feel, think, and do.

One of the easiest ways to be effective is to suggest little changes that make the congregation's property more attractive and useful. Beware of walking on people's toes and stay away from harsh judgments in this. A fresh approach goes sour if it bypasses accepted procedures or fails to consider people's feelings. But offered in the right spirit, small changes can improve the quality of life in most congregations. Giving the church office a large indoor potted plant (if the church secretary likes the idea!) may improve everyone's experience of being in the room. A similarly fresh, responsive attentiveness is useful in every leadership arena, particularly for tasks that seem dull.

Be Governed by the Head and the Heart

Both "head" and "heart" are required when you investigate what is necessary to provide a caring context, make the necessary effort, and celebrate when members of the community grow in spirit and in truth. Often, this synthesis of our thinking and feeling can lead from either-or options to new possibilities.

Howard Thurman, whose extraordinary sermons and exploration of spiritual life have influenced tens of thousands of Christian and Jewish clergy, once put it to me this way: "When it comes down to a question of your head or your heart, go with your heart. It is so much older." Some might claim that Thurman overstates the case. If so, it is because the message is so badly needed in a culture where violation and greed turn many hearts to stone. God created us thinking *and* feeling creatures. Accountable leaders learn to weave these two threads together honestly instead of segregating them from each other—as the title of Thurman's autobiography asserts, *With Head and Heart* (1979).

Integration of thinking and feeling is enhanced by exploring a subject in more depth. Move from sharing opinions to sharing the experiences that forged the opinions. With important issues, discuss their *context*, spending enough time for the group's wisdom to surface slowly. This helps clarify everyone's understanding and often reveals opportunities nobody realized.

Resist the Temptation to Become Polarized

Actively resist the temptation to become polarized over issues or personalities, within yourself or with the congregation. People who succumb to polarized attitudes elevate their point of view above the common good and render themselves blind to whatever goodness resides in those they oppose. Some mix of good and bad is usually found on both sides of a given disagreement.

This need for perspective is clear to us all until we find ourselves stubbornly at odds with someone. Disagreement does not have to create enemies, however, if conscious good will and a common purpose transcend the disagreement. Differences of opinion will always exist, for which we can be thankful. But an exercised imagination discovers ways to affirm the congregation's basic solidarity, whatever disagreements individuals have with each other.

Resist polarizing tendencies by holding up everyone's gifts, and learn to value those who do well what is difficult for you. Working together means saving each other from the misplaced hope of being all things to all people.

One Saturday morning in a neighborhood church, a pastor arrived early in order to set up the chairs for an all-day meeting. He turned on the coffee and otherwise prepared for the day. The leader of the deacons also arrived early. This man, a city bus driver by profession, quietly walked around the church. Standing in each doorway, he raised his arms up and out (like a tree in the springtime), bowed his head, and prayed for those who would come through these doors in a few minutes. The organizer and the one offering prayers need each other in guiding the worshiping community.

Seek the Truth About the Particular and the General

Seek the truth about the particular and the general, drawing from the wisdom of both conservative and liberal perspectives. In other words, resist the culture's tendency to polarize everything. Seek out goodness wherever it can be found. Pay attention to each member *and* the whole congregation. Combine prudence and risk taking, order and imagination, while you serve God and the community.

Years ago, in a small rural church where I was a summer intern, the council was trying to write next year's budget and simultaneously deal with a neighborhood problem. Teenagers, with no other place to go, would gather on the church steps each Friday and Saturday night and get drunk. Calling the police seemed an inadequate response, and alternative solutions were studied. A proposal was made to bring a mobile trailer onto the property and hire a youth minister to use it in setting up meaningful activities for the neighborhood youngsters.

The problem with the proposal was that it put the budget in jeopardy, threatening a $3,000 cost overrun. After considerable debate, a relative newcomer put his hand up. His flowing white hair and ruddy complexion made him look like Colonel Sanders. In fact, he recently had purchased a Kentucky Fried Chicken franchise and moved into the neighborhood. The council obviously respected his judgment, as he had been elected moderator for the coming year. But he had not yet addressed the youth problem. When he put his hand up, at least one of the assembled silently concluded that the youth ministry was doomed, condemned by the generation gap on the altar of financial prudence.

The man stood up and, as expected, made a strong case for fiscal responsibility. But he went on to make a stronger case for the need to move forward in faith even when you do not know where the resources are coming from. He concluded that a church budget that consistently balances each year is not a faithful budget. The vote was called when he sat down, and the new youth program became a powerful influence in that neighborhood. The church did not have to search far for the money to fund the new ministry, which is probably what our Colonel Sanders lookalike understood. As a natural leader. he understood the need and the context, and he had the courage to take a position and make it "safe" to support. By standing for responsibility and championing a calculated risk, he helped empower the church to do its appropriate ministry.

Prepare to Be Resilient

Finally, prepare to be resilient when the road is bumpy, treating your prayer life like food. Do not despair if you discover yourself in the middle of unhappy, troubled situations. Such is the stuff of authentic family and community life. The people and agencies mentioned in this book and others like them can help. More important, the gifts of the inner life,

buttressed by the spiritual resources of your tradition, including scripture and prayer, can provide the light when you find yourself in a long
dark tunnel.

A minister I know tells the story of accepting a call to a small, healthy
church in a rural California community. It seemed to be a congregation
without any serious problems except for a weak choir. Six brave singers
gathered each Sunday, but none of them could read music! The new pastor made a habit of sitting in a particular chair in her study for a half hour
each day, praying for the congregation and its ministry. Often, her prayers
turned to hope for the choir.

One Sunday, two years into her tenure, a stranger came to the pastor
after worship. She was a newcomer to town, she said, had a graduate
degree in choral music, and was looking for a home church. The pastor,
surrounded by parishioners leaving the sanctuary, exclaimed, "I've been
waiting for you! Could you stay a few minutes, until people leave, so we
can sit down and talk?" Several years later, the church's four choirs,
including the original, offered a concert to the whole town.

○

Mineo Katagiri, a retired pastor to pastors and one of the wisest of the
many readers who improved this manuscript while it was being written, said to me, "Don't forget that the church has a unique mission. We
are called to a relationship with God and to live creatively in a society
gone mad."

This particular mandate indeed sets the worshiping community apart
from all other communities. Building a relationship with God together is
our reason for being. This is an audacious, even outrageous notion, as theologians remind us through the centuries. Yet it draws us together, giving
us a vital reason for being and aiming us at what we might become. Leaders help along the way, leaning on some shoulders and offering a strong
shoulder to others.

As we have seen, knowing how to lead accountably has become more
complex and difficult. To the degree that we remain committed to the purpose and faith that draw us together, and to the degree that we do our
best in bringing imagination, persistence, and responsibility to the task,
the children of God will be faithfully served.

REFERENCE

Thurman, Howard. *With Head and Heart.* New York: Harcourt Brace, 1979.

INDEX

Abingdon Press, 17, 109, 117
Abrahamson, James O., 15, 25
Abuse: addressing, 153–183; approaching
  subject of, 168–169; aspects of, 151–
  224; and clergy misconduct, 185–208;
  community resources for, 169, 219–
  220; emotional, 162–163; extent
  of, 153–154; and healing process,
  170–171, 209–224; indicators of,
  159–166; issues of, 155–166; learning
  about, 176–179; litigation on, 29; pastoral response to, 166–173; policies
  prohibiting, 211–212; proactive strategy toward, 217–221; and protection
  for pastors, 171–173; resources on,
  167, 179–183
Accountability: and abuse, 151–224; and
  administration, 59–150; aspects of,
  1–58; attitudes for, 225–229; of governing board, 45–58; and law, 29–44;
  meaning of, 7–13; and responsibilities,
  3–27; and standards of care, 11–13
Accusation, risk of false, 198–199
Adams, Carol, 178, 180
Administration: accountable, 59–150; of
  congregations, 61–80; of employment
  practices, 115–133; of financial management, 81–113; learning about,
  74–77; resources for, 77–80; and secular nonprofits, 76–77; and service
  providers, 135–150; training for,
  117–118; vision-driven, 62–65
Afterpastor role, 215
Alban Institute: and abuse, 177; and
  administration, 61, 67, 68, 70, 117;
  and clergy misconduct, 202, 204,
  215–216; and congregational health,
  210, 215–216; and governing boards,
  53, 57; and responsibilities, 5, 14, 18,
  19, 23, 24, 25
Allegations, responding to, 212–217

American Association of Fund-Raising
  Counsel 87, 99, 102, 104, 105,
  106, 110
American Association of Pastoral Coun-
  selors, 167, 179, 204
American Bar Association, 147
American Institute of Architects (AIA),
  111, 143, 149
American Psychological Association, 191
Americans United for Separation of Church
  and State, 41, 42
Americans with Disabilities Act (ADA) of
  1990, 128–129
Anderson, David E., 37, 43
Anderson, Leith, 75, 78, 111
Anthony, Michael J., 56, 58
Architects, service provided by, 143
Aristotle, 22
Ashton, Debra, 111
Audits, annual, 85–86
Avena, Erica W., 69, 78

Bakker, Jim, 32
Balmer, Randall, 39, 43
Bangor Theological Seminary, 66
Banks, Robert, 69, 78
Barna, George, 108
Barnhouse, Ruth Tiffany, 202–203, 205
Barton, Ronald, 191, 205
Battered women, 163–164, 171
Baylor University, 41, 42
Bear, Euan, 178, 180
Beck, Melinda, 191, 205
Behrens, William C., 14, 27
Believe the Children, 178, 179
Bergstrom, Richard L., 109, 111
Bernardin, Joseph, 198
Berry, Jason, 205
Bloss, Julie L., 17, 40, 43, 123, 129, 130,
  131, 132, 150, 213, 224
Bond financing, 97–98

231